Listening
with the
Ear *of the* Heart

Listen carefully, my child, to the master's instructions, and attend to them with the ear of the heart.

~ Proverbs 4:20, as quoted in the prologue to
The Rule of St. Benedict

Listening
with the
Ear *of the* Heart

Writers at St. Peter's

Edited by
Dave Margoshes & Shelley Sopher

St. Peter's Press ★ Muenster, Saskatchewan

© Individual works are copyright by the author.
© Compilation copyright by Dave Margoshes and
Shelley Sopher, 2003

All rights reserved. No part of this book covered by the copyrights herein may be reproduced or used in any form or by any means — graphic, electronic, or mechanical — without the prior written permission of the originating publisher, if previously published, or by the individual author if previously unpublished. Any request for photocopying, recording, taping, or storage in information storage and retrieval systems of any part of this book shall be directed in writing to Access Copyright, 1 Yonge Street, Toronto, Ontario, M5E 1E5.

Front cover: detail from the painting *Dancing with the Moon* by Randy Senecal, OSB. Reproduced with the permission of the artist and St. Peter's Abbey.
Cover and book design and page layout by Betsy Rosenwald.
Text face is Minion; Contributors' Notes are set in Syntax.
Printed in Canada by St. Peter's Press.
Bound in Canada by Provincial Bindery.

National Library of Canada Cataloging in Publication Data

Main entry under title:

Listening with the ear of the heart : writers at St. Peter's / edited by Dave Margoshes and Shelley Sopher.

ISBN 1-896971-24-5

1. St. Peter's Abbey (Muenster, Sask.)—Literary collections. 2. Muenster (Sask.)—Literary collections. I. Margoshes, Dave, 1941- II. Sopher, Shelley.
BX2529.M83L57 2003   810.8'0382   C2003-911024-9

St. Peter's Press
PO Box 190
Muenster, SK S0K 2Y0

Available in Canada and the USA:
Fitzhenry & Whiteside
195 Allstate Parkway
Markham, ON L3R 4T8

The editors and publisher gratefully acknowledge the financial assistance of the Saskatchewan Arts Board.

SASKATCHEWAN
ARTS BOARD
SINCE 1948

Contents

Foreword xi

Introduction xiii

Patricia Abram
 Gathering the Family 1

Susan Andrews Grace
 For Brother Thomas 2
 from *Joy of the Proper Tool* 3

Kimmy Beach
 Three in the Morning 4
 Eggs 7
 The Hermit 8

Madeleine Beckman
 Foxtails, etc. 9

Jacqueline Bell
 Marysburg, Saskatchewan 11
 St. Peter's, Muenster 13

Sheri Benning
 Wolverine 14

Erin Bidlake
 August's Tomatoes 16

Ronna Bloom
 * 17
 Dry Season at the Monastery: An Inventory 18
 Vow 19

Annette Bowers
 Alone Donna is Weak, Together with Mary, She's Strong 20

Beverley Brenna
 Pipe Organ 22

Laura Burkhart
 Walking into the Sky: Writing the Canadian Prairie Landscape 23

Alison Calder
 Hunger 32
 Wind in the Pines 33

Anne Campbell
   Lily and the Light   34
   Trees Take Account of the Air   39

Warren Cariou
   Chapter One from *Lazarus*   40

David Carpenter
   At Night, the Writers   55
   A Piece of Quartz Crystal   57

Sara Cassidy
   If Light Was Suddenly New   70

Hilary Clark
   No Time   72
   Moment   75

Marlene Cookshaw
   St. Peter's, Thanksgiving   76

Gloe Cormie
   Eight Sage Writers Journey to Quill Lake   78

Lorna Crozier
   The Divine Anatomy: 1. *God's Mouth*   79
                              2. *His Feet*   80
                              8. *God's Bones*   81
   A Prophet in His Own Country   82

Lynn Davies
   Approaching Vespers   83

Degan Davis
   Saint Peter's Abbey   84
   Confessions   85

Adam Dickinson
   Vespers   86
   Father Demetrius's Bees   87

Sharon Abron Drache
   Chapters Two and Three from *Ritual Slaughter*   88

M.A.C. Farrant
   The Mirror   98

Dorothy Field
   Jew in the Abbey   100
   Here in the Monastery   102

Hold Out 103
Ora et Labora 104

Linda Frank
When Doves Cry 105
The Doorway of St. Scholastica 107

Myrna Garanis
Roads Rise Up 109
Stay Among the Trees 110
A Day Very Much Like This 111

Connie Gault
The Fat Lady with the Thin Face 112

Sue Goyette
On Building a Nest 127
Meadow 129

Heidi Greco
No Wallflowers Permitted 130

Frances Greenslade
Skellig Michael 133

Catherine Greenwood
Monk Love Blues 142

Maureen Scott Harris
Ghazal for the Evening Games 144
The Next Morning, St. Peter's 145
Walking in Saskatchewan with Rilke 146
A Walk by the Dugout 147

Julia Herperger
St. Peter's Abbey 148
Brother Basil 149

Trevor Herriot
On Mount Carmel 150

Gerry Hill
North Central Baseball League Semi-Final, Muenster Red Sox vs. Melfort Brewers, July 23, 2001 156
Prayer for the Sun 161
Vow 19

Kitty Hoffman
Ghosts 162

Maureen Hynes
  Clang   169
  Dance Pavilion   170

Barbara Klar
  Three Weeks   171

Myrna Kostash
  Demetrius: A Saint in Progress   172

Judith Krause
  Retreat   177
  Devotions   179
  Wolverine Creek   181

Katherine Lawrence
  Please And   182

Ross Leckie
  Danceland   183
  Lady's Slipper   184

Tim Lilburn
  I Bow to It   185
  Touching an Elephant in a Dark Room   186
  Hawk   188

Jeanette Lynes
  Silence at St. Peter's Abbey — Morning   190
  Silence at St. Peter's Abbey — Night   192
  Day in Town: Humboldt   193

Hannah Main-van der Kamp
  Why Prairie Barns Are Red   194

Dave Margoshes
  Triumph of the Light   196
  The Photographer's Eye   198

Mary Maxwell
  A Wise Heart   199

Don McKay
  Vespers   201
  Northern Lights   203

Arlene Metrick
  February in Saskatchewan   204

Erin Michie
   St. Peter's Ghazal   205

Jane Southwell Munro
   Great Horned Owl   206
   Crows   208
   Frog   209

Brenda Niskala
   from *Stagline*   210

Jacqueline Osherow
   Saskatchewan Sonnets   212

Miranda Pearson
   A Week in an Abbey in Saskatchewan in the Middle of February   214
   Thaw   215

Elizabeth Philips
   Below   216
   Wild Mint   218

Alison Pick
   Wildflowers   219
   Washing Meditation   220

Ruth Roach Pierson
   Below "Imponderable," A Yellowed Iris   221

Joanna A. Piucci
   Communion   223

Marion Quednau
   Osmosis   224

William Robertson
   Sainthood   227
   Hunting Truffles   228

Mari-Lou Rowley
   1st Confession   230
   2nd Confession   231
   3rd Confession   232
   4th Confession   233

Allan Safarik
   Sanctuary   234
   First Winter Storm   235
   Witness   236

Brenda Schmidt
   Bone Fragment #5   237
   Out of the Elements: Shed #1   238

David Sealy
   Seance in the Far Garden   240

Steven Ross Smith
   from *fluttertongue 3: disarray*   242

Birk Sproxton
   Lines, Written in Country Graveyards   244

Yvonne Trainer
   St. Peter's Abbey   248
   St. Scholastica   250
   What Makes This   252

Paul Tyler
   Saskatchewan   253
   Seventeen Poets in a Caravan of Various Trucks and Cars Head into the Wetlands   254

Elizabeth Ukrainetz
   At St. Peter's   256

Guy Vanderhaeghe
   Things as They Are?   257

Bernadette Wagner
   Calling   283
   Specimens from the Abbey 2002   284

Joanna M. Weston
   Sunrise Walk at St. Peter's   285
   Two Cemeteries   286

Christopher Wiseman
   Dead Angels   288

Jan Zwicky
   Study: Aspen   291
   Small Song: Blue   292
   Study: Reeds   293
   Small Song: Prairie   294

Contributors' Notes   296

Permissions   305

Foreword

In 2003 St. Peter's Abbey celebrates its one hundredth anniversary as a Benedictine monastery in Canada. St. Peter's has had a long tradition of fostering education and the arts in Saskatchewan; it stands in a longer tradition of Benedictine monasticism which has fostered religion and the arts for more than 1,500 years.

I visited several abbeys in Germany in 1999. The first was our grandmother abbey in Metten, Bavaria founded in 740. The other two abbeys were in Vienna and in Salzburg, and both of them were also over 1,000 years old.

Common to all three abbeys is a rich history of culture and the arts. At Salzburg, Mozart's father worked for the abbey, and the church organ which Mozart himself played is still in use. All three abbeys have extensive libraries; I was particularly struck by the library at the Abbey of Metten. It is not only full of books, but it is also beautifully decorated. The monk guestmaster said that since monks spent a lot of time in the library, they thought they should make it a beautiful and inviting place.

Monasteries have had a close relationship throughout history with the creative arts. It was the monasteries that set up scriptoriums to copy and preserve the classical works of the ancient world in the dark ages of European history. It was monasteries where beautiful Gregorian chant was sung as a prayer and where science, literature and painting both enriched the lives of people of that era and made their lives more humane.

It is with great joy that I introduce this volume of literature which was produced over the past twenty-five years at St. Peter's Abbey. It has become an annual tradition — a tradition we look forward to — to have writers and artists from Saskatchewan, and far beyond, come to our abbey every winter and summer. In the 1970s and 1980s, these gatherings often involved baseball or volleyball games between the monks and the writers. More recently it has been badminton that has stretched our muscles, if not our minds.

I'm proud that St. Peter's is a place where the arts continue to thrive and to be fostered. I'm proud that St. Peter's can be a place of quiet where the creative energies of so many writers and artists have been able to flower and bear fruit. It's not only the quiet, mind you. I think it's also the cookies, the friendly staff and the wide-open spaces and animals at the farm.

As I read through some of the work in this book, I thought, "Thanks for the memories." More importantly, I want to say to all the writers and artists, "Thanks for making Saskatchewan the bright spot that it is in the literary and artistic circles of Canada."

Peter Novecosky, osb
Abbot, St. Peter's Abbey
Muenster, June 2003

Introduction

When we want to get away from it all for a while, our minds often turn to St. Peter's Abbey. The Benedictine monastery, which includes a working farm that raises much of the food served to residents and guests, University-of-Saskatchewan-affiliated St. Peter's College, and a press that publishes the Catholic newspaper *Prairie Messenger* and books such as this anthology, lies on the other side of Wolverine Creek from the village of Muenster, about an hour's drive east of Saskatoon. It's quiet, serene, contemplative — qualities that make it an ideal place for writers and artists.

Our own individual involvement with St. Pete's, as it's affectionately known to its admirers, is through a writers and artists retreat held there for two weeks every winter and six weeks in the summer by the Saskatchewan Writers Guild. The colonies, as they're called, have been held at St. Peter's for close to twenty-five years. The monastery offers ideal conditions for both writers and artists wrestling with the demons of fiction or poetry, painting or photography: no mail, no newspapers, no meals to cook, no dog to walk, no kids to ferry — you get the picture — no distractions.

The writers and artists who come to St. Pete's leaven their days by browsing in the abbey's well-stocked library or taking long walks through the gardens, meditation pathways and surrounding countryside, with its lonely stands of black spruce and occasional sloughs, pausing to feed peanuts to the tame chickadees — bold enough to come to an extended hand — and enliven their evenings with beer, wine and conversation, and sometimes spirited badminton games in the gym, where they are challenged and often beaten by Abbot Peter Novecosky, the abbey's athletic and outgoing headman.

Some also join the monks occasionally at prayer services in the abbey's stylish new church, its light-refracting stained glass windows reverberating with music from an impressive handmade organ, or make pilgrimages to St. Peter's Cathedral across the road, to view the Imhof paintings. Sometimes we rove farther afield, to Humboldt for an ice cream cone or a bit of shopping; to Manitou Springs to take the healing waters at the spa; to Danceland to let our hair down; to the Quill Lakes to bird-watch; to Mount Carmel to view the sunset.

The seasons influence our activities, as they influence those of the abbey. The winter sees more indoor activities including fiercely competitive Trivial Pursuit games with Father Demetrius, the guestmaster. In the summer, colonists nibble raspberries, watch with fascination the bees and sometimes even help out with farm chores. One summer a few years ago, colonists gawked as a film crew turned a story written at the abbey ("The Fat Lady with the Thin Face," by Connie Gault, which appears in this collection) into a feature film called *Solitude*.

Writers and artists value the sense of peace they feel here. Some believe that geographical locations can soak up the energy of events; for a hundred years this place has been a focus of spiritual activity, producing a deep-rooted sense of peace. That peacefulness — call it spiritual or something else — and the subsequent feeling of timelessness it evokes is especially nurturing to the creation of art. Life is simple here — everything extraneous falls away and you're left with what is important. For the writers and artists, that is their creative work.

That work is valued, as is all work to the Benedictines; they see work as another form of prayer. The monks work at a variety of tasks such as physical work on the farm, teaching at the college, or washing up in the kitchen. That they value the creative labouring of writers and artists adds to the welcoming atmosphere; often our society tends to devalue that type of work, and therefore the people who produce it.

The Benedictines came to Saskatchewan at the start of the last century, along with thousands of German Catholic settlers migrating north from the US, establishing St. Peter's in 1903. Behind them was a monastic tradition that dates back to the first abbey established by a monk named Benedict — later to be made a Roman Catholic saint — in Monte Cassino, Italy, around 530. St. Peter's is the oldest Benedictine abbey in Canada, and one of only three in the country where the monks continue to wear the traditional black habit.

The relationship between the writing community and St. Peter's has expanded in recent years. While the Saskatchewan Writers/Artists Colonies began here in 1980, the Sage Hill Writing Experience, in collaboration with St. Peter's College, has been holding month-long poetry colloquiums in the fall since 1995. Saskatoon poet Tim Lilburn, who has been teaching creative writing courses at the college for years, along with poets Don McKay and Jan Zwicky, organized two week-long workshops that brought together writers interested in nature. And recently a two-year creative writing diploma program, under Lilburn's guidance, has been available at the college as will be a distance MFA in creative writing with an environmental slant.

So, when we conceived this anthology of writing from the abbey, it quickly became apparent that there was an abundance of work to choose from, not only work that was written here but that is set or in some way evokes this place or its landscape. Seventy-six writers contributed ranging from Governor-General's Award-winners Lorna Crozier and Guy Vanderhaeghe to many writers you will likely be encountering for the first time. All of them were touched in some way by their experience — whether one-time or on-going — at St. Pete's.

In the pages that follow, you'll find stories and poems about monks and the monastic life, writers and the writer's life, root cellars and groaning dining hall tables, country walks, wildflowers, endless prairie sunsets, bold chickadees, nearby dance halls. You'll read about religious conversions, moments of doubt, renewals of hope.

More than that, you'll find yourself drawn, as were the writers who found brief refuge here, into the quiet, the serene, the contemplative, the magic of St. Pete's.

~ Dave Margoshes & Shelley Sopher,
St. Peter's Abbey, Muenster, June 2003

Patricia Abram

Gathering the Family

I don't go to Ukraine. I travel west to Saskatchewan, to the prairies where Ukrainians marked the land with their plows, their hands. I breathe in this place that echoes the treeless steppes, fertile soil of your native country. I travel to a monastery, to the quiet of St. Peter's, to write this story down, as history, as myth. Like monk Nestor centuries ago. One afternoon I walk the fields, the miles of wheat, blonde on blue sky. It's harvest time, *koliada*. Time to gather in the crop. The fields have been cut, but windrows of wheat lie like lines across a yellow page. I fall to my knees and dig my fingers deep into this earth, its black like the richness of gold. I smell its scent, its meaning, wrap a handful of soil in a kerchief as you did when you left your motherland. I sift through the scatter of stalks and find unbroken shafts, gather stalk after stalk, walking down row after row, till my hand aches and can hold no more. Till I gather in the *didukh* as our ancestors did many years ago. Gather in the last wheat sheaf, the soul of the family. And I bring it home.

(1996)

My time at St. Peter's was a deeply enriching experience in relation to both my writing development and my connection to my Ukrainian heritage. During my stay, I worked on a poetry manuscript which explored the lives of my Ukrainian ancestors, specifically my grandmother and grandfather, who emigrated from Ukraine in the 1920s and whom I never knew. The college library provided a wealth of resources on Ukrainian history and culture — books I had not been able to find elsewhere. One day I even took a bus into Saskatoon and visited two Ukrainian museums, where I learned much about the immigration journey to Canada, and the customs and life of the land left behind. However, it was the peace of St. Peter's Abbey surrounded by endless fields of wheat and endless sky, and one special walk through those fields, which led to the generation of my poem "Gathering the Family." That walk became a symbol of my time at St. Peter's.

Susan Andrews Grace

For Brother Thomas

Ordinary is for those who have time
not for people who must live
quickly in joy
steeping a liquor of blessedness
roundly
lightly
dancing in the kitchen.

Not many know this.

(1986)

I wrote the "Joy of the Proper Tool" poems, many of them set at St. Peter's, in the summer of 2000, returning from Las Vegas, where I was living at the time, to Canada by car, travelling the plains and thinking about them and how they are being altered by North American human behaviour. Returning to St. Peter's for a colony was poignant as ever because it is a crucible for my creative life: a place to which I have been returning since early childhood with many happy memories of family get-togethers, dances and ball games. "For Brother Thomas" was written during a much earlier winter colony, when Brother Thomas was the cook and he joined us for a celebratory supper.

Susan Andrews Grace

from JOY OF THE PROPER TOOL

[2]

Newly dead monks buried,
their work undone & agendas

underground with them.
The maze goes unmowed.

Chickadees chitter in the pines and spruce
alight on blue-green looking for a Francis,

dusk and time bullies
Benedictine magpies.

[11]

Now you see how wrong:
turn the round corner

unlikely larch,
cedar maze leads to a clearing

the hermit's house, tiny glade
its yellow perfection, undone.

Nature's so often like this gap
unthinking itself, moving along

self-forgetful: it's all in the short-term.
Glaciers missed the Cypress Hills

bristle cone pines, beachy things
sand, gravel and shells up there.

(2000)

Kimmy Beach

Three in the Morning

let the door close against
my left hand   Catherine and I
whisper across the courtyard
two identical orange farm kittens
cross our path   their aim to trip us up

click of my flashlight

we enter the hundred-year-old building
now housing the laundry   art studio
unclaimed spirits of dead monks
let the screen door creak
closed against my left hand
through the glass to my right a light burns
in a room beyond   habits hang
drying shadows of men turning
in small rooms

my flashlight beam shows a staircase
facing me   take it down   walk
on the left   avoid creaks   swing
the metal door open   a kitchen
dusty with moonlight   turn right and through
the refectory door
monk chairs monk tables quiet
till breakfast   to our left   cookie jars
white tins masking tape labels
chocolate   oatmeal

gingersnap
these are why we're here
we may have them anytime we like
there are buckets of gingersnaps
ice cream buckets full of them
in every guest lounge
but these are the ones we want   the ones
we cannot have   the monks' cookies
Catherine pulls the tin from the counter
removes the lid   fishes
out two cookies
she takes one into her mouth
places the other in mine

we stand just so   ginger molasses
honey lodge in our molars

the Co-op bag a sudden brittle echo
fill it   two dozen
gingersnaps   only gingersnaps
cover our tracks move the remaining
cookies so they will appear more
smooth the flour ring
left by the tin's bottom

we'll not meet the keen eyes of the
baker tomorrow morning
we like her
her easy chat   hands of flour
there is no returning them
she will know

sugar and cinnamon stick to doorknobs
I leave a gingerprint
as I let the door close against my hand

now I lie on my belly on Catherine's bed
my sin melting
like these crumbs on fingers   tongues
my heels kick
at heaven

(1999)

Poetry Colloquium with Robert Kroetsch. There I met four talented chicks with whom I am still in daily contact. Two of these women, Catherine Greenwood and Heidi Greco, have books coming out, and the other two, Holly Borgerson Calder and Rebecca Campbell, aren't far off. I finished my first book in a tiny room in St. Scholastica, the former convent. I may never have sent it off if not for Kroetsch screaming at me every day over breakfast to "get that goddamn thing in the mail." Though I was there to finish *Nice Day for Murder*, I spent a lot of time writing poems about the abbey and its residents, several of whom are now close friends. These poems are from that collection, currently entitled *Monastery Crimes*. It may or may not become a book. It doesn't matter. I had fun writing them. Since my first visit, I've returned seven times. I can't stay away, nor can I properly state the influence of St. Pete's on my writing life. I'll just say that I am the successful writer I am, in part, because of the time I've spent there and the people I've spent it with. I am more productive there than anywhere else. Maybe it's because I don't have to cook or pay the phone bill, but I believe it's more than that. Sometimes I'm a working guest: making beds in the morning for my keep, and spending the rest of the day writing, feeding chickadees, or playing some Tragically Hip on the juke box while drinking cheap wine at Kenny's bar up the road. Thanks, St. Pete's, for the friends I've made and kept over the years: those of the genus monk and otherwise.

Kimmy Beach

Eggs

rubber boots scuffing
the gravel outside my dorm
Brother A calls up
returns from collecting eggs
they fill the wire basket on the front
of his bicycle
comes to the window
I ask him to save me a nice
brown egg for breakfast

I have explained a dozen times I am
childless by choice and will remain so
my joy does not penetrate his
single-minded prayer for me
after vigils we say the Hail Mary together
on the back porch
my wine glass hidden behind the stoop when
I hear him shuffling toward me
arms full with icons

after vespers today
though I try to refuse it
(you have given me too many presents I say)
he gives me a green plastic rosary
faceless white Christ crucified
pictures of the Holy Mother
pamphlets with the correct wording of
the Our Father
a prayer that I will someday have children
and find joy
where she walked and slept

(1999)

Kimmy Beach

THE HERMIT

(for Robert Kroetsch)

Robert, you had a lot of notions
yessir a lot of romantic notions
about the monastic life
you tackle solitude
in a hermitage back of the abbey cemetery
try it for a week
that's all you can stand

we wonder how Sister Suzanne did it
this holy shack where you go stir crazy
she spent twenty-nine years
in contemplation and prayer
sending regular memos to the abbot
complaining about how much noise
the tractor makes

today you find two Catholic medals
on your pillow you swear
were not there yesterday
Robert, nuns must get lonely too
I think Suzanne's making
a pass at you from where she
fell asleep in Jesus

(1999)

Madeleine Beckman

Foxtails, etc.

She vowed to learn the names of all
the grasses where she walked and slept,
the yellows, greens, the purple
reed, blue grama and the rest, like
mistresses revealing undergarments when
the moment's right;

yes, she'd study the trees, or, at least the ones
giving shade or shadow to her days and nights,
those under which she'd sit and wander
in her mind, drift into infinity, down aisles
of tall, stately pines, poplars, aspen, a universe
into which she'd disappear, as they bowed
in the wind or fold like palms
in prayer above her head;

but what of the clouds, the songs
of birds and insects, beyond magpies and
dragonflies (those even she might know)
unlike the wild carrot wasp or willow sphinx,
unlike the minerals deep in marshland soil
rich with mushrooms, scary in their hues, like
the skins of snakes: rust, lime, oxblood red
pigments like those searched for by painters
to fill their frames with saskatoons and fairy bells,
with prairie buttercups and pussy toes, berries
blossoms, vibrant as life: delicious and deadly;

she needed to begin, find charts, books on species,
phylums, but wait, what was that aria she just heard?
she needed to know, learn composers' names,
beyond Mozart, Strauss, Stravinsky; she didn't want
to overlook all the schools of architecture, the forms
of verse she loved, but did not know by heart;
ashamed, she needed to confess (if only to herself)
she didn't know her favorite tea — was it Ceylon? Or
the wine she liked to drink — Syrah?

and what of her beloved kitchen tools
used regularly but without a proper name, not
just thingy or whatchamacallit; or
the dozens of elaborate fonts designed
throughout the ages; methods of printing:
lithograph, serigraph — etcetera, etcetera
would no longer do;

her head began to throb, pulse —
dendrites, axons, neurons clashed, and
looking up to relax her retinas,
the stars and planets gazed back, the
Milky Way smiled, and she knew
she'd wonder more than ever know;
there was a term for this dilemma,
no doubt.

(2002)

Were it not for St. Peter's Colony, "Foxtails, etc." would never have been written, while sitting under a tree looking out over the fields of planted corn. I was feeling blessed for the invitation to St. Peter's and blessed for the beautiful day. I was also feeling overwhelmed and a bit frustrated that there would always be so much I wouldn't know. A sense of urgency came over me to try and consciously learn, absorb and be able to name as much as possible — from that moment on.

Jacqueline Bell

Marysburg, Saskatchewan

This church gives them something to work on,
something bigger than this small town.

Men who've lived here all their lives
Replace the bricks and rotten wood around
stained glass windows.

Inside — a statue from Italy, St. Conrad.
His hands, painted wood with veins so real
you expect birds to arrive. He could feed the hungry,
fondle the rosary hanging at his rope belt.

Come freeze-up, services move in a southerly direction —
to the arena. While in the unheated church
purple cloths of the confessional whisper in frigid air,
scarlet echoes by the altar.

*   *   *

Leave the church, a procession of pines
lead down the lane to the cemetery.

All the graves face east, as if they would still be here
dolls in old chests, glass eyes recording each sunrise,
What strange faith —

                and here, all the babies' graves — so many.

How did they go on then, back to fields
just five feet past the poplar that marks off this place
taking the coldness of the gravestones inside them.

Kraus, Mueller, Weiland, Bittman.
Here, the Eischen twins — alive three days.
How to hold them, brief as water running back
to this land. You used words like breaking, broken by it too

    all these babies —

the stone reads: *his memory lingers with us still*
and maybe he does too — it feels possible here:
smell of pine, a low glow in the wheat, light in the field.

They came and made it their place,
land beaten like a dog — only its bones here
plowed under. Wild grasses staging a comeback
along the borders

    With this wind, I thee wed

How did they learn to go on
gripping each other so tight in winter —
you would like to believe

or not, maybe turned away in the bed, shoulder to back
looking out a window — outside going on too long

    a land like deer in the bush, at twilight

they knew how to hunt, took what was needed
with hands blunt as axe heads

and sometimes hungered for more

    a breath of wind, a blessing on sweaty foreheads

        cool as holy water.

(2000)

Jacqueline Bell

St. Peter's, Muenster

We wrote into the night fields,
into the wind, the cornstalks, the straw.
Wrote until our fingers felt used, our brains
couldn't find words. We wrote to the edge of sense and then
Tim said *keep going* and so we did. Our keen eyes
like harriers. Everything we gathered into us, arms weeping:
the snowgeese — how they lift, games of pool in Muenster's bar,
the crane's dance, each other, monks in their robes and how we loved
our tiny gossips, and after, even the dining hall, its sickly green walls —
we will love that too, in absentia.

Who's to say what we do is wrong, or right
how we choose to live — our lives, obsessions.
How we stand on the glittering night field
stars in our mouths, shining
beacons to each other   yes   come   a little farther.

Tim said   *write into it, write your tiredness, your hunger*
bring out your dead
and we will:

they will rise singing, rise from the dirt spitting straw,
they will be reborn in crows, carried on raven's wings,
they will be cranes, croo-crooing us to sleep.
They will feed chickadees in the silent forest,
taking our hands and leading us gently into the fields.

It is dark   here   this way.

(1995)

Sheri Benning

Wolverine

Fall. When scraped-bone
fields show us the empty
cathedral-air behind breastbone.

Shrew sounds of leaves,
bleeding at a pace the eye can't hold.
As a child standing in willow kindle,

grasses the yellow of grandma's dying arms,
watching geese till a sky made more blue
by the radiance of decay,

asking for a sign —
*if you are there, spell this
in the furrow of geese*

and always unable to decode their flight,
to find the equation, a basket to heap meaning,
grandma's apron full of chokecherries, small questions,

why in death the smell of estrus?
But soon the geese over Wolverine,
the creek that dog-tails our land.

Standing in the wake of passing,
mind made small by another's height,
left with the imprecision of loss —

strewn chokecherries, their bee-sting taste.
Learning we reckon only through
loss: the place that we begin.

(2002)

I grew up on a small farm close to St. Peter's Abbey. Three of my great uncles were members of the monastic community — Fathers Xavier, Leonard and Edward. My grandfather, who was also a monk until Father Leonard introduced him to my grandmother, helped plant the copse of evergreens west of the college. When he moved out to his new farm southeast of St. Peter's, the first thing my grandfather did was plant a shelter-belt of evergreens reminiscent of the abbey. And when my father started farming on his own, he took an evergreen with him, transplanted it in what we, as a family, will always think of as our home. I can never say how much the college and abbey have affected my writing; St. Peter's is so deeply part of who I am. A few years ago, my mom and dad were forced to make the hard decision to sell our farm. Before leaving, a friend and I took a small evergreen and transplanted it at the abbey in the clearing of a poplar bluff facing southeast. It just seemed like the right thing to do.

Erin Bidlake

August's Tomatoes

august's tomatoes
are september's poetry

is what I would tell my grandmother
if she was living, just as
yesterday's raspberries are
tomorrow's jam and last week's cukes
are next week's relish
and so we are nourished
by the pains we take
to set aside plenty, feast
on just enough

(2001)

This poem was written at St. Peter's after visiting the cold cellar one evening. The enormous jars of canned preserves and heaping piles of potatoes made me think of my grandmother, who was originally from rural Saskatchewan, and who had died a few years earlier. Having survived the awful drought of the 1930s, she tended to stockpile food, and in her lifetime she managed to preserve two lifetimes of jams and pickles. I was raised in New Brunswick and didn't have the opportunity to visit the prairies before she died. While at St. Peter's I felt a strong reconnection with my roots.

Ronna Bloom

*

The rooms
    with the writers
        on either side of mine

The curved shoulders
    of the cedars
        on either side of the path

The knowledge
    that each is focussed
        on their task: writing, reaching, sleeping

and that between these trees
    within these walls
        infinity

(2001)

Ronna Bloom

Dry Season at the Monastery: An Inventory

There was the path to the cemetery,
all the stones the same. The maze
of trees around the graves, an inner
hedge of pine an outer one of cedar, trimmed
shoulders hugging the path. Me, the single walker.
There were the raspberry rows behind the maze
almost ripe; the wildflowers clinging
to the garden fence, free for the taking.
There was the tenacious hold of their stems.
There was the statue of Mary on a nearby mound,
the words, *Consolatrix Afflictorum*. There was the sage
pulled fresh from the hill, green like a wing.
There were Saskatoon berries, high up and blue.
A little dry. Not a great season, she said
as she filled my hand. There was
the freshly oiled road, slick and stinking.
The dry one we were on.
There was the dust behind the car and
the rocks hitting it. There was the cracking
of the rocks against the glass, the dust like smoke.
There was being alone there and waiting.

(2001)

Ronna Bloom

Vow

Dance,
you have taken your vows
drunk wine before the altar —
are one.

How the bells,
ring on ring,
are overlapping each other
with song,
pushing and shoving,
bongbongbongbong.

Yes, you are married!
The long engagement
is ended, the garbage strike
is over. Rejoice — we are
back to work tomorrow
in our robes and jumpsuits.

And so.

The peonies are finished.
Their pink heads fallen over
too heavy from rain
like the faces of drunk brides
smashed into the earth.
They have the dark
icing on their faces,
and the long stems of their shoulders
are slumped.
Surrender.
The wait is over
and we no longer mind.
As long as we're here,
we are all married to the world.

Annette Bower

Alone Donna Is Weak, Together with Mary, She's Strong

Donna was tired, road worn and estrogen deprived. She'd taken up the cause in January of 1942 and inspired the world during wwii. She'd been retired since the 1980s. She'd travelled the world and arrived at St. Peter's Abbey for a restorative retreat in the monastic setting. But ever since she arrived, she'd heard the call and she could no longer block it out, even when she turned off her hearing aid.

Donna opened the secret compartment in her suitcase. She put her foot on the toilet lid and wriggled her toes into the red tights. She surveyed her puffy ankle and remembered that Cat Woman had been referred to as a bitch just because she didn't have ankles. Soon Donna might fit in that category if her diuretic didn't kick in. She continued to pull the spandex over her calf, which looked like it belonged to Bessie's last birth and she was ready to bawl. Her womanly thighs had more dimples than a waffle, but soon they were smooth and firmly sheathed in the red stretched casing. Donna gave one last monumental hike over her rounded belly, which was like a loaf of white dough that someone had forgotten to punch down.

Donna reached for the one-piece strapless stay-enforced royal blue leotard. No matter how many repetitions she did with the barbell, her triceps still sagged like batwings. The word pendulum took on a whole new meaning when she struggled to position her breasts in the formed bra cups.

Her peaches and cream complexion was dried and curdled. Her blue eyes lost their magnetism behind her bifocals. Donna reached for the silver tiara studded with rubies and garnets and placed it in her thick gray hair.

She bent over and pulled the black leather thigh-high boots over her long slender feet. She stretched the gold cinch belt around her waist. She stood with her arms akimbo and booted feet astride. Not bad, she acknowledged. When she'd put all the separate parts together, it still made one powerful body.

She opened the medication packet and stuck the estrogen patch to her upper arm. Then she added the protective heavy bracelets to her forearms and she put on her silver earrings whose stone balanced the scales of justice.

Ever since Lois passed on, Clark didn't have the strength to put on his suit. Batman and Robin were searching the caves in Afghanistan and so the time had come for the soldier of Aphrodite, the goddess of love and beauty, to return. It was time for Wonder Woman. Donna Troy was ready. She twirled her magic lasso as she strode confidently through Severin Hall guestwing. She nodded briefly to Father Demetrius, the Benedictine monks' guest master. He dipped his head briefly. Donna saw the corners of his mouth pull upward and his eyes twinkle before he bent his head in prayer. She was glad that he'd had a lot of experience with writers and artists as guests and therefore her behaviour was still within the pale.

Donna climbed behind the wheel of her rented Ford Tempo and headed onto the highway. She slowed through Muenster, past grain trucks on the highway and left holiday travellers in the dust. She parked at the base of Mount Carmel. Donna trod along the pilgrimage path, past the Stations of the Cross and ascended the summit and saw Mary, with one arm supporting her child and the other offering a scapular, a protection against eternal fire. Donna turned to see hundreds of miles of horizon; she breathed in strength from the grandeur of space. The time had come to combine heroic Amazon power with the watchful grace of the Lady of Mount Carmel, the blessed lady, the queen of peace. The world needed both myths, Donna and Mary working side by side again, if humankind was to survive this next century.

(2002)

During my first writers' colony at St. Peter's Abbey, I went for a walk on the beautiful grounds. I sat for a moment to enjoy the peace when suddenly the bricks began to vibrate as the bells in the tower above my head summoned the community to prayer. This was my first indication that this place was not simply as it appeared and I'd better pay attention. During that time and subsequent colonies, as I enjoyed the comforts and hospitality of the abbey's guest wing, Severin Hall, and St. Scholastica residence, walked the halls of the college, watched the employees at St. Peter's Press, strolled through the farm and attended vespers, I observed the Benedictine monks, priests, and the community engaged in the Benedictine life. The safe environment offered me a place to expand ideas and to refine my goal to create simple stories about the struggles and glories during the journey of life.

Beverley Brenna

Pipe Organ

(for Father W.)

how it goes together   eleven hundred pipes
the lead   the zinc   the maple   a secret
between him and God, this decade of his work
uncurling like the tuba pounded straight
all sixteen feet, to hold a single note;
and at the altar listening past the ripened bells
for each tone balanced, pure, the passion in him
stronger than the clay he's made of
lacking all the stops for now   but someday
when the console's finished   just you wait
he thinks the sound   the sun   in the patient church
he dreams of gold from straw

(1998)

Laura Burkhart

Walking into the Sky:
Writing the Canadian Prairie Landscape

In February of 1999, while attending a writers colony at St. Peter's, I had the opportunity to convene a "round table" of three Canadian prairie writers, Lorna Crozier, David Carpenter and William Robertson. I wanted to know if and how they thought their writing was influenced by the prairie landscape — so evident just outside our windows in the abbey's Severin Hall — and whether there was a uniquely prairie voice in literature here. The winter wind and bells calling the monks to vespers formed the backdrop for the discussion.

Lorna is a Saskatchewan-raised poet currently teaching at the University of Victoria. Dave, recently retired from teaching at the University of Saskatchewan, writes fiction, essays and poetry. Bill is a poet and fiction writer who teaches through the Gabriel Dumont Institute. Both Dave and Bill live in Saskatoon. [All three have work in this anthology.]

One of the significant insights for me that arose from this discussion was how much the weather and climate informed the thoughts and speech of all three writers — Lorna even titled one of her early books *The Weather*. Saskatchewan people, writers or not, love to talk about the weather, its power to change lives and communities, its unpredictability. These writers are so immersed in the landscape they may not even realize how much it affects them. I don't believe a group of Toronto writers, or Maritime writers, or Quebeçois writers, would have had this same conversation.

What follows are excerpts from our discussion.

I started off with a quote from Wallace Stegner's *Wolf Willow*: "I may not know who I am, but I know where I'm from." Stegner, who spent his early years around Eastend, in southwestern Saskatchewan, went on to attribute that knowledge to a sense of landscape "scored into me by that little womb-village and the lovely lonely exposed prairie of the homestead."

I told Lorna, Dave and Bill I saw in their writing this kind of evocation and reflection as well, and that I sensed that the prairie is very much alive in their own writing. I asked them to talk about how they think this happens — what is it about this particular landscape that calls so urgently to be written about and written from and written into?

DAVE: Well, Bill and Lorna have spent more time in Saskatchewan than I have. This is my adopted home. I think when I write something, say set in Alberta or set in Saskatchewan, it feels to me quite different. And when I refer to Alberta I refer to an imagined Alberta of course, and an imagined Saskatchewan, reconstructed by me the writer. I grew up in Alberta at a time when oil was struck at Leduc and there was something in the atmosphere that I've never ever felt here, that whatever you wanted you just went out and got it.... Coming to Saskatchewan, where, in my humble opinion, no one really does believe in the future, it's a very different atmosphere.... So, I had to kind of court the province. It took me many, many years to feel as though this is my home, and this is a place that I could set a lot of the fiction that I write in, and the personal essays and stuff like that.

LORNA: I was born in Saskatchewan and lived here for forty years. I really do believe that the place we are born, the landscape that you know as a kid, gets into your very blood and bones and constructs the structure of your cells. [Poet] Eli Mandel talks about first place, first word, first dream, and where you have those things they are forever going to shape how you see the word and how you articulate what your relationship is to language, how you shape your poems or fictions or essays or whatever. This place for me has always been a great and wonderful mystery, even though I was born here.

I remember the first time I was interviewed on *Morningside*, Peter Gzowski said, "Why does so much good writing come from Saskatchewan?" — the perennial question. I used to say, tongue-in-cheek and kind of smartass, "Well, you know, the place is so empty we fill it with words." I remember [the late Saskatoon editor] Carolyn Heath saying, "It's the sound of the wind in our ears all the time. And that's like the sound of the sea. It's continual, and it creates a rhythm and you write songs and sentences out of that rhythm."

I was riding once to see my mom who lives in Swift Current. I always have to fly to either Regina or Saskatoon and either rent a car or catch a bus, and I just enjoy that ride so much now that I'm living on the coast, that drive into openness. And I was thinking, "It's not that it's empty," which has been what travellers who have passed through here have always said. "It's that there's a sense of waiting, that something is about to show itself." And I really felt that. I always try to sit in the front seat of the bus if I can, to the side of the driver where you get that big expanse, and I thought, "Something is about to appear." And it could be an angel, it could be a hawk, it could be a snowy owl, but it's that sense of always being on the verge of something of import, a premonition. And I think I'm always trying to get at what that is and get that feeling into words. And it's not writing *about* the landscape, but it's writing about grieving for my father, loving my lover, missing my cat, whatever, and the landscape and that sense of the mysterious is there waiting to be spoken.

You know, you can't live here without looking up. And Stegner makes that other wonderful comment… "When you live here, you're not a humble people. You're both small and not small, because you're the only upright thing in the landscape. And you're a poetic people."

And I think he really touched on something there. Eastend is the same kind of topography and so on that surrounds Swift Current as well. And Shaunavon.

LAURA: Which is where you grew up, Bill.

BILL: Well, actually, I moved to Shaunavon at the start of grade eight, and for me, it was one of the first times I ever felt at home. And I didn't know why. I didn't understand it except that I knew I was a small-town guy and we'd been living in Nanaimo, which I hated. But I think it was the power of my father's personality that meant even though I was born and raised in different parts of Japan, and Ontario, small-town Ontario, sort of that Gothic stuff of Alice Munro, and small-town Jack-Hodgins-style Vancouver Island, northern Vancouver Island, wildcatter country, my sensibilities didn't feel in alignment until I was in Shaunavon. And I realized of course that my father — you could be living in the lap of Mount Fuji, but if your father is constantly telling you stories of Depression-era small-town Saskatchewan, then you're imaginatively formed by: skiing behind the car in the ditch — "and then my hands froze to the rope and I got dragged on my knees across the curve" — and Uncle Don going out and his mom giving him one bullet and saying, "Go get us a rabbit, we only have one bullet," and playing hockey with horse turds and things like that. That was what I grew up on, and my father told us those stories over and over again. So despite the fact that my mother and her parents ministered to the Haida Indians on the Queen Charlotte Islands and up in Bella Bella and Bella Coola and my mother spent years of her life working with the Chinese, some of it in the tunnels of Nanaimo, because of my father's strength of personality, what we grew up on was cabbage soup and Watrous, Saskatchewan. And my grandfather trying to make a go of it there. So when I came to Saskatchewan, this was where it was.

LAURA: You just sort of answered my second question, which was about Saskatchewan people enduring and being so resilient. Edward McCourt, when he writes about the dust bowl in the Thirties, says

> the survivors now took a kind of defiant pride in showing the world their strength to endure, without flinching, the worst that Nature could do to them. For the people of Saskatchewan, that nine-year sojourn in the dust-darkened wilderness was a genuinely traumatic experience which has left its mark not only on those who actually lived through the Dirty Thirties, but to some degree on their descendants.

And you touch on that in one of your essays, Dave, about how we're such resilient people here in Saskatchewan and we can take anything that Ottawa throws at us and that kind of stuff. So I assume you agree with McCourt's —

DAVE: I'm attracted to his statement. I think there is a terrific resilience out here, and I've heard an awful lot of people say that they take a kind of — oh, maybe a kind of dark, perverse pride in absorbing all of the atrocities from Ottawa and having a football team that never wins any games and having the worst weather in Canada. It's almost as though they're survival snobs in Saskatchewan, whereas in other parts of Canada I think they have rather haughtier reasons to be snobbish. My grandparents were Saskatchewan people; my parents were Saskatchewan people; and I'm sure I've inherited an awful lot of that perverse pride in all the atrocities that come our way from the weather and the politics.

LAURA: This kind of history that we carry, as Lorna said, in our very cells — how is that reflected in prairie writing? Or is it? Is it just something that's sort of inside, and doesn't really —

LORNA: Well, in my own writing, it comes out in the Mrs. Bentley poems, which of course is based on that wonderful novel by Sinclair Ross [*As For Me and My House*]. But part of wanting to write that was not just my admiration for him, and the novel, but to get my parents' stories about the Depression on paper. And, like Bill, those stories were told endlessly and I was bored to tears with them, over and over and over and over again, right? Until I read this book by Walter Ong, *Orality and Literacy*, where he mentions oral people keep repeating the story, keep it alive by telling it again. And I thought, "Maybe that's what my mom and dad are doing" (particularly my mom). She had to keep repeating it because she wasn't a writer, and, you know, not an intellectual person, so the story kept getting told. But part of writing that book for me was to save those pieces from my family, my cousins, my aunts, my grandfather, my mother and father, and when you grow up with people who grew up in the Depression, you really do feel like you were there too. I mean, what is memory and what is reality? Half the time I think I remember something but I've invented it. Or sometimes I think memory is real, whatever. Anyway, it was important for me to be able to honour, I guess, that time, because if we have a mythology here, our defining mythology is the Depression. And the bad weather, but that's the epitome of bad weather, nothing worse can happen.

*   *   *

LAURA: Carolyn Heath talks about that regional kind of writing. She says you can tell Ontario writers because they're wordy and they take this high moral stance. She compares prairie writers to maritime writing, which I think is really significant, given the history and the hinterland kind of stuff. She says, "Prairie writing is sparse, understated, ironic, flecked with black humour." So if this is an accurate reflection for the most part, and of course it's a generalization, how or why do you think the prairie landscape — interior, exterior, social, topographic — has impacted on the form or structure as well as the content?

LORNA: I remember reading that essay by Carolyn, and I disagreed with almost everything she said. One of the things that really annoyed me about the essay, and I had a chance to talk to her about this, was that she was trying to identify a single voice. Not only a single prairie voice, but a single Saskatchewan voice, and just list them. How are you going to fit even the three of us? Throw in Anne Szumigalski, throw in Guy Vanderhaeghe, throw in Liz Philips, just toss all these people in a pile. If you just look at poets, our line length is different, our diction is different, our rhythms are different. We may go back to some similar stories, and some similar descriptions of place, but I think that any sign of a healthy literature is that the voices that are heard are the ones that have a stamp of uniqueness about them too and are not just espousing some common view or form. I think one of the advantages of being an underdog is that we're all extremely aware of what's going on somewhere else. Whereas the same is not necessarily true of writers who come from the centre. They often don't know the exciting stuff that's going on in the margins. But I think because we know all that, we're experimenting with different forms, the content that we write about is sifted through.

LAURA: So would you say there's more freedom, there's more space to do that kind of experimentation?

DAVE: The temptation to be trendy is much less on the prairie, I think, because in a very physical sense at least we're somewhat remote from the trends and so I think that a certain kind of originality, or maybe the better word is eccentricity, can flourish in a province where towns are far apart and where writers really have to get together now and then or they feel isolated.

BILL: On the other hand, one of the things that Carolyn Heath said there about the sparseness, I completely disagree with that as a person who has walked miles and miles and miles of this province, with either a gun in my hand or a fishing rod. I would say that this is an incredibly lush province. It's just a different lushness than what you get in the Kootenays or what you get on Vancouver Island or what you get in Ontario some places. It's just different. I have no truck with these people who say that there's nothing there. They're just not looking very hard, that's all.

DAVE: I've been thinking about that essay by Carolyn for a long time, and I've tried to be fair and say, "In what sense can I agree with her and in what sense do I disagree with her?" If you look at literature as the phenomenon of the impact of environment and landscape upon consciousness, I think maybe she has an argument. But Lorna will turn that around and do the opposite thing. She'll write "The Sex Life of Vegetables," where you can see the impact of the writer upon the environment, in this case the vegetables. And so if you look at certain kinds of books, Stegner's not a bad example and Sinclair Ross is not a bad example, or "The Wind Our Enemy" is not a bad example of a poem, there's lots of examples — W.O. Mitchell's first book, *Who Has Seen the Wind?*, for instance — you can probably see the sparseness, you can probably see that there's a kind of similarity. In Sinclair Ross's *As For Me and My House,* you get a very dry physical environment, and it seems to spawn a kind of dry spirituality, a spiritual stinginess in the people of the town, and an emotionally dry atmosphere. The whole book is a sexual tragedy. But I think that's because Ross, writing when he did, was very sensitive to his environment and we see the impact of the environment upon the writer.

LORNA: And that was fifty years ago.

Dave: Yeah. And so many writers now are turning that around, and you're going to see maybe the same landscape turned funny, or grotesque, because the writer has now insisted on imposing his or her imagination upon the place that he or she imagines.

Bill: There's so much room to do it in. I can't help but think that when Alice Munro writes about Ontario gothic, there's only so much room there to push your imagination around, because those towns have been there for a couple of hundred years and they ain't going anywhere. But around here we can't help but see that whereas, for instance, when Lorna and I go from Saskatoon to our hometowns, the grain elevator's gone in Stewart Valley. So the landscape continues, the wind our enemy that Dave's talking about, continues to move things around. Everywhere you go things are constantly changing. There's always a state of flux. And in that environment I think we have this unbelievable luxury to push things around ourselves. We don't have to be hemmed in by mountains, pushed into a corner by any big trees — you know, you can do anything you bloody well want, in a sense.

* * *

Laura: In one of her essays, [Alberta writer] Aritha van Herk says the point of view will change depending on your vantage point, if you're writing from the top of the hill or the bottom of a coulee. And your voice, the voice that you were just talking about is different from the previous generation of voice. So actually, Lorna, when you were saying you disagreed with Carolyn and gave all these examples of difference, yet they're all at the same time saying something uniquely prairie —

Dave: That's true

Laura: — even if it's from the top of a hill or the bottom of the coulee or beside a stream.

Lorna: But what is that, though? What is that, if we're saying that? What is uniquely prairie about the thing that they're saying? And the same thing about form. I can remember — was it Anne Szumigalski or Carolyn Heath? — said once, I think it was Anne, who said she thought people on the prairie wrote longer lines. And of course that was just completely silly. It isn't true. It's something you'd like to believe, but it just ain't true.

DAVE: Rudy Wiebe said novelists on the prairie write longer novels and he said that while he was in the midst of writing a very long novel.

LORNA: Well, balderdash, right? So I always feel slightly suspicious when we come to try to make such generalities. Especially as a writer, I think, they make me nervous. Maybe some critic someday will come upon these things, but I don't know that I want to know about them.

LAURA: Is it just a different way of entering the landscape of relationships and reflecting that in your writing?

LORNA: I think it creates a certain solitariness, and perhaps a certain spirituality. Because we're walking into the sky all the time. And that's probably a terrible generalization and cliché too. When [poet] Patrick [Lane] first came here — he comes from the Okanagan, which are very high hills, they call them mountains — one of the first things he said which I thought was so sharp was, "You don't have to climb mountains to live here, you live on top of them already." Because that's the view we have, we have that long view. And maybe that makes us think about certain things more than people in other places, I don't know. I don't know if that's true. Again, it's like I'd like our lines to be a long line, because it would be a lovely parallel.

DAVE: I'm going to make a bold statement, that maybe, just maybe all three of us could agree that although we inhabit a rather global world, as readers and as writers, we suck up all the sources we can find from all over the world, there may yet remain something behind, residing in our writing, that reminds our readers of where we are from. A flavour of Saskatchewan, perhaps, a flavour of the prairie perhaps — in my recent writing, more than a flavour — but there's this centrifugal influence to move out into the world and see what it can teach us and come back and write about it and there's this sort of centripetal impulse going on in all of us as well that takes us back to that first place, in my case it was ravines in Edmonton, and then coming to Saskatchewan. Only now do I feel comfortable writing about Saskatchewan.

LAURA: Stegner calls it imprinting.

BILL: I think one of the strongest impulses that we ever come across in literature is the impulse to remake paradise. And personally I think we've got a heck of a better shot at it here where there's so much more openness than —

LORNA: [*laughing*] I love your Saskatchewan chauvinism, Bill. I think we've got a great shot of it but I don't know if it's better than anywhere else.

BILL: I'm not saying better, no, I just feel that if I want to recreate paradise for myself, which seems to be such a — it's been there since Genesis, there's this incredible impulse to — I mean, people talk about it all the time, "It was like Paradise. It was Edenic." It's there all the time. We have this huge need as human beings to find our way back to this garden that was taken away from them or something, or we lost. And boy, I tell you, I go out into northern Saskatchewan or southern Saskatchewan and I feel as if it can't get much closer than that. And if there's a price to pay to live here, which is the isolation Dave was talking about, perhaps, the *perhaps* lack of community, then I think there are huge benefits to be gained by living here, which is being that much closer to that garden. I think.

LAURA: Can I ask one final question? If you're talking about landscape, to you is that a noun, a verb, or a metaphor?

LORNA: [*laughing*] All of the above.

DAVE: For me it's a catch-all noun, it means the look of the land, the part that we've tamed, the part we haven't tamed, it means the people who live there, who have this sort of abiding connection to the landscape. It could mean the city, the cultural landscape. It could be the rural cultural landscape. It's a word that contains everything that surrounds you and influences you and deflects your voice to what it is, you know — I say deflects because I came here from somewhere else. I had to unlearn Alberta optimism to get into the old-fashioned Saskatchewan despair [*laughter*]. Paris gave us impressionism, Berlin gave us expressionism, Saskatchewan gave us depressionism.

LORNA: I don't think I ever write about landscape, and that would be one way to answer. I never write about that. It's what's here. You know, I think we're doing what everybody does everywhere, with a few writers who don't pay attention to place, but most of the writers that I read, that I adore and go back to, are very place-centred. Wherever that is [*others agree*]. And they write about the great things, but they always write about it with their feet firmly planted on the ground that they know. And they can take tremendous leaps once they've got their feet there, but they always fall back and leap again in that spot. And I guess that's what landscape is to me: the place I leap from and land on.

(1999)

Alison Calder

Hunger

I want to roll in sage
I want to smell of it

I want to tear it to pieces
and throw it in the air

I want to eat it
I want to graze

I want to dig like a dog beside it
I want it to grow out of me

(2002)

Spending time at St. Pete's gave me the space to get back into my writing. I had put poetry aside, for the most part, while I was doing my Ph.D. and then starting a full-time academic job. Attending the Poetry and Silence Symposium that Tim Lilburn and Don McKay facilitated at St. Pete's made me realize that my poetry was still there, just ignored. I wrote a lot. I came back to St. Pete's the following summer, hoping that the muse (and the cookies) were still there. It worked. My poem "Hunger" came out of a particularly beautiful evening, when those of us in residence drove out to the shrine at Mt. Carmel and watched the sun set. As we drove home, a huge orange moon appeared and hung over the field to the east of the abbey. The ditches were full of fireflies. It was pretty great.

Alison Calder

Wind in the Pines

Wind in the pines sounds like traffic
and already I'm ashamed of my senses,
mistaking very air for mere mechanics.
How to make our way without direction.
Sisyphus rolls his rock, he's always at the top, we
at that moment with him when breathing is believing.
Sisyphus knows things could go either way:
the torture's not the labour but the possibility.

The world is a good place. I believe this
like my grandmother continued to believe
the china dog her parents' parents brought from England
was priceless, though when she went abroad
she saw them row on row in Portobello junk shops.
Unreasonable. But there you have it:
hope, flying in the face of proof.
How can you hope against hope? You have to
move to make a path.
I'll add my shoulder to that rock,
I'll take a china dog out for a stroll.

(2001)

Anne Campbell

LILY AND THE LIGHT

LILY LOVED MONKS. She had loved them ever since she had been taken by her parents to visit her father's brother at the boy's school where he and the other monks worked and taught. She loved their sombre robes, their solid way of walking and the way their faces would suddenly light up when they laughed, which was often. She loved them working in the garden, going to chapel and laughing at supper. It was as simple as that. She loved everything about them.

She loved arriving at the college, always about 3 o'clock on hot August afternoons when the prairie was quiet. She loved the moment after the car stopped before the family got out when she thought everyone felt they should sit a minute before breaking the silence.

Her mother would get out first, then the little kids; last would be Lily's father, then Lily. Her mother would set out to find Brother Abbot, the head of the school. He was sixty, thin, with sandy white hair and glasses. Often he was in his office or in the little lounge area nearby. He would be pleased that the family had come and he would send someone to get Uncle, or tell them where Uncle was working and the family would find him themselves. When Uncle came into the lounge with someone who had gone to find him Lily thought he looked like the Protestant, Martin Luther, she'd seen

---

One of the monks at St Peter's Abbey, Brother Ozwald King, was my uncle and my godfather; thus, since I can remember I've felt part of the abbey and a kind of ownership. As a child I visited my uncle at the abbey most summers as my family made its way north to visit grandparents, parents of my father and John, become Ozwald. The story "Lily and the Light" sprang from the memories of those visits, from the sights, sounds and feelings of the abbey and, in particular, from the land and sky surrounding it. The deeper more silent part of the story seems to me to explore something about differentiation, or lack of it: salient mystery. My poem "Trees Take Account of the Air" was evoked by the silent, seemingly still, yet stirring, monastery grounds. At St. Peter's, though there is much activity, with farming, gardening and teaching, there seems to be always space for silence, and in this silence, the trees, or air or quiet of the day can be apprehended as gift, not taken for granted. At St. Peter's there is always enough time.

pictures of at school. She loved his plain face and square looking head with brown hair around the edges. She was always surprised to see him when he walked in and to think that he was her uncle. He seemed to Lily to have something about him that wouldn't let you look away and to be very large even though he was no bigger than Lily's father. When the family found him themselves he would be fixing something electrical in the kitchen or making tables or repairing desks in his shop.

In the kitchen Lily loved the huge stainless steel bowls the sisters mixed cake or bread in, the long counters and the mixing machines and the huge ovens and how clean it all was.

At suppertime Lily and her family and Uncle ate in the dining room that the boys used during the school year. After supper Uncle showed them the gardens and they walked around the college grounds looking at the trees and shrubs and flowers and at the wheat fields beyond that were yellow and ready for harvest. Sometimes Uncle showed them a plan for a new building the monks would build, or the motorcycle he was working on. Uncle was the only grown person Lily knew who rode a motorcycle on the roads after supper when his work was done.

When they walked back to the main building together it was very still with the wheat and sun mixed together like apricot dust. The family would have tea and cocoa with the monks and when everyone was talking Lily would slip out to have a look inside the empty classrooms. There were pictures of the King and Queen of England on the front walls above the blackboards. Desks sat on yellow hardwood floors with blackboards around the walls and that was about it. Lily liked the plainness; the absence of all the things that were usually in classrooms. There were no cutout shapes in construction paper of green shamrocks or red hearts on the windows; no pictures of birds or flowers of different nations; no extra tables or books or papers. Lily thought when school was in session, it still wouldn't be cluttered. Some monk would stand at the front of the room with something to say and the boys would listen. Like that.

The family slept in a big dormitory; each person with a bed of his own and a big quilt covered with heavy cream-coloured cotton. One night Lily heard her mother say that Uncle had had a spell that summer. He seemed fine to Lily. If Uncle had had a spell, Lily liked him that way.

Mornings the family would have breakfast, then drive around looking at the countryside; sometimes the sisters packed a lunch for them and then they would picnic by the side of the road under the trees at noon.

They were always back by suppertime and Uncle would eat with them again in the boy's dining room. Sometimes Uncle wanted to go out and work on his motorcycle even if his brother and family were visiting, and if he did Lily would go along with him to his shop. She would sit on a sawhorse in the doorway, leaning against the wall in the sun watching Uncle work inside the same light. Sometimes he looked up from the motorcycle and out into the fields. Sometimes he looked for a long time and Lily thought then that Uncle looked like he belonged there, in the dusty wheat light and the warm evening air.

In the morning Lily's mother might say that Uncle had had a spell the night before. Lily thought he looked the same as usual when they had lunch with him at the college instead of driving around the country and having a picnic. Lily's mother said that the spells made Uncle tired, and sometimes he slept during the afternoon. So it was, summer after summer. Visiting the college, and Uncle, and continuing their holiday.

When Lily was eleven her class studied China in school. They read *The Good Earth* in Literature and Mr. Follow discussed China in Social Studies. They talked about the Yellow River and its influence on the people and about the old Chinese teachings and how they affected the people and a bit about the revolution and how that was to change things, and they discussed whether it would or not. They talked about the religions of Taoism and Buddhism; Buddhism, Mr. Follow said, taught the Chinese to let things be and do not get upset about things that couldn't be changed. He said in Canada we are taught to get upset and change the things we don't like. Elmer Larsen stood up and said that his mother said Buddhists were heathen. And that ended that. Mr. Follow didn't argue with Elmer about what his mother said.

Lily looked in the dictionary for the meaning of the word Buddha, but found only the explanation, "the enlightened," which didn't tell her anything, only gave her a picture in her mind of something glowing. That was April and over the next few months when Lily felt things were not going her way she would think of Mr. Follow's words, "... let things be and not get upset ..." She wondered how a person could not worry. One day at recess she went and stood beside Mr. Follow's desk. When Mr. Follow looked up she told him she had looked for the word Buddha in the dictionary and found that it meant "enlightened one." She asked him how that fit with what he had said about Buddhism teaching taking it easy and not worrying. Mr. Follow said enlighten meant "shed light on" and Buddha's teaching shed light on ordinary things so that people could see them better and enjoy them more and not worry so much.

That summer the family was transferred to another province and Lily's mother said this might be the last summer they would be able to visit Uncle for some time and then she said she wondered how his spells were and they didn't seem to keep him from skating in winter or riding his motorcycle in summer, at any rate. Lily asked her mother what happened when Uncle had a spell and her mother said he just got very still and sort of "blanked out" for a minute. Lily could always imagine how Uncle looked, especially when she thought of him in his workshop fixing his motorcycle when he looked up and out into the sun. A person seeing him like that might say he was "blanked out," but it seemed to Lily he was "blanked in." Blanked in, to wheat dust and warm sun and the stillness of those evenings. But the more she thought about it, the more Lily thought that what she had seen might be what the others called a spell. She thought about it over the next few days: that what she had sometimes seen might be a spell. Then she thought that if it was a spell, what was it a spell of? A spell of being in the air and colour and smell of the night? A spell of being out of thinking? "Blanked in" or "blanked out"? "Blank out" sounded like "clunk" to Lily. Stopped, up against a wall. And Uncle in a spell seemed more like part of everything there, with no walls.

Then it was time to go. The family packed up their things to move and set out to see Uncle on their way. When they got to the college it was the same as always. Lily's mother found Brother Abbot, laughing, dusty with chalk even though school was out. He said Uncle was resting, tired from the night before. The family went to settle into the dormitory and Lily was left in Brother Abbot's lounge to wait for Uncle. He came into the room in the same surprising way. Suddenly there; large and hard to look away from. He said hello and that the family must be on their way to their new place. Lily said they were. She was sitting in a big chair and Uncle sat down on a bench across from her looking like Martin Luther again. Lily and Uncle sat in Brother Abbot's lounge in the light coming through the windows and Lily thought Uncle looked fine. Mr. Follow's words about things looking different in light came into Lily's mind. As the two of them sat there, Lily looked at Uncle. It came to her that she cared for him very much and a picture of that caring came to her, wheat-coloured and clear. She looked at Uncle again and it came to Lily that all of her caring for him could fit through one tiny pore on one of his hands.

She got up and walked over to Uncle. She took both of his hands in hers and pressed them hard to the right side of her face. He stood up then and together they walked outside and waited for the family. When the family arrived they all walked together to see the grounds. They had never seen the gardens in the afternoon with Uncle before and they looked different; rosier with a breeze stirring slowly through them. Lily thought it was nice that they were able to see Uncle in the garden in the afternoon like that, before they went away and wouldn't be back for some time.

(1982)

Anne Campbell

Trees Take Account of the Air

1. Walking   early morning across the monastery yard
                  air breathing   breeze
         ruffling dark poplar trees,   already

                    I've walked our country road,
                         eaten eggs coddled for breakfast,
            found a monk who's found a tape recorder,
                       my new song waiting to be sung,

                      "Light works as an anointing material,
                    works its way, works its way   into my body…"

2.
                        the day barely begun   but alive I hear
       leaves   almost name
          the feeling   on my face   they are trying
              to say: listen,   you are happy. This rustle I take to mean content.

3.   Trees do not let you down,   oh their leaves bend,   and
                  daily   they shake out   their grief,   but
only the rarest of tornado can fell one,   pruned well they withstand
                         even
                                this;
             Trees I think of as   answers,
                                   love
            in   solitary monastery   air.

Warren Cariou

CHAPTER ONE *from* L AZARUS

Tuesday, June 14
St. Joseph's Benedictine Abbey

THIS IS NOT A CONFESSION. No direct line to the Almighty, no appeals for absolution. I will spare the Lord my attempts at honesty, because they aren't the same thing as truth. As soon as I understand the truth I'll be ready to confess, but in the meantime I can only do what the bishop has sent me here to do: pray and rest and meditate, and stay as invisible as possible. This last humble duty would be easier if the monks could give me one of the hermitages on the south side of the abbey grounds, but for the moment all of these meagre dwellings are occupied — perhaps by other clergymen seeking escape from their parishioners. The hermit's life seems to be enjoying a renaissance these days. Maybe after lunch I can convince the abbot to build a new subdivision of shacks in the northwest quarter. I'd like one overlooking the pasture, so I can watch the cattle grazing in easy oblivion as I wrestle with the question of what I am.

 I count it as a blessing that the bishop sent me here. Perhaps I'm even thankful for Father Remy's treachery in reporting my troubles to our superiors. At breakfast today a retired deacon was explaining the Church's doctrine that abbeys and convents do not exist in the world. They are a different space altogether, an alternate universe maybe. That might be why I feel like I've done a rope trick, climbing out of my former life into a new one where none of the old encumbrances apply. Such is

---

St. Peter's was an important part of my writing life long before my first publication. I attended several summer colonies there in the late 1980s and early 1990s, and while I didn't write about the abbey at that time I knew that someday I would. When I began working on *Lazarus* in the winter of 1996, I realized that the abbey would be the perfect setting for the frame of the story, so I came back to St. Peter's for the colony that summer. I remember that when I wasn't revising the story, I paced around the abbey grounds, imagining how my main character would experience the place. I recall he liked the raspberry patch nearly as much as I did.

my hope in any case, though I know that the dark shadow of my own doubts has followed me here, and I worry that Lucius Drake's rumours of my so-called miracle could arrive at any moment.

As an extra precaution I have gone incognito, signing in under my dead father's name, pretending to be a civil servant like he was. No one has disbelieved me so far. The best thing I can do is keep to myself — which is why I want a hermitage. For now, I try to enjoy the place from the safest vantage points. I stay in my room during the day, or I walk out to a secluded prayer hut in the forest south of the barns. Even from these enclosed spaces I can sense the gardens ripening around me. The flowers are everywhere. And when I see the monks out in the fields wearing their coarse monastic robes as they hill potatoes or pick raspberries or uproot thistles, I could forget what century it is.

I could forget many things. But not belief. The belief of others, that is. It confronts me every moment, in the brassy tolling of the chapel bells, the smell of incense in the hallways, the very presence of these buildings. All of it rests on an unquestionable foundation of faith.

How do we know what to believe? I envy those who have no need to ask that question. They are either saints or fools, but both possibilities seem preferable to the agony of unknowing that inhabits me now. That night, three weeks ago, something happened between me and Lucius Drake, but even though I was there I don't understand it. I was a witness, but only in the legal sense. Lucius has become a different kind of witness, spreading his message around the countryside like an old-time preacher. And Guadeloupe has disappeared. I'm left alone to decide the truth about what I've done.

Two years ago I married Lucius and Guadeloupe in a secret ceremony, and I have never forgiven myself. Father Remy had explicitly forbidden it, but I did it anyway, perhaps because I knew he disapproved, or else because I was intrigued by the thought of clandestine activities. The couple had been to Father Remy's office earlier in the day, pleading with him for a church wedding. They had already been married three days earlier in a civil ceremony at the Calgary airport, where they had met for the first time. She was a mail-order bride. Lucius had been looking for a wife for years, but no woman who had actually met him would consider it. Guadeloupe's parents didn't know any better. They sent her from Mexico because they had fourteen other children and they thought this one, the beautiful one, would have a better life in another place. She arrived in Calgary wearing her cotton wedding dress and toting a trunk full of burnished black pottery that her family had sent as a dowry. Only one small urn survived the trip, she spoke almost no English, and when she got to Immigration she saw her reprobate husband for the first time. She was eighteen years old; he was forty-six. He was also a lumbering, unwashed wildman who smelled of dogs and had never been to church in his life. He looked nothing like the pictures of American cowboys she had seen in the movie magazines that she and her sisters had adored like sacred relics. He was more like the villain in a Mexican soap opera. She embraced him politely but turned her head away involuntarily when his bearded mouth moved toward her face.

And then when she saw that the marriage ceremony didn't involve a priest, she began her prodigious weeping. When they came to me three days later the tears were still coming out of her, and she was so dehydrated that her face was wrinkled up like an old woman's.

This was the only time Lucius ever gave in to her demands. It took him a long time to figure out what she wanted, since they couldn't speak each other's languages, but eventually she made him understand that she didn't consider them married until it had been sanctified by the Church. Lucius didn't understand the fuss, but he was so frustrated by the weeping that he finally took her into town for a second marriage. I heard them down the hall in Father Remy's office, Guadeloupe sniffling and sometimes repeating a short prayer in Spanish, Lucius demanding to have a wedding then and there. Father Remy refused — which must have taken some backbone, given Lucius's belligerence and his reputation for settling scores. Father Remy said they would have to take a marriage preparation course, which would take eight months, and he said Lucius would have to consider converting to Catholicism. There was a storm of shouting and foot-stomping and Spanish litanies, and I was beginning to enjoy the trouble he'd gotten himself into, when the couple suddenly left his office and appeared in the doorway of mine.

Lucius was a huge man, his head the size and shape of a pumpkin, his limbs post-like, and his posture almost comically malevolent. His face was lit with a permanent glowering, his eyes inflated with amazement or rage, like a professional wrestler on TV. But it wasn't Lucius who convinced me. It was his tiny, rumpled bride, cowering under his arm and looking at me through the film of her tears with an expression of unshakeable faith. It was not supplication. She wasn't begging me for help. She already knew I was going to help, and she was thanking me in advance. I was so unnerved by her certainty that I went along with it. Not then, not with Father Remy listening down the hall, but later that afternoon, when he had already retired to his bedroom with his customary magnum of sacramental wine. I was trimming the cedar shrubs in front of the church, and they came by in Lucius's ancient International half-ton. He stopped on the edge of the road and waited for me there, his bride staring out the open window with a sibyl's dark conviction. I put down the hedge trimmers and walked to the passenger door and opened it for her.

"Park on the other block so he doesn't see you," I said to Lucius, and he nodded and took off in a maelstrom of dust and blue smoke. Guadeloupe and I were left there on the roadside, and I didn't know what to say. She wouldn't have understood me in any case. But she placed her tiny hand on my elbow, and smiled broadly, so I saw the row of fillings on her lower molars. She trusted me. I led her into the church and we waited at the altar for Lucius.

I was too nervous to appreciate how ridiculous the whole scene must have been. Lucius standing at the altar in his workboots and jeans and plaid lumberjacket, looking up at the crucifix on the back wall as if it was about to tumble down upon him. He sniffed at the remnants of incense in the air, and stood with his hands in his pockets. He had bought a huge white cowboy hat in Calgary for the first wedding, and he wore it again now, brazenly, right up to the altar. When I told him he had to take it off, he cringed and glanced nervously at the crucifix again before prying it off his enormous head and placing it on the carpet beside him. In those surroundings, which must have seemed bizarre to an irreligious man like him, I was temporarily his master. He wouldn't look at me, only at the crucifix or else at the statue of the Virgin in her crèche beside the pulpit. He even seemed wary of Guadeloupe, since he saw that she too knew something about this strange and lurid place, and perhaps he suspected that she could use it against him.

I sensed the power I had over him, and it was so gratifying that I tried to prolong my preliminary instructions. Here was Lucius Drake, the scourge of Windfall — gambler, drunkard, criminal — trembling before me on the lowest step of the landing. I had to make the most of it.

"Mr. Drake," I said. "Your wife is a Catholic. You may not have known that yesterday but you know it now, and you're going to have to accept it. That's why I have a condition. I can't perform this service unless you make a solemn promise here before God that you will bring her to this church at least once a week to attend mass and to receive the sacraments."

He was confounded by this proposal. His forehead produced a fantail pattern of pudgy creases, and his eyes lost their focus, as if he was attempting some impossible computation. When no solution was forthcoming, he exhaled heavily and glanced over at his grinning bride, who had no idea what we were talking about.

"Okay," he said finally. "I promise."

"Before God?"

"I promise before God to bring her if she wants." He spoke haltingly, as if it was he and not his wife who knew only twenty words of English.

I went on with the ceremony then, at a frenzied pace, elated that I had humbled him. He repeated his vows in the same empty tone as he had spoken his promise. Guadeloupe knew how to say "I do," and she said it ecstatically and more often than necessary. Finally I pronounced the blessing on their union, in the slightly disapproving echoes of the empty church. I felt giddy with transgression and with the knowledge that I had extorted a bargain out of Lucius Drake. I watched their awkward kiss, feeling suddenly that it was perverse to be the only onlooker. There should have been a burst of applause at that moment, and a blinding crescendo of flashbulbs, but there was only the rustle of Guadeloupe's dress and a surprised moaning sound from the depths of Lucius's chest. I was embarrassed, as if I had been spying on them in the honeymoon suite, and I fled back into the sacristy without waiting for them to finish. As I moved down the dingy passage toward the rectory, I heard Guadeloupe calling out her thanks in Spanish.

I will give Lucius credit: he lived up to his promise which is more than anyone could have expected. He never set foot in the church again, but Guadeloupe arrived every Saturday for seven o'clock mass. She sat in the front pew just below the pulpit, and then after the service she knelt next to me in the dark and said her confession in Spanish. This was our arrangement from the beginning. "In Spanish, *Espagnol*," I said to her the first time. "God will understand." She often spoke for many minutes, and with loud defiance, as if she was wrestling with each sin as she pronounced it. Sometimes I understood a word or two, but after a while I stopped trying to make sense of the sounds and simply let them envelope me. As I came to know more about her life with Lucius, I began to think of her confession as a song, an epic hymn of pain and isolation. Sometimes I wept as I listened to the flow of her syllables. I couldn't imagine what her sins might be, that they could call forth such a deluge, wave after wave that encompassed me in sorrow. Most probably it was not her own sins she was recounting, but those of her husband.

I came to depend on Guadeloupe, to look forward to the sound of her voice in the confessional. Maybe it was a kind of catharsis, or an exaggerated sense of compassion for someone so unhappy. But even more, I felt responsible for her. It caused me endless torment to know that I had made her suffering possible, but at the same time it put me in the gratifying position of being her confidant, the only person in the world whom she could trust.

I offered to give her English lessons after confession, and Lucius often allowed it, when he was off drinking or gambling somewhere and didn't want to bother picking her up. Sometimes we sat in the rectory kitchen reciting verbs until midnight, and several times I had to give her a ride back home because Lucius didn't come to get her at all. She never told me she was in anguish, but I could see it in her eyes, and in the way she was so extraordinarily grateful for even the most banal kindnesses — a cup of tea, a tin of cookies to take home. When I gave her an English Bible to practice her reading, she broke into tears, and then apologized half a dozen times for drawing attention to herself.

She gave other hints about her desperate situation too. Once she told me she had been having recurring dreams about a black wolf that followed her everywhere. It was a brief but terrifying scene, and she trembled when she described it: moonlight, and the river enclosed in fog, and the black wolf walking toward her across the water. "Like our Lord," I said when she told me, but she was certain it was not Him. "El lobo, he's eyes are shine like stone," she said, and pointed to the yellowed zirconium in her wedding ring. Since the first time she had dreamed about the wolf, she had been terrified to go near the river, which was only a few yards from their house. Lucius sometimes forced her to go down there simply because he knew she was afraid.

Gradually I learned more about Lucius's vicious temper, about his drinking, and the people he called his friends. She never said outright that he had done anything illegal, or else I would have had grounds to send the police in there and take her away. I should have tried it in any case, if they would have listened. Everybody knew that Lucius ran more than one shady operation, but he'd never been charged with anything except impaired driving. He didn't seem to fear the police at all. He ran moonshine to the men who worked out at the pulp mill, among others, and he just sold it off the back of his truck like they used to do in the old days. Twenty bucks a gallon for everclear so potent it almost evaporated before you could drink it. The pulp mill boys lined up for it, but none of them ever drank with Lucius or even talked to him much. He was beyond their comprehension.

People were scared of Lucius because they thought he was crazy — which was not an insupportable conclusion. He had earned an undying reputation as the district loony the summer he'd started his infamous Bird Zoo. It was seven or eight years ago. The highway near his place goes north toward the provincial park, and he must have thought he could capitalize on the tourist traffic, because near the bridge he put up a sign that pointed down the back lane toward his yard and said simply "Bird Zoo 1 MI." He has always considered himself an entrepreneur. He slapped together some makeshift chicken-wire bird cages in his front yard, and there he displayed his collection of bedraggled magpies, robins, grackles and starlings, along with his prize attraction: a breeding pair of pheasants he had taken from Lenny McKay in lieu of a moonshine debt. Luckily for the birds, a weasel put them out of their misery before the second year of the operation. This shut down the business even more effectively than the SPCA could have done.

Lucius's dogs were another reason that people shied away from him. He was known as "The Dog Man" because he owned at least a dozen of them in various states of mutilation, and they followed him everywhere in a pack. I don't know how they survived without him when he went to Calgary to pick up Guadeloupe. The were the walking wounded, each of them missing some essential part: an eye, an ear, a leg. He had more sympathy for canines than for any human being. People took their injured dogs to him, and he performed impromptu surgeries on the kitchen table. He was the best amputator, stomach pumper, porcupine quill remover, and general dog doctor in the district — better than any of the veterinarians, but best of all, he worked for free. Just for the love of dogs. As his reputation spread, people started dropping their lames and strays in his yard, and he always took them in.

Lucius had been The Dog Man for years already when Guadeloupe married him, and it was clear when she arrived that the dogs considered her a threat. They never attacked her, but sometimes they herded her around the farm like a lost sheep. She took it especially hard when she saw that Lucius was kind to them, because it showed her that he was capable of human feeling. She thought there must be something wrong with her, that he preferred to give his affections to a pack of maimed dogs instead of to his own wife.

There wasn't anything I could do, legally, until Guadeloupe was willing to leave him. I told her she was a landed immigrant now, that she had rights and didn't have to depend on Lucius for anything. I said I could take her away to a place where the bad dreams would stop. But all she said was "I am married." As if she had expected such a life from the beginning and was now resigned to it. To me, it sounded like a reproach, because I had allowed her to marry him, knowing what I did. If I had refused, as Father Remy had, she probably would have gone back to Mexico.

Finally I became so distraught at watching her misery that I suggested she seek an annulment. I dared to hope that the marriage had never been consummated, though I was too embarrassed to ask Guadeloupe for confirmation of this hypothesis. Lucius was such an unappealing oaf that I imagined he was somehow beyond sexuality. But even if the consummation issue was a lost cause, I had come up with another loophole. There had been no witnesses at their wedding, and that was enough of a technicality to render it invalid in the eyes of the Church. A petition based on this obvious omission would make me look like an idiot before my superiors, but I was more than willing to undergo some ridicule to save Guadeloupe. Unfortunately she didn't want to be saved. She knew what annulment meant — she had obviously already looked it up in her little blue dictionary — but she shook her head when I proposed it, and looked up from her hands into my eyes. "They will take me away from you," she said. That ended all discussion on the matter.

I kept my silence for a while after that, but still I continued to worry. I watched her for signs of pregnancy. If she were to have a child, she would be linked to Lucius forever. The words I had recited at their wedding ceremony came back to me like a malediction: "You will accept with joy the fruits of your union, and baptise them in the Catholic faith, and raise them in accordance with the laws of the Church." I wished I had left room for another loophole. Of course I couldn't tell Guadeloupe myself about the hazards of pregnancy, but I asked one of the ladies from CWL to talk to her about the natural methods of family planning that are sanctioned by the Church. She never did have a child, so perhaps those arcane rituals worked. Or maybe her barrenness was the one consolation that the Lord sent to mitigate her suffering. A miraculous non-conception.

Unfortunately, the state of Guadeloupe's womb was the only thing in her life that could be considered miraculous. During the second year of her marriage, her situation stabilized at a particular dull level of pain and indignity, and she seemed to be moving through her life like a sleepwalker. She ceased to be amazed by Lucius's brutishness, his anger, his drinking. It all began to seem normal to her. I knew this was the most dangerous time of all, because it was possible that she might give in and become like him. She might lose faith in the Church and in me. So I told her to fight against him, to stand up for her rights, to do everything in her power to change him instead of allowing him to change her. I admit it: I set her against her husband. After being foolish enough to marry them, I tried to break them apart.

I had no idea how dangerous this might be until three weeks ago, when I received a phone call from Guadeloupe in the middle of the night. I was asleep, and I walked out into the hallway to get the phone because Father Remy is half deaf and he sleeps without his hearing aids. I recognized the voice immediately, but understood nothing. All I knew was that she was terribly upset. I tried to talk to her, to make some sense out of the sounds coming at me through the receiver, but it was like her confession: all sound, no meaning. I hated to let go of the phone, but finally I did, and then I struggled to get dressed and ran out to the car.

It was a long drive, more than twenty miles, but I goaded the old K-car up past its redline and crouched forward in anticipation as the farm lights whipped past me on either side like shooting stars. I concentrated on the road, connecting the stream of yellow dots that disappeared beneath the hood, and I tried with rank desperation to avoid thinking about what might be happening at that moment. I had no idea what Lucius might be capable of. I was responsible for everything. I swore that this time I was not going to quibble about legalities; I was going to take her away from there without any further hesitation.

When I turned off the highway onto their rutted laneway, I was almost afraid to go any further. Maybe I should call the police, I thought. But I had already decided, and this time I was going to force myself to go through with my decision. The car bounced along the shadowy road like a shopping cart on a motocross track, but I kept the accelerator down, and finally I crested the last hummock and came into view of their yard light. Guadeloupe was there, outside, leaning against one of the empty bird cages. She was unharmed as far as I could tell. I stopped the car and waited there for a second, wondering where Lucius and the dogs had gone. Then I got outside and walked toward her. She met me a few steps from the front door of the house, and stood between me and the building as if to stop me from seeing inside.

"He has going to hell," she said. She was backlit by the feeble kitchen light which shone through the screen door. I stood apart from her, trying to see her eyes. She had sounded so wild on the phone, yet she was almost serene now. I heard the κ-car's engine ticking as it cooled.

"Who?" I said. "The wolf? El lobo?"

"No," she said. "Him."

As she spoke I saw her eyes, and they were full of darkness like a deer's, and I stepped forward to embrace her, my fingers interlocked behind her waist as if in prayer. I felt her small breasts against me, and her legs through the thin cotton of her dress. She held me too, her forearms crossed behind my head, pulling my face down toward her shoulder. The smell of Lucius's cigarettes in her hair.

"You will forgive," she said.

It was an unmeasurable time, a time that would have a before and an after but no connection to either of them. The kitchen light diffracting through her hair like a comet. I couldn't speak. My legs began to shiver, not from cold. She was whispering again but I didn't register the words, only the general shapes of them. There had been a party. Adeline Lajeuness and a man named Percy and another one. Cards. Moonshine. Something unpardonable.

"*Imperdonable,*" she repeated more loudly. "He said to me things, he did to me things. Now he is in hell."

"What do you mean?" I said. I loosened my grip on her waist and tried to step back so I could look at her face, but she wouldn't let me. She held on tighter to my neck. I felt her rib cage pulsing like a bird's. Through her hair, in the dim space of the kitchen, I thought I saw something move.

"I hit him," she said, and finally loosened her arms from my neck. "With the gun. You will forgive?"

"You haven't — "

I broke away from her then, and ran toward the screen door. She didn't follow. I opened the door and stepped into the room, my shoes loud on the hollow floor. Lucius was laid on his back across the spindly table, his treadless yellow bootsoles facing me and the rest of him receding toward the far wall like a wide-angle photo. The boots, the curving planetary mound of his plaid belly, and in the far distance a spray of crazy bristles from his beard. Both arms were cast over the side in a gesture of irrelevance. His dozen dogs were crouched near his right hand like diffident apostles, unsure if they should lick the palm. They wore the badges of their own multiple wounds, their contusions and amputations and missing organs, but they hadn't considered that their healer might be vulnerable too. They glanced back and forth from Lucius to me, licking their black lips in consternation.

"Lord save us," I said, but I still didn't move. Three chrome chairs were overturned, and an old lever-action rifle was braced against one of them, the barrel pointing above the dogs' heads. The whole place smelled of disinfectant-grade moonshine. I heard the screen door swing open behind me and felt Guadeloupe standing there although she didn't touch me.

"He was a devil," she said.

I stepped toward the table, on the far side from the dogs, over the chair and the gun. My leg brushed against his hand, which was stiff. The head was leaned back on the Arborite, the rimy mouth wide open as if awaiting a tonsil exam. The left eye was half open, so Lucius looked like one of his dogs, piratical and squinty. The wide white tract of his forehead was interrupted by a gargantuan knob that protruded above his right eyebrow like a nascent horn.

One of the dogs keened as I bent over to listen for breath at the toothy cavern of Lucius's mouth. I looked back down the body toward the metallic worn-through toes of the workboots and saw Guadeloupe framed between them, still holding the screen door open, watching almost nonchalantly. I've seen a lot of corpses in my time as a priest, and I knew without checking for a pulse that this was one. No sign of respiration. I could sense the frigid inertness of the body without even touching it.

"May the Lord Jesus Christ have mercy on your soul," I said, reflexively, and drew a sign of the cross in the air above his head. I couldn't help thinking about my own role in this. First marrying them, and then turning Guadeloupe against her husband. Coveting her. The magnitude of my sins rose up in my mind with dizzying force, a whirlwind of iniquity that engulfed me so suddenly I almost cowered down against the body. Guadeloupe's eyes, and the questioning eyes of the dogs, and the baleful Polyphemus on the table squinting up at me.

"Forgive me," I said, and placed my hands over Lucius's face, and closed my own eyes. But I didn't see darkness. I saw a vague misty nimbus surrounding an empty shape. It looked almost like the Horse Head Nebula, except this shape was a human form, head and shoulders ensconced in light. Lucius's pate was resinous and cold. The skin around his wound was so taut it seemed that some kind of volcanic excrescence was about to burst forth. The empty shape came closer. It waded through the light, down and down, toward a place behind my eyes. When it arrived there, I felt something hot and fugitive flooding down my arms and into Lucius's face.

I pulled my hands away and stepped back, kicking an empty moonshine bottle with my heel. It spun like a lobbed hatchet or a throwing star, something deadly, ringing against the nailheads that protruded from the floorboards, and it stopped with the open screw-top pointing at me. I held my hands away from myself, palms up, like a scrubbed surgeon. I almost expected them to be stained, but they were as white and damp as ever. I glanced at Guadeloupe, who was staring behind me at the corpse, her eyes all pupil, her fingers clenched on the edge of the screen door. I was going to say something, but didn't. A sound interrupted me, a sound like the wings of crows in the distance, approaching in their black and shapeless cloak to smother my words. It grew louder for several seconds and then stopped abruptly with an almost flatulent burst, a hideous piglike snort cut off and the crescendo. I turned around involuntarily, despite my furious desire to keep staring at the screen door, and I focussed on the body in time to see Lucius swimming his maddened way into a sitting position. Guadeloupe said something in Spanish. Lucius edged forward on the table until his feet swung freely. He took another breath, shook his head three times, and then he recognized his wife. He gazed at her with idiotic adoration.

"The Lord is with thee," he said, and smiled childishly, his eyes suddenly gushing with tears. At the sound of his voice the dogs broke into thunderous exultation, and they all sprang toward his lap with slavering jowls and frantically wagging tails. It looked like he would be torn apart, but he fended off the horde with quick thrusts of his feet and blithe breast-stroke motions of his hands. The smaller dogs caromed away like deflected hockey pucks and tumbled to the bottom of the pile. The larger ones recoiled back onto their haunches, howled, and jumped again. Lucius kept pace with them, his limbs pumping rhythmically as if he was trapped in a crazy new-fangled exercycle. But he didn't speak to the dogs or give them any sign of recognition; his eyes were all for Guadeloupe, and he aimed that blissful smile at her as if bestowing a gift or benediction, his copious tears dangling from his beard like jewellery.

Guadeloupe had been standing motionless with one hand on the screen door, but suddenly it slammed shut and I glimpsed a swirl of her dress as she fled toward the river. I burst out the door after her, leaving Lucius to contend with the dogs. There was a rectangle of light on the wet grass and after that only murky half-tones and the shocking face of the moon and the blur of movement that had to be Guadeloupe. She was faster than I would have believed. I dodged a birdcage, a sapling, a prehistoric tractor. My feet seemed to make no sound, and the howl of the dogs quickly receded. I lost Guadeloupe in a stand of trees and slowed down to get my bearings. In a few steps I saw the river below me, a fan of moonlight on the rippled water. I stopped, listened for something other than the quick flow of my own breathing and the muted din of the dogs. Nothing.

"Guadeloupe?" I called. "It's only me. Father Silvan. Don't be afraid."

She didn't answer, though I knew she had to be close enough to hear. My eyes had adjusted to the dark and I could see that there were only about twenty trees in the bluff. If she had run across to the next clump of poplars I would have seen her in the moonlight.

"Come with me in the car," I said. "I can take you to a safe place, a place where you won't be afraid. You shouldn't stay here anymore."

I saw a quick movement from behind one of the poplar trees near the edge of the river bank, and I was just beginning to smile when the moon made a sudden swoop in the sky, down to the water and back up, and I heard a noise like an apple dropped on cement. Something had struck my head. A rock. It tumbled to the ground at my feet.

"Go!" Guadeloupe hissed. Another rock bounced off the tree I was leaning on. "You are my bad dream. The wolf. It is you!"

I shrank behind the tree, pressing my shoulder against it and standing as straight as possible to minimize the angle. I bleated her name but she didn't answer. My skull was throbbing above my right ear where the rock had hit, and I reached up to check for blood. I felt a dampness on my scalp, and the beginnings of a lump, but it didn't seem serious. I heard Guadeloupe moving again in the bush, probably gathering more rocks.

"I'm trying to help you," I pleaded.

She appeared suddenly beside me, brandishing a huge leafy stick the size of an uprooted sapling. Her face was outlined in the moonlight, her once-demure features clenched in grim ferocity.

"Only a devil could do what you have done," she said.

I had been preparing to reason with her, to negotiate, but now I hesitated. Her certainty unnerved me. What *had* I done? That empty shape was still lurking inside me somewhere. I could feel it prowling in my body like a piranha in a bowl.

"I didn't — " I said, but couldn't complete my denial. To say anything more about it would be to give it a life of its own.

"You did," she said, and pushed the sapling toward me, shaking a cluster of foliage in my face. I tried to wrench it away from her but ended up with only a handful of leaves.

"Devil!" she yelled.

Our scuffle was interrupted by the sound of Lucius calling Guadeloupe's name. He said it as if he had never pronounced it before, which may well have been the case. He had always called her Lou until now. Guadeloupe and I turned toward the house to see his colossal silhouette crowded into the doorway, a clamour of dogs behind him. He peered back and forth across the yard and repeated her name again like a bird call.

Guadeloupe took a quick breath as if she was going to answer him, but before she could speak the dogs made a concerted rush at Lucius and pushed him out into the yard. They flowed around him as he stumbled in the grass, and when he stopped they kept running toward Guadeloupe and me, moving as a single being, a dozen-headed mongrel Cerberus that stretched out into a serpent as the larger dogs pulled into the lead. Even though each of them was missing something, they all had their jaws and most of them still had teeth, which were visible in the moonlight as they barked and growled and bayed across the yard. Lucius ran behind them, waving his arms and trying unsuccessfully to whistle while hyperventilating.

"Hurry!" I said, and I grabbed the sapling again and tried to drag Guadeloupe toward the car. She followed for several steps, but then she let go and I was catapulted toward the stream of dogs, stumbling nose-first over the quackgrass with a severed piece of poplar dragging behind me like a travois.

"I hope they kill you," she yelled.

I didn't have time to plead with her again — the lop-eared doberman was nearly upon me, and I swung the sapling around to defend myself. I was still twenty yards from the car. The dog bounded straight for the end of the stick, clamped its jaws onto it, and flailed its head around like a frenzied shark. The sound was horrible. Two other dogs caught up with the doberman and snapped at the stick. It would only be a second before they figured out that I wasn't connected to it. I had a momentary vision of my own leg caught in such a hopeless tug-of-war, my foot swinging back and forth like a kite in a tornado. I dropped the sapling and fled.

The large dogs stayed with the stick, but the second wave — those with short or missing legs — saw me making my escape, and they raced across the yard to intercept me. Five steps from the car I tripped on a kamikaze terrier and only regained my balance when I banged into the passenger door. I yanked on the handle and wedged myself in, but as I did I was savaged by a three-legged beagle that clenched onto my right ankle and wouldn't let go, as if the mutt believed it had found its own lost leg and refused to relinquish it a second time. I had to reach down and pry the dog's mouth open, risking further injury from the flurry of snapping jaws that surrounded the beagle. I succeeded, and shut the door quickly, and slid across the seat to the driver's side. Lucius and Guadeloupe were no longer visible, even when I switched on the headlights. Nothing but dogs and empty cages in the yard. Maybe I should have waited, but my ankle was bleeding and my forehead ached and I couldn't even begin to think about what had happened. I started the car and spun out of the yard, mulching two long strips of grass behind me. I kept looking at the rearview mirror for Guadeloupe, but she was gone. I haven't seen her since.

(1996)

David Carpenter

At Night, the Writers

It's after midnight in the kitchen
thirty-one below and the popcorn's all gone
the sink is full of wineglasses and mugs
writers   slumped around the table
like a bunch of old shoes
all worn out but the tongue
words are getting harder to come by
like the sound of a tommy gun
laughter erupts in staccato bursts
the conversation rolls over
silence threatens
dread silence

One by one the words are slipping off to bed
the writers watch them go
now they're leaving in groups
the nouns detach themselves from the verbs
mumble their way out the kitchen door
mutter down the dark hallway
reluctantly the modifiers follow
expletives still want to party
they and the indefinite articles
will be the last to go
and then the writers

All through the winter night
in a storm of letters
they flounder after lost words
letters stick to their brains like fridge magnets
no no no you don't understand
it's *words* I'm looking for
the writers in pajamas
standing beneath the windows
of their favourite lost words
holler *Stella! Stella-a-a-a!*

Morning comes too soon
I wake to the clang of cathedral bells
dislodge from my teeth
just the husk
of a kernel of corn

(2001)

I was on the Saskatchewan Writers/Artists Colony Committee with Anne Szumigalski when we first visited the abbey in the early winter of 1980. We fell in love with the place, reported back to the committee, and it was adopted as one of our retreat sites. Little did I know, back then, that I would spend so much time writing out there. I've walked the mazes for twenty years and I never tire of rediscovering the flora and fauna and reacquainting myself with the brothers and fathers who host us. Best of all, I get more serious writing done out there than in any other place in the world. Every member of the community works at the abbey, and so do we (when we're not playing badminton). St. Pete's is a place where work is sacred.

David Carpenter

A Piece of Quartz Crystal

SATURDAY, AUGUST 3. Grey rags drift across the prairie, nebulous and dull as dryer lint. Not clouds today but *nuages*. Draw out the word for several yawny seconds. Perfect day for reading instruction manuals.

SUNDAY, AUGUST 4. Light rain. A sky of leaden gloom. Ideal conditions for brooding over the death of summer.

MONDAY, AUGUST 5. Great grey layer of slutswool ranged all the way down the horizon. The clouds have the precise shape and woolly texture of dreams from a sheep's brain. On such days the sheep fall asleep counting clouds.

WEDNESDAY, AUGUST 7. Dreamt last night of Lake Louise. That eighteen-year-old feeling. No clouds today. Deep sky blue from stem to gudgeon. A clean slate, you might say. Perfect day to begin something.

Let me begin. I am at St. Peter's Abbey. No negotiations at the gate. You just knock and then a-walk on in. The presiding spirit of this version of paradise is Father Peter. A few years ago he was running the *Prairie Messenger* and fiddling with computers. But wasn't he the guestmaster then? And wasn't he the captain of the abbey's baseball team? And didn't we see him on a tractor, heading for a field of potatoes?

Now he is the abbot. Peterabbot, they like to say. Yesterday he was either in Brazil or just returned from Brazil. Perhaps both. There is no general agreement. Peter is like Chicken Man. *He's everywhere, he's everywhere!* Everywhere smiling in his black soutane, everywhere fierce in his badminton shorts. Everywhere like his Boss, the Cloudsmith.

At this precise moment, Peter is at vespers. This is hard fax, as they say in the news business. I know, because I am there too, singing and taking notes in my pew.

The holy men chant beneath the arched ceiling of a high chapel, which hums beneath the great blue vault of the sky. Priests and monks in black robes. Most of them are over fifty, many over seventy, a handful over ninety. Their voices are faint, strong, discordant, rich, on key, off key, everyone's voice a few minutes out of sleep and echoing like voices in the catacombs.

This cathedral and this abbey are one mile east and south of the town of Muenster, Saskatchewan. The prairie all around Muenster is grain and willows from horizon to horizon — all except for the vast canola fields of squinting yellow. And of course our little atoll, St. Peter's. It is run by Benedictines, who are famous throughout the world for their hospitality.

The abbey is the size of a large farm. It has forests with mazes, big meadows with wildflowers and apiaries for the annual honey harvest. It has a ravine and a pond in the woods next to the railroad tracks and a series of pig barns and corrals for horses, pens for chickens, a patchwork of fields for vegetables and sizable orchard for berries and apples and plums — all this grown and processed by the brothers and fathers. They even make their own wine from the fruit in their orchard.

There's a baseball diamond and a track for runners and an academic college and a cathedral in the middle of the property. Where, right now, the Benedictine brethren are still at their vespers, and so am I, this evening's token sinner.

I don't smirk about my status as a non-Catholic. An agnostic, actually. I don't feel as though I'm a secret agent for nonbelievers. I'm always humbled by the openness of these Benedictines, who play host to so many artists and writers, year after year. They don't just tolerate us; they spend time with us. Willingly, I suspect. They don't catechize, but their doors are always open.

If you want to pass the time watching clouds, you need only wander along one of the mazes out to where the trees stop and stand at the edge of the prairie. Or you can climb up to the bell tower and gaze out at the copper light of August. You can't do this in Saskatoon unless you live in a high-rise. And in a high-rise you can't smell the wind coming off the grass bringing in the scent of aspen rot, the residue of last week's mown hay, the musky perfume of the sloughs.

Coming here is my August ritual. All through the year, though August is the best time, artists and writers come here to finish work and to recharge their batteries. They are lodged in what used to be the convent, a small brick residence surrounded by high carraganas. It has ten monastically spare rooms and a small chapel with a pump organ. This chapel has now become a library. Each writer is given a room, to live and work in. In addition to their rooms, the artists are given studios on the top floor of the college. The meals are cheap and wholesome and the clouds are free.

When you arrive at the convent, you haul your stuff into your room, hoping for one that's shaded from the ripening August sun. The room will be a plain little space with a crucifix on the wall and perhaps a religious motto or two. The walls will be painted in absolutely the wrong colours — pick your worst. The little bed will have a grass-green polyester coverlet. You strip off the coverlet, wrap it up and place it in your closet.

The process of unpacking in a holy place is under way. It's a delicious process, so you don't mind dragging it out. You *want* to drag it out. Unpack your clothes. These are very casual. A sweater for hailstorms and their chilly aftermath. Shorts for hot weather, badminton and volleyball. Sweatpants and jeans and T-shirts, all the ragged clothes that proclaim to your fellow writers and artists that you are a real casual guy and not the slightest bit bourgeois. Lift out the books, stack them in the bookcase. Place the laptop on the big table, printer right next to it on the small table. Connect them.

Oh, you are going to be inspired in this place.

That crucifix. Is it going to make you feel sinful or something? Shouldn't you place it in one of your drawers? Bring it out for inspiration when nothing else works? No?

Leave it there.

Your manuscript, the big one, the one that glows in the dark, the one that will put you over the top this time. Put it next to your books on the shelf where (the room is so small!) you can reach it without having to leave your chair. Your wooden plain straight-backed chair. Seat of wisdom for the next three weeks. Place this manuscript, for good luck, between Munro and Shields.

The pens and Scotch tape and erasers and push pins and paper clips and your Donald Duck stapler and your elastics and bottle of White-Out, all the things you can find in a writer's desk drawer: put them in the drawer that comes with your table.

Your special totem. Hmmm.

(Pause for contemplation.)

This is the lucky object with which this year's manuscript seems to be bonding. You know: the little soapstone loon, the freeze-dried scorpion, the rubber shrunken head from your adolescence, the rusty wobbler you flung into the cattails to catch your biggest pike, the hair jewellery from your weird sweet aunt. You place this object on top of your glowing manuscript that lies between Munro and Shields and you pray that it will bring luck all through the night as you dream. A pagan prayer, of course. About as Christian and selfless as the prayer uttered by a boxer who wants to dismantle the fellow in the opposing corner, who is also praying.

This year's totem is a piece of quartz crystal from a mountain cave somewhere west of Lake Louise.

Hmmm.

Warren Cariou carries himself taut and humming like a bowstring. Right now he's shifting furniture in the next room. He wants to beat Father Peter in badminton. So do I. He wants to complete work on a novella. So do I. He knows that this time he'll connect with his Muse in a way that he's never connected before.

So do I.

My novella. This is a story I've been working and reworking since 1988. In fact, it has elements of a story I wrote in 1965, finished in a dishevelled first draft and never sent off. Thank God. Each version of this story calls on my memories dating back to 1960 and 1961, when I was a carhop and a cab driver in the mountains. I've forgotten most of what really happened back then, but I retain a vivid impression of who I was and an equally strong impression of a parallel existance. *A young man I could have been.*

He grew up in Edmonton. He played a ukelele. He did impressions of James Stewart, Arthur Godfrey and Premier Ernest C. Manning. He had no politics at all, which made him fair game in various quests for the possession of his soul. Ardent socialists and zealous capitalists claimed him for their own. As always, he listened. *The less government the better.* Yeah, why not? *Universal medicare.* Now there's a neat idea.

Almost no one noticed or remembered him from these years. He was a terminal romantic, but not a good bet for romantic lead. He was built for yearning and not for love. A head full of romantic dreams and a body full of hormones, sustained by beer and cheeseburgers. This year's chronic innocent. A listener, a brooder, a follower. He had a tendency to go moralistic on all questions that required a gift for complexity or a measure of worldliness.

I (he, we) arrived at Chateau Lake Louise in early May of 1960. A sodden, snowy day. For the first time in my life, I gazed up at the Victoria Glacier. A great grey amphitheatre as big as a galaxy, booming with avalanches and obscured by clouds. I must have experienced some prairie-boy wonder at that scene. The highest reaches of the chateau merging with the gloom of low-lying clouds — and it just disappeared! All day I kept off the chill with mugs of coffee, breathed in the larchy air and became a great openmouthed yearning happy fool. Mountain madness.

My nickname at that time was Scale, a derivative of Scaley Carp. I bore this name patiently because I was so insecure that *any* nickname was welcome.

It happened like this. Mike McNulty and I were having a gab outside the main door of Chateau Lake Louise. I admired McNulty because he owned a small green sports car called a Sprite and because he was a cynic. He tolerated me because I was deferential to a fault and because he thought I was funny. It was early August, probably around midnight. We were tired. It was the end of a late shift, and McNulty was waiting for a man whose car he had brought up from the parking lot.

McNulty said to me, "Are you going down to the roast?"

"Where?"

"Great Divide Campground. It'll go on way past midnight."

"Nah," I said. "I'm bagged. You going down there?"

"Guess not. Kinda late."

Then McNulty added, "The Lake O'Hara girls will be there."

I shrugged. I had no idea who the Lake O'Hara girls were.

At last the man came down for his car. He was tall, well built, about fifty. He had a florid face and wavy silver hair. He wore a white dinner jacket and he was a little tight from his revels in the hotel. He looked at us.

What he saw was a pair of carhops. We both wore blue serge pants and jackets with the Grayline crest on the breast pocket. We both had brush cuts shaved very close. McNulty was a small dapper fellow — so dapper, in fact, that even in his Grayline blues he looked like a Harvard Blueblood. I was taller, gormless version of McNulty. Perhaps we were both gawking at this distinguished fellow, this playboy.

He was obviously a playboy, the real McCoy. For one thing, he looked like he could *afford* to be a playboy. And although he smelled a bit like a distillery, we were not really put off by the man. Perhaps we should have been, but he was what some of my friends referred to as a neat guy.

The man fixed us both with his glazed eyes and said something like the following: "What I wouldn't give to be as young as you fellas. Up here with all these girls. Take my advice. For God's sake, have all the fun you can when you're still young enough to enjoy it."

The man had spoken with such sadness, such embarrassing candour, that I had to wonder if he weren't an American. But American or not, his words hit home. Even McNulty, who was an intellectual snob and scoffed at everything as a rule, went silent when the man drove off. This neat guy in the white dinner jacket was the approximate age of our parents, and in one short speech he had told me everything my parents had feared I might learn away from home. In my shallow repressed undergraduate heart, I must have harboured a secret desire. It was contained in this man's hedonistic message. He smelled of gin, he was a self-indulgent playboy, he looked like he was born to cause divorce and heartache — he had these sad occasions written all over his face — but he was *carpe diem* in the flesh.

This is an August memory. It has a peculiarly August poignancy to it. The summer is dying, the nights are getting cool. Youth is dying. There's a late night roast at the Great Divine Campground. The Lake O'Hara girls have come down for it. The Lake O'Hara girls.

You guessed it. McNulty and I were gone in a flash, down to the Great Divine.

Well past midnight, I found myself sitting by the campfire between Judy Waitress and Judy Chambermaid. They were both from Nanaimo, BC, and this was their first time down from the lodge at Lake O'Hara to Lake Louise.

"Where, exactly, is Lake O'Hara?" I asked Judy Waitress.

"Hold it still," she said.

She was pouring beer, meant for me, into a very large milk-shake container until it was two-thirds full. Then she made me hold the container steady so that she could turn my beer into a porch-climber by adding about a glassful of Jordan's Branvin port, which sold back then for ninety-five cents a bottle.

Judy Waitress was, of course, a waitress. She had freckles and long brown hair that was very curly and beautiful and out of control — chaotic hair that she complained about and tossed over her shoulders as though someone with no brains at all had imposed it on her. She was almost unbearably cute.

"Lake O'Hara? It's this beautiful lake up over there." She pointed to a star that twinkled somewhere above the Great Divide.

"There are two ways of getting to Lake O'Hara. You can walk from the front of the Chateau Lake Louise all the way to the top of the Victoria Glacier, elevation eleven thousand feet, and basically ski downhill until you crash into our lodge."

"Which Mr. Ford frowns on," said Judy Chambermaid.

"Which Mr. Ford frowns on. Or … you can pay five dollars and take the alpine bus up the road."

"Which Mr. Ford *doesn't* frown on," said Judy Chambermaid.

"Which Mr. Ford doesn't frown on," said Judy the Waitress.

The second Judy (Chambermaid) was, of course, a chambermaid, and she wore a heavy wool sweater with a snowflake design. She had short sensible hair, which was also beautiful. We three settled into our porch-climbers so nicely that all the world became a wiener roast and we the only people that mattered. The Lake O'Hara girls had become beautiful before my eyes. Their presence took the chill out of the night.

Why were the older, more experienced guys not buzzing around these girls? Why hadn't they cut them out of the herd before I arrived? Why was I allowed to come so close to such perfection? I don't remember. If beauty is indeed in the eye of the beholder, well, perhaps I was the only beholder. Or perhaps, as often happened up there, the supply of girls exceeded the demand. Or perhaps the Lake O'Hara girls, having checked out the other Grayline drivers and having found them to be a pretty randy crew, well, perhaps they found me to be a pretty safe bet. Nonthreatening. Perhaps even "cute," under the right circumstances (night vision, porch-climbers).

Along came the driver of their alpine bus and mentioned to the Judies that he was heading back up to Lake O'Hara.

"Are you Mr. Ford?" I said to the fellow.

"No," said Judy Chambermaid, rising from her picnic bench. "This guy is Bob Big Bus."

I shook hands with Bob Big Bus, who seemed like a nice fellow. At this stage of the proceedings (one porch-climber too many) almost everyone at the campground seemed a nice fellow or gal. But I was missing the point. Bob Big Bus was telling the Judies that this was their last chance to ride home with him. That is why Judy Chambermaid was now gathering her things together. She smiled tenderly and knowingly.

"We have to go," she said.

"Now?" cried Judy Waitress. (My, but her freckles were fetching!)

"Now," sighed Judy Chambermaid.

"We just got here," cried Judy Waitress.

"You've been saying that for the last two hours," sighed Judy Chambermaid.

"C'mon," said Bob Big Bus. "Rally"

"I'm too tired to rally," said Judy Waitress. "The might is but a nolecule."

She rose to her feet and gave me a little hug. "Well, Scale, it was real."

Until this moment my nickname had been a thing to be endured. But coming as it did from the lips of Judy Waitress, this name seemed suddenly a term of sweetest endearment. She tossed back her great wonderful mane of hair and made as if to follow the other two back to the alpine bus.

"You can't go now," I said to her.
"I have to."
"Why?"
"I told you."

I must have seemed a bit of a slow learner to Judy Waitress. She told me again. About the alpine bus being the only vehicle allowed up the road etcetera. But I was hearing a man in a white dinner jacket saying something about gathering rosebuds while ye may.

Apparently I made a speech. I have witnesses. The speech was delivered to Judy Waitress but was loud enough for the equally impaired lot around the campfire to hear. My speech was impelled by Eros and porch-climbers, and to anyone with even a touch of rhetorical subtlety, my words could likely have been consigned to the cliché bucket. But porch-climbers do not, as a rule, tend to sharpen the critical faculties, and my small audience found no fault with my entreaty to Judy Waitress. I spoke to her of such things as the fleeting of the summer, the brevity of youth and beauty (the grave's a fine and private etcetera), the fact that if she went back to Lake O'Hara I might never get to know her more intimately —

"Know me more intimately?" she said.
"I don't even know your real last name."
"Oh."

I spoke of memories in old age. I constructed a hypothetical scene, AD 2020, when she was in her twilight years, speaking to her grandchildren, recounting to their young ears this very crossroads in our lives. And would she say to little Annie and sweet Deirdre *No*, we did *not* stay behind at the Great Divide Campground to get to know each other? We went instead back to separate cold bunks divided from each other by a huge eleven-thousand-foot glacier? No? We only *wished* we had stayed together at the roast? Or would she say to this wide-eyed gathering of burgeoning youth… (dramatic pause) *Yes*. Yes, to keep the party going. Yes, to getting to know each other. Yes, we said yes to life itself.

I remember some applause at this point in my speech. It would be so like me to insert this moment of glory into to my account and later call it memory. But. Applause, yes. I remember applause of the porch-climber *carpe diem* variety.

"You don't understand," said Judy.

By that time she was the only Judy left at the campground because Bob Big Bus had given up on her and driven off into the night with Judy

Chambermaid and the other Lake O'Hara girls. I must have realized that I would have to do something responsible to set Judy's mind at rest.

"I've got an idea," I said.

She looked at me with the sort of exasperation one feels in the presence of the irrepressible. *You don't understand.*

"No, seriously," I cried. "I have the answer. McNulty!"

"Maybe he's gone home," said Judy.

"He can't be gone. His car is still here."

"I don't see what —"

"McNulty! *McNulty!*"

I roamed up and down among the rows of necking couples sprawled around by the fire, some of them rolled up in blankets and thrashing sleeping bags.

"Have you seen McNulty?"

"Bugger off."

"Have you seen McNulty?"

"He drowned in the Bow River."

"Have you seen McNulty?"

"# % * * !"

"Have you seen McNulty?"

"Piss up a rope."

After interrupting enough rutting youth to retard the illegitimate birth rate for the entire valley, I just gave up and sat with Judy by the fire. I know we did some cautious kissing. She always closed her eyes first. It was almost too delightful to bear. And then, from a blanket near our feet, there came a voice. Female, exasperated. "Are you the guy looking for McNulty?"

"Well, yeah —"

"Don't touch this blanket!" cried the same voice.

Judy pulled me back before I had revealed anything too scandalous beneath the blanket.

"What exactly do you want from McNulty?" said the voice.

"I want the keys to his car," I said. "Emersion of missy."

"Emersion of Missy?"

"A mission of mercy, you retard," said Judy.

She got a bad case of the giggles and we both lost it for a minute. A long, bare arm emerged like a moray from the folds of the blanket, jingling a set of keys before my eyes. I took the keys.

"Thank you," I said.

"You're welcome," the voice replied.

"You see?" I said to Judy. "You see? Hey?"

She bent over as though to look at her shoes and shook her head *no no no* until her entire head was obscured by her hair.

When she came up for air, she was still smiling. "You don't understand, Scale."

And then she gave up trying to explain anything to me and we went off into the bush and necked and partied and fell in love and sent a large animal crashing through the underbrush and got lost. Then we found our way out back from the bush and continued to party with the last of the partiers and did a long chorus for McNulty, who was still missing in action:

> *we know what you're doing*
> *we know what you're doing*

All things considered, a pretty good night.

When Judy and I piled into McNulty's Sprite we were both perilously close to sober. It was pretty cold. I wheeled the little green car off from the campground and away from the Great Divide. In the space of fifty feet we had crossed over from Alberta to British Columbia. To Albertans with notions of high living and elegant lifestyles, British Columbia was the Promised Land. Maybe to the expectant capitalists of the world Alberta meant oil revenues and fast bucks, but to us it also meant hard work and harder winters. British Columbia meant leisure. Lotusland. Luxury.

Driving west with Judy next to me in the Sprite, I had a vision of moving out to Vancouver Island and settling forever in the bosom of Lotusland and in close proximity to the bosoms of my new love. I saw my entire future as though the mayor of Nanaimo had handed me the key to the city. I turned to Judy and realized that I was too sober to say what I had to say.

"Scale, are you feeling okay?" she said.

"This is the happiest we'll ever be for the rest of our lives."

"Just watch your driving. The turnoff's about a mile up the road."

I said again, a sad three AM drunk. "This is the happiest time of our lives. We have to live. Live!"

"Isn't that what Gooch said in *Auntie Mame*?" said Judy. "'Live'?"

"Live!"

"Live!"

"Live!"

"Turn there!"

I wheeled the little Sprite up a gravel road.

"Slow down! There's a gate!"

I hit the brakes and ground to a gravelly stop just a foot or two from a bright silver obstruction.

"What the hell is this thing doing here?"

"I told you!" said Judy.

"Yeah, but how do we get up to Lake O'Hara?"

"Remember what I said?" You either have to walk in or ride with Bob Big Bus."

"Oh."

"And now I have to walk up the trail in the dark. If I don't, I'll miss my morning shift in the dining room. Jeez."

"I'll walk you home. No sweat."

"No."

"Yes. I mean it. You always walk your date up to the door, right? Even in Alberta."

"No. You shouldn't. It's okay."

"I *mean* it. *I'm going to walk you home and that's all there is to is.*" It was great sounding like such a take charge sort of guy.

"I mean, what if you ran into a bear or something? Seriously. I am going to walk you home."

"Well, Scale, that's real nice of you."

"Aw."

We got out of the car, and Judy went off into the bush. I thought she was just going for a pee, but when she came back she was holding a couple of large sticks she had broken off from a dead tree.

"You might need one of these," she said.

"What for?"

"As a hiking stick. It's mostly kind of um … uphill?"

There was something vaguely apologetic in her tone.

We began to walk up the trail.

"Ah, Judy?"

"Yes?"

"How far is this?"

She looked straight ahead and said, "About eight miles."

"Eight miles? One way?"

"I told you."

Eight miles in the dark along a gravel road, mostly uphill, at three in the morning is certainly one way to get to know a person more intimately.

Trudging up the steepest hills we had little breath for conversation, but each time the road levelled off a bit, we found out all kinds of things about each other. I only wish I could remember them, because whatever we said to each other seemed quite important at the time.

I remember what we didn't talk about: we declared a moratorium, for as long as it remained dark, on any bear conversations.

We rose higher and higher along the road towards the very top of the treeline, and by four or five in the morning we could see our breath. At last a trace of light began to rise back in the direction of the Alberta Rockies. We stopped to drink from a waterfall on O'Hara Creek. We were somewhere beyond weariness, but when at last we rounded the corner between the warden's cabin and Lake O'Hara Lodge, we both cheered.

Just as the sun was rising I found myself leaning against the door frame of the O'Hara staff cabin, smiling into the face of Judy Waitress. I wonder if morning hadn't begun to undo the night's mischievous work. We did exchange addresses, I remember that. And she gave me a piece of quartz crystal she had found in a nearby cave as a keepsake.

In a few minutes I would be going back down the hill, eight miles, to McNulty's Sprite. Perhaps I just smiled at her and she at me. Adventurer to adventurer. And then she made her excuses and said that she had to change into her waitressing uniform, so we said goodbye.

I need a rest, and so I found a bench overlooking the lake and just for a moment closed my eyes. I breathed in. A breeze greeted my nostrils. It had come all the way down from the glacial heights of Wiwaxy or Cathedral Mountain and descended like the breath of God to the alpine meadows, picking up the exhalations of each moist organism in all the gurgling alpine places; it had breathed through the forests of larch, tamarack, juniper and pine. The fragrance was more delightful than any I had ever given myself over to. It smelled green.

I opened my eyes. Down by the shore of the lake was green. A green as green as Scarlet O'Hara's eyes, green as all Ireland. A pale greyish-green around the edges of the shoals, a ponderous green in the middle. The breeze descended on the water, a cloud passed over the rising sun, and suddenly the water was turquoise. The cloud passed, the sun returned, and the water was several shades of green.

Judy and I kept in touch over the years. She was my first love. This lake granted me my first glance at perfect beauty. She and the lake are forever intertwined, a part of my green remembering.

I realized then that I might never see her again. She would go back to Nanaimo to attend Malaspina College or UVic and live among the coastal mists and exotic vistas of Lotusland. I would return to the Prairies. I wasn't a man with plans of his own; I was still somebody's son.

Perhaps I walked all the way back to McNulty's Sprite with this in mind. All the way back to my side of the Great Divide. Waking up, like Bottom, to the memory of a perfect dream. Whatever else I thought about, one thing was clear: my future lay on the grey side of the Great Divide.

When people move to Saskatchewan from somewhere else they sometimes acquire a lost look. I know that look. I wore it from the moment I moved into my apartment in City Park in the summer of 1975.

"Do you miss Alberta?" people would say.

"I miss the mountains," I would say, remembering my mountains at Lake Louise. I miss Lake O'Hara. I miss my dream of moving to Lotusland, the one I never allowed to happen. I miss 1960. It was a very good year. I miss Paradise.

Nothing is quite so boring as people who wish they were back home where the real action is. Nothing is quite so sad as people who wish they were somewhere else. And so you move on, and so, one night lying on a hillside in the Qu'Appelle Valley you and your beloved are gazing up at a meteor shower. You have the intimacy you had so often yearned for, and you are reminded of something that happened thirty-five years ago in the mountains....

An eighteen-year-old boy at the wheel of a green Sprite turns to a tired girl with freckles and says this is the happiest we'll ever be for the rest of our lives.

You wonder why, if he is so damned happy, his tone is so sad. And you realize, of course, that he was wrong. You have probably known this for some time, but tonight beneath the throbbing prairie cosmos, you are sure. Anyone with any brains at all would know without thinking that Paradise is right here. On the hillside. Beside this gal.

Or, believe it or not, in this monastery. Gazing at this manuscript. Held down by this piece of quartz crystal. Today.

(1995)

Sara Cassidy

If Light Was Suddenly New

  if light was suddenly new   the ocean   would hang above us
        the sky   swim through the valleys
we'd cheer   compose dirges   for each ripe bruise
   sustained by the fall leaves   if light was suddenly new
      every cow in the pasture   would be as different
  as Margaret Thatcher and Ella Fitzgerald

  if light was suddenly new   our skin
    would praise cocoa   plums   rice   strawberries
      ivory would rebecome bone   and night
would be so lost   it would rub up against truth
      follow it around

    if light was suddenly new we might not need
the word love   we'd crack egg after egg
to find out how it happens   the roots in the field
    would be partners   in any dance
       stones might be surface all the way through
      stars would be travellers
we would put out dishes of water   to help them home

  if light was suddenly new
     we might never stop touching
    a mouthful of pear   could make us happy forever
we'd care for the moths at the window as if
    they were our own eyelids
     we would sun ourselves
blameless   as the water where Narcissus drowned
    lapping at the wind

(1996)

I came to St. Peter's for a three-week fall poetry colloquium, after having spent most of the summer working out of logging camps, as a tree planter, where I was invariably the only woman. I noticed the row of men's boots inside the abbey doors, the small cities of condiment jars on the dining hall tables (including, thank goodness, Cheez Whiz) and knew I had stepped into another organised community, again one of men. Only, here, women were warmly welcomed, food was grown, animals were tended, and the game of pool was pursuit rather than pastime. The one moment of awe I remember from my logging camps days came in a logger's rapt description of virgin rainforest (which ended, in growled surprise, "Then we go in and destroy it all"). At St. Peter's, awe was like the weather, always present, and generous. Whether perching one afternoon on a haystack, reading books with the poet Barbara Klar, or swooning with two other poets under the northern lights as we tried to collect ourselves with scientific explanations, or blinking at row upon red-blooded row of canned beets in the cellar, those three weeks seemed to live, rather than pass, in a world that had been redeemed. Brother Andre leading the goats across the grass beneath my window seemed to be keeping up that redemption. This is the only poem that ever "came to me," as easily as thinking. After a full St. Peter's day, I'd lain down to sleep, but the first few lines struck with such persistence, I finally got out of bed, crossed the room to the desk and wrote them down. Every time I snuggled back down under my covers, a few more lines set in. I'm glad now I didn't say "to hell with it" and dive into sleep, because the poem now gives me a small way to say thanks to St. Peter's.

Hilary Clark

No Time

7/27/02

The pull, thunder up, negative
air — alarm bells for penitence.

I have no time for time, I have
no mind, at least not human.

Aspen, little hissing tongues.
The victims shimmy their wings.

The grass is long in our poems —
tea musty, saskatoons shrivelled.

"Casta Diva" — empty head, a voice
ascent. Lights out.

7/28/02

Canola struck to abstraction, chartreuse
under thunder. Trucks whizz by.

Those colonists — like ants all over
the abbey! Sunday bells, cloud cover.

Write the word "hieroglyph": black ink,
first yellow aspen leaf.

The master's in his bell, singing
4 PM, 4 PM, grey sky, grey sky.

Black habits — breeze stirs much
more than leaves.

7 / 29 / 02

White sun will thunder, corn shafts
thrust up, high on aether.

Two minds drive the volvo, two-faced
over the dusty roads of Humboldt.

Fade to pillow-white, sleep's impress,
deep. Where are the birds?

Diving chickadees, no crumbs —
Where on the prairie shall I hide?

"For the day will fall, though jewelled
with water," she wrote. Then erased it.

7 / 30 / 02

Blue sky already reversed to white.
Mourning train, no one in the garden.

Mirror has a double chin, a flaw
where my mouth is. *Croccck* — two crows.

White upon white. Wind carries mind
clenched, surrendering,

clenched. Chickadee ruckus in the pines.
So many books, 70 hours and counting.

Corvus, black points pixillate the hour.
Just take one breath, then another.

7 / 31 / 02

A woman's face, no moon since full
on Mount Carmel.

Monks beat up empty boxes, Mack trucks
rev and rerev up the highway.

At 3 PM sleep blows in, like snow
over Red Deer. July 31ST, note that —

Too much tea, clouds cycling on caffeine.
How will I change my life?

Small corners of the night, coyotes
crying, bereft. Another death.

Two odes to St. Peter's:
Summer: Mosquitoes and storms, peonies heavy with rain. You grab handfuls of saskatoons as you walk, keep an eye on those crows. Distractions — wild lilies, roses, canola in the blue distance. Monks tinkering with tractors. But you write, and walk, and mark the bells, and write, then sit on the back steps in the sun. Colonists in the grass, gin and tonics before dinner. The luxury of not washing up, but sinking back into a poem until dark. Until the last draft, the last supper, the last, lingering walk.

Winter: The monks rise in the dark. After breakfast, with fresh coffee, you have hours to sound and scan another poet's lines, mark the bells, inhabit the music. Hours to pencil-scratch, to type and delete, delete. You go to lunch flushed with words. Hours to walk but back in twenty minutes pursued by hungry chickadees, stinging, wind chill minus 40. A nap instead, then wine before dinner. Hours diminishing — another poem, another — until that bleak morning when the hours are spent, and life calls.

Hilary Clark

Moment

I would delay the first stroke —
                        but here the moment
breaks
     on its own urgency —
                      full

then empty, save a line of hours
neatly tolled

the first stroke, first moment
                      missed —
still resonant

a hand gathering the air.

A story knelled of death and rain,
wet lilies in her arms

rain on our skins, a lust —

I would delay the sense, but in the holding
lose it
      one drop, another, sliding down the glass
          her earth-stained face

wind gusting over graves and peonies

our black-shrouded hours —
     crows, yellow leaves
 in June
       oh, hold —
            a stroke past solstice,
slipping —

(1999)

Marlene Cookshaw

St. Peter's, Thanksgiving

*… happiness,
when it's done right,
is a kind of holiness*
      ~ Mary Oliver, Poppies

Go to the far side
of the stack of bales.
The cat will abandon your ankles
at the barn of the yearling pigs.

Make certain the sun's well up
and your shoulders teased loose
by a night of manoeuvres
on the sprung floor of Danceland
an hour south.

The Olson Orchestra's *Yellow Bird*
has nothing on the voluptuous yawps
of the abbey pigs,
near market weight now,
who loll in godly satisfaction
on their sisters' flanks, or
root their bedding till straw
dusts their eyelashes

gold. Such bliss that the morning lies down
for the honourable sky.
The silo fans catch their breath
while poplar leaves shiver
the fall hedge. Mingle, they say. Ask

one of those old men to dance.
Or that lightfooted matron
in lurex shirt, defying the mirror ball
for magic. The last
of the crop is taken up.

One pig straddles her neighbour
en route to the trough.
A young woman with oatstraw hair
jumps her partner, is
jitterbugged into the air.

High-centred. Squealing. The pleasured
sift of the wind through young fall rye.
It's the birthday of the musical twins

and everyone sings. A foursome in seven-step
wheels like a glittering carriage
through splintered light.

Find the bale already shaped
to your body. Move in, snug
under the cantilevered stack,
bedded, overhung, taken in
by the bunched, the gathered,
the fall-silvered mass.

Rub your head in it.
Line the cuffs of your jeans.

Let the abbey bell ring ten times.

"St. Peter's, Thanksgiving" was written near the end of a three-week stay at St. Peter's in October 1996. The Sage Hill Poetry Colloquium was my first taste of the deep affirmation offered in a dedicated writing retreat and the pleasures and friendships birthed in a writing community. It was a reminder too of the haunting prairie landscapes and northern lights I'd grown up with and left behind for rainforest twenty years before.

Gloe Cormie

Eight Sage Writers Journey to Quill Lake

Stubble fields
subtle jazz
coil along the prairie road

Then the twangy tugging
music of Sarah Harmer

We rustle up prairie dust
sparked with sun &
dappled shadow

Our trail of tires —
red with desire

Fields of unshaven skin
bristle Naples Yellow spikes
vertical flashbulbs on the wide
black expanse   John Deere tractors
smack sunlight at us

Our two trucks & a car
move like one dusty caterpillar —

On the gravel road   bucolic bulls
lift their grazing heads to see the action —
a cilia-tickling version of Sarah's
Summertime and the livin' is easy ...

Fish jump in the fall water of Quill Lake
anticipate our visit.

(2000)

Lorna Crozier

The Divine Anatomy

1. God's Mouth

That prairie sky you rhapsodize
is one huge yawn. He's bored
with what you're doing here.

Like a tone-deaf kid
who's been told
he carries a tune in a sieve,
God mouths the words.

The animals of course
can hear him. Look at that dog
who stares into the night,
his ears on fire —

it's God's great singing.

(1999)

I couldn't write without St. Peter's. I've been going there for too many years to count. Now, because I live on Vancouver Island, I need to get back to the monastery at least once a year to see the sky, to breathe the smell of dust on grass just as it starts to rain, and to hear the wind-roar of that big cottonwood outside our residence. All of my books have begun in that special place; poems seem to be waiting for me there if I'll just give them the right kind of attention. A chickadee in the palm is worth two in the imagination. I wish I were there right now.

2. His Feet

It's his son's we're familiar with,
long and pale, pegged together.
God prefers the black
foot of the magpie, each toe
distinct and deftly clawed.
Other times he wants
a millipede's multiplicity.

When he walks as human,
under his robes his big toe
is fat as any sea lion,
his little one, blunt and pink
as that famous pig
crying all the way home.

What a journey! Gone so long,
no matter how many feet,
how many soles
he wears out and makes new,
he can't remember the bend
in the road by his mother's house
or the river where she bathed him.
He can't remember she used to
kiss each toe.

(1999)

8. God's Bones

His bones are light,
they are light walking,
light sitting
and standing still.

If he dies
you can't bury them.
Light slips out of
any darkness. In pine
it becomes the pine;
in oak it gathers in the grain.

If he dies
you cannot cremate them.
They are fleshed with fire,
fire-fattened.

Even the smallest bone
in his inner ear —
there's enough light
for the whole world
to read by.

(1999)

Lorna Crozier

A Prophet in His Own Country

The gopher on his hind legs
is taut with holiness and fright.
Miniature and beardless,
he could be stoned or flooded out,
burnt alive in stubble fields,
martyr to children for a penny a tail.

How can you not believe an animal
who goes down head first
into darkness, into the ceaseless
pull of gravity beneath him?
What faith that takes!

I come to him with questions
because I love his ears, how perfectly
they fit, how flat they lie against his head.
They hear the inner and the outer
worlds: what rain says
underground. The stone's praise
for the sparrow's ankle bone.

Little earth-otter, little dusty Lazarus,
he vanishes, he rises. He won't tell us
what he's seen.

(1999)

Lynn Davies

Approaching Vespers

Order for the eye in the long elm boulevard
and its timely shade, the trimmed cedar,
rough spruce in parallel rows.
Beyond the abbey, the roads cut grids
under a sky so big I wonder if it'll fall

like a blanket or in pieces. Two magpies
chase a cat past Mary in her shrine. Bells
call the monks to their late afternoon prayers.
Timing and breath for a hundred years
on this square of prairie. Feet mulling the gravel,

we bring our histories too. One side chants,
the other responds. Brothers industrious
as the ants working the peony buds. My untrained
ear, surprised at the single chanter. Later, the owlet,
ookpik-fat and whistling on the ground.

(2001)

I attended the 2001 Conversation and Silence: A Symposium on Writing and the Natural World. I walked, talked, listened, wrote, went dancing and bicycling, fed chickadees and kittens, and only missed vespers once. I wrote "Approaching Vespers" when I got home. Those ten days at St. Peter's still feed my thinking and writing.

Degan Davis

Saint Peter's Abbey

Confessions
are the most brittle
art:

you are not writing a letter
to your father
years after his death

or to your friends
who may love you through
where you've gone or not gone;

perhaps we should all come alone
to some place where time
is measured in belief

and where after there are bells
there is long silence,
and no one asks anything of you

but you.

Before I came to live at St. Pete's, I had spent three and a half years in Japan. In those years, I inched closer toward a deeper understanding of the Buddhist sense out of which Japanese culture has arisen. In particular I began practicing shodo, or "the way of writing." This calligraphy gave me an insight into a more meditative side of Japan. In fact, when I began to look around me, it felt as if there were two worlds that existed where only a physical or surface one had before. The second was, of course, an inner space, a quiet contemplative world. At St. Peter's for a poetry colloquium, among the rows of trees, the bells and the slower, quieter life, I felt myself entering another place where the physical world was only surface. Daily I met those who prayed, wrote, contemplated, taught, painted, and practiced their own "ways" of being, within the walls of the abbey. In the four months I lived there, I divided my time between working and writing,

Degan Davis

Confessions

I went into the forest
and put my hand out
to the birds
like a perch.

I had no peanuts or seed
but one landed
though I held
nothing.

I have often worn myself
loudly
to the city,
walked through streets
like an accomplishment.

I want to give you
nothing
but my hand

and for you
to take it.

---

and spent many hours walking in the paths around the Mary shrine, singing the psalms with the monks at vespers, searching through the library and perusing the vast array of mystical and sacred literature. Shortly before my departure, I came upon a room that had been used by one of the many religious groups that St. Pete's hosted. On a blackboard I was shocked to find an otherworldly writing, which was both completely foreign to me, and which I could read. It was such a surprise to see this language in a small room in the middle of the prairies, that it took me a few moments to realize why I could understand most of the words: it was Japanese. I ran and got my dictionary to read the rest, then wrote down my ramshackle translation in my notebook. I've lost that note, but I remember the blackboard contained the characters I had practiced many times: *ai*, love, *shizuka*, quiet and, *shin*, heart.   (2000)

Adam Dickinson

Vespers

The first difficulty is air,
its empty rooms, its cupped hands.

Breathlessness is a trap
sprung in the throat,

wearing clouds
on the inside of the voice.

Prayer makes such high cheekbones of the air.

By wanting, by wishing,
the breath assumes a flesh of ears

in the diminished chords of dusk.

But like all earthly faiths, there is only the heat
of having already spoken.

I visited St. Peter's in 2001 as part of Conversation and Silence: A Symposium on Writing and the Natural World. I remember very well the walks I took around the abbey, through the gardens and woods mulling over the provocative theoretical discussions that were taking place. During my time at St. Peter's it was difficult not to appreciate the overwhelming sense of resonant intersection between questions of the spirit and questions of the physical, phenomenal world. These poems have their genesis in various encounters with the rhythms of St. Peter's, be they the rhythms of prayer or those of the apiary and farm introduced to me by the generous monks.

Adam Dickinson

Father Demetrius's Bees

All day over the canola,
small prayers for the sun.
If love could quit its veins, its chemical language,
the airy transmogrification of trembling hands,
the clots that build dark hills in the chest,
it would be these small sparks, these lanterns
that explain plants to each other,
that return home at night,
and write the first desires of things
in moonlit sugar.

Because we cannot simply stand in the sun,
because, in reality, there is no single honeysuckle,
no hummingbird tuning the valves of the heart,
they work in the name of abundance, of gift.
To live is to stick to things, honey in the hands,
the simplest wish crowded with wings.

It is said that when the beekeeper retires,
he becomes allergic to the venom of bees;
What love asks so much?
All day over the canola,
the fresh wax of introductions,
the first deposits of fat
in the catacombs of the heart.

(2001)

Sharon Abron Drache

from RITUAL SLAUGHTER

CHAPTER TWO

THE VAN WEAVED ITS WAY northward through the city on to the autoroute leading away from Montréal. Baruch and Faigele sat together behind the Hasidim. Usually women sat separately, but Baruch was permitted to sit beside his sister since his dress as well as his attitude indicated that he was no longer a follower of his sect. Four rows in front of them were filled, three men in each. With their black coats and broad-rimmed hats, they formed a dark, mysterious barrier. Curious drivers in passing cars peered up at the bright yellow bus with its bold, black lettering in English and Yiddish: *Datschlav, Québec.*

Just beyond Vanier, at a junction indicating the road for the twin cities of Claremont-Ste. Justine, the little bus turned off the autoroute into the service area of an isolated Texaco gas station. The McGill student came to the rear of the vehicle to check the baked goods stored beside Faigele and Baruch.

"What a fuss they'll make if these baskets aren't sealed properly," he complained. "Last week, the wrapping on one of them was loose and the corner of an onion bun slipped into view. I nearly lost my job." Tightening the wax paper and tin foil packaging, he asked Baruch, "What do you think of these Datschlavers?"

"Ask my sister."

"Sorry, I'm not allowed to talk to the good women. Not even to your sister or the rebbetzin. Rules, you know, rules."

"I thought my sister and the rebbetzin were special."

The student snickered. "They're special, all right. I don't mind," he said, "neither does the old lady, but your sister here, she gets a little lonely." He addressed Faigele, in almost a whisper. "You do get lonely sometimes, don't you, sister?"

Faigele looked pleadingly at her brother. Perhaps he would speak on her behalf. But he had been away for so many years. What could he possibly say in her defense?

"You'll see what I mean when we get to Datschlav," the driver nodded. "Won't be long, now." He closed the back door and paid the gas attendant.

Soon they turned on to a winding dirt road. For a few miles Baruch could see only flat land and spruce trees appearing against the low-lying Laurentians. But several bends in the road later, the Hasidic village loomed as unexpectedly as ever on the otherwise deserted country road. The community had grown since Baruch left. There were only thiry-six houses on Datschlav's main street, *Rehov Zion*, then. Baruch counted many more homes, perhaps a hundred, forming a giant square, as formidable as any urban facsimile with a central boulevard enclosed by massive, wrought iron fencing. He could hardly recognize the gardens, planted when the village was established. Individual hills proffering the rebbe's favourite herbs had spread wildly, each variety bearing a sign in Yiddish: fennel, hyssop, sweet cicely, coriander, and marjoram.

Only a few minutes earlier he had read road signs in French. Mature linden trees, like leafy sentinels, lined the pathways used for pedestrians. Park benches faced cultivated rose gardens bordered by white pansies. Baruch thought the boulevard in its final fall bloom appeared to be the only lavish aspect of the Hasidic town until he saw the yellow stucco *yeshiva*, a modern structure at least four times the size he remembered, and the slaughterhouse, expanded in length and breadth to the size of a city shopping centre. Green pastures flanked the two-storey emporium, painted white, trimmed with blue, bearing two signs: *L'abbatoir Datschlav* in yellow, transliterated Yiddish; *Richard Vincennes* in Roman, blue.

The girls' and boys' schools as well as the two buildings housing the ritualaria (one for men and one for women) were yellow stucco, like the holy of holies, the *yeshiva*. In the parking lot beside the slaughterhouse stood a fleet of fifty white trucks, bright crimson curtains hanging in the windows. From the distance, the vertical and horizontal line-up looked to Baruch like a giant cross. He laughed to himself at the absurdity of the Christian image.

"Not the Datschlav you knew, is it?" Faigele asked.

"It's incredible," Baruch answered. "Quite incredible."

"The white trucks, everyone of the fifty is refrigerated," Faigele told him, "and the transports over there, near the slaughterhouse, a hundred of them, all have freezers. You won't believe this, Baruch, but Datschlav delivers *glatt kosher* meat to twenty-seven smaller Jewish communities in Ontario and Québec." She pointed again to the parking lot. Baruch looked in amazement at the trucks shining in the afternoon sun. "And that's not all," Faigele said, "those transports carry *treyfe* to cities and towns as far west as Fort William and as far east as Chicoutimi...."

"So, the Datschlavers must have some money?" Baruch said.

"Money, what do we need money for? We live simply. Look at *Rehov Zion*. Are the homes not as modest as you remember them?"

Baruch had to admit they were. "I don't understand," he said. "You are making much more money than you need. What are you doing with it?"

"Dear brother, do you remember the negotiations with Richard Vincennes when the Datschlavers bought this land?"

"Of course I remember. Months of meetings before Rebbe Mendel Yehudah agreed to let Richard Vincennes remain on his parents' farm to act as a mediator between us and the neighbouring Gentiles."

"But the rebbe wanted Vincennes to keep his distance, to be available only when *we* needed him," Faigele added, stressing *we*. The bus stopped at *Rehov Yakov*. Baruch looked out his window and saw a huge, ivy-covered wall.

"That's where he lives," Faigele said. "In a moment, you'll see the house." The bus passed a driveway fringed with meticulously trimmed cedar leading to a grey stone mansion with leaded glass windows. Wrought iron balconies decorated every second floor window and a spacious veranda on the first floor extended into the front garden. Vincenne's home was extraordinarily luxurious compared to the other Datschlaver residences. Looking back at the drab houses and religious buildings on *Rehov Zion* and finally over to the slaughterhouse, Baruch felt wretched and uneasy.

He recalled how his father had tried to teach him the art of the ritual slaughter, how he had insisted that Baruch accompany him to the abbatoir. He could see his father in the basement of their home sharpening his knives on the grey and black whetstones, his father's index finger nail filed especially to test for sharpness. Again and again he passed this nail over the rectangular blades to make sure there was no flaw that could cause the animal pain. He told Baruch: "One day, these knives will be yours ... watch and learn, my son."

He respected his father too much to tell him he would never use the knives. The shining blades would rust were they left to him.

CHAPTER THREE

The bus pulled up in front of Rebbe Mendel Yehudah Kasarkofski's house. Because he had been away these many years, Baruch thought he should see the rebbe first to ask permission to return for this short, one day visit.

Frima, the rebbe's eldest daughter and his former betrothed, greeted him at the door. How well he remembered her while she obviously had forgotten him. She had the same buck teeth and persistent acne of her youth. To her added misfortune, she also had several holes marking her face, the result of the grotesque creativity of chicken pox she had suffered as a high-strung teenager. But what struck Baruch most was her dark brown head scarf. She was such a homely woman whose best physical attribute had been her curly, blonde hair. Now, he surmised, it was gone. Like his sister and all the other married women, no female was exempt. Frima was as obese as ever, her unkempt bulk contained in a red-flowered dress with long sleeves and a tightly buttoned collar. Each flower had a thin, green stem winding onto its neighbour, forming a vine puffed out by her generous girth. Although she wore black stockings and the skirt of her flowered dress was long, her chubby calves still showed, making her feet look like they were planted only with great difficulty inside her cumbersome oxfords.

Several men already waiting to see the rebbe were seated at the oval dining table at one end of the living room. Frima invited Baruch to join them. Meanwhile, the rebbe's other daughters, Shaindel, Rifkeh, and Rachel joined their sister at the cupboard, giggling fiercely, while their mother, the rebbetzin, strode into the room. A towering individual, she wore a brown-flowered dress, similar in pattern to Frima's. Her head scarf, also brown-flowered, had a wide beak projecting over her forehead. Looking more like a policewoman than a rebbetzin, her scrutinizing eyes and frowning visage added to her authoritarian arsenal. Scrupulous devotion to Datschlaver law had honed her naturally superior demeanor and the padding in the shoulders of her dress further accentuated her charismatic armour. She feasted her judgmental eyes on the men gathered about the table before heading directly for the rebbe's office.

Although she made Baruch feel very nervous, he took advantage of her absence to study the room he had not seen for so long. Still the same white, Italian provincial furniture trimmed with gold: the tables crowded with ornate china, painted with romantic pastoral scenes, totally inconsistent with the Datschlaver way of life. Their rigid philosophy didn't blend with this middle-class décor. He stared at the floral appliqué-cut velvet six-seater sofa and each of the four matching chairs covered with clear plastic. He could see the silver zippers running up the sides of each piece of furniture holding the covers in place. The room was so full that one could pass through only by careful, painstaking navigation. Baruch, of course, knew that the furnishings and other ornaments were gifts to the rebbe and his wife in appreciation for their services, honouring the rebbe's abilities as faith healer and miracle worker.

A plastic runner going from the hall to the dining table and a second runner extending from the rebbetzin's chair at the head of the table to the rebbe's office already bore the brown smudges of the day's traffic. (The streets of Datschlav were not paved.) Under the table, a red-flowered rug completed the unharmonious décor.

After a quarter of an hour the rebbetzin returned with a ledger similar to but larger than Krakower's. She placed it on the white damask cloth which was covered with clear plastic like the sofa and chairs. In the middle of the table sat a large comporte of aqua porcelain, the plate part supported by three plumb cherubim which was itself filled with waxy fruit. She opened her book and began taking attendance.

"Meir Rabinovitch."

"Present."

"Please write here what you wish to discuss with the rebbe," she droned.

Rabinovitch, a seedly looking chap, wearing a blood-stained apron, stoop up. "*Nu!* What should I write? I've come about the kill."

The rebbetzin ran her index finger down an open page. Raising her pudgy palm, she pointed at Rabinovitch. "Wait a minute, mister," she said. "Let me see your hands."

Sheepishly he held them out, his fingernails caked with dried blood, the skin stained with reddish-brown blotches.

"I'll write," announced Rebbetzin. "How many minutes, Rabinovitch?"

"Ten, maybe fifteen at the most."

Rebbetzin carefully recorded the time in her ledger. "Thank you," she nodded. "Moishe Shatsky."

A scrawny man in a navy three-piece suit scurried from his seat at the end of the table. Taking Rebbetzin's pen, he wrote, "Gas for the lorries. *Five minutes.*" Hastily bowing to avoid eye contact with the rebbetzin, his yarmulke flew as though a mischievous imp had propelled it from his head on to her lap. The lady jumped to her feet, standing so quickly that her chair fell over. Shatsky rushed to pick up his cap which had fallen to the floor and to restore her chair to its upright position. The flustered rebbetzin sat down again to resume her roll call. "Reb Lazare Lichtenstein."

Reb Lazare wore traditional garb, a black brocade waistcoat, a satin *shtriemel* trimmed with red fox. When Rebbetzin called his name, he stood slowly, taking off his broad fur-trimmed hat, placing it on the table. Still, his head was covered with a white crocheted skull cap. Two gold and silver tassles in the centre caught the noon sun streaming through the living room window.

Reb Lichtenstein silently paced the distance of the oval dining table before he gave his answer. With his eyes fixed on the men, first Meir Rabinovitch, next Moishe Shatsky, he actually dared to stand so close to the rebbetzin that he could whisper in her ear.

Delighted with himself, he stood back, checking his own black book which he took out of his waistcoat pocket. "Thirty minutes," he repeated aloud to everyone present. Feverishly he computed costs for cattle shipments from Passover to the Jewish New Year. "That includes time to discuss the Manitoba shipment," he added.

Not many Datshlavers were allowed such a lengthy audience with the rebbe. Shaking Reb Lazare's hand, Moishe Shatsky curled his thick lips upward in approval. Rebbetzin sighed, taking a deep breath. It was time to address the stranger.

"Monsieur," she said to him, "your name, please."

"Bartholomew Bessette," he replied.

Humph, she thought. Certainly not a Jewish name. Who is he? What does he want with Rebbe? Strangers are usually accompanied by Richard Vincennes and they sit quietly while he speaks on their behalf. For instance, the municipal tax collector, Monsieur Blanchette from Claremont-Ste. Justine, Vincennes speaks for him. But this stranger pranced in here as if there were no question about his right to speak alone with the rebbe. "I won't allow such impertinence," Baruch heard her mutter.

She rubbed her chin where several grey hairs sprouted and strained her half-closed eyes (no woman worth her Datschlav salt ever looked directly at a male unless he was younger than thirteen) to study his face, announcing candidly to those assembled, "Looks Jewish, this stranger! Monsieur," she at last said to him, "what is your business in Datschlav? The rebbe, he only speaks to Jewish people. Understand?"

"I am a Jew."

"Ah, you have changed your name? You are for some good reason a self-deprecator? But look at you, the way you are dressed… certainly you are not an Hasid… are you really Jewish?"

Baruch nodded, glowering proudly. "Inside I am a Jew." And yes, he thought to himself, I do dress differently, but look at them, in black from head to toe, with the exception of the red fox trimming their hats. Dull conformists… anti-life… joy haters. Their women in sexless, grey dresses are gawking mischievously at me from the hall. Only Frima and her mother dress differently, although grey would suit them too. Their baggy, flowered dresses are even uglier than the drab, joyless garments that the other women are wearing.

Baruch adjusted his green serge tunic, abruptly tugging at the long cape sleeves trimmed with rabbit fur. Rebbetzin, occupied with consulting time slots for the day's audiences with Rebbe, cast a furtive glance away from her ledger, resting her gaze on his thick mauve sash, tied loosely about his waist. From the sash's macramé tassels swung at least a dozen rabbit's feet. The man was mad… an alien… certainly not a believer. She concluded that his eyes were not centred properly and that he might even be a murderer.

Agonizing about what he could possibly want from her husband, she decided to conduct a preliminary investigation before granting him an audience.

"Maybe you'd like something to eat, Mister? A glass of tea, perhaps?" The stranger's eating habits might yield some important clue about his character. Rebbetzin prided herself as a wonderful hostess. She had already served the other three men, happily sipping from their glasses of tea with floating slices of lemon and enjoying the accompanying poppyseed cookies. Reb Lazare dunked his expertly in his tea.

"I baked them myself," she said proudly. "You should eat, Mister, after your trip. Such a trip." She raised her eyebrows.

What trip? He had travelled only twenty miles north of Montréal. Besides, he'd had breakfast at Ben's that morning, not to mention the meal Danny Wintrob had treated him to the night before in the Maritime Bar at the Ritz Carleton: *soupe à la tortue, scampi au pernod, salade romaine avec petits morceaux de bacon…*.

"You eat kosher, Mister?"

He felt a lump rise in his throat. He could lie to her. "After a fashion," he hedged, awkwardly.

"So, you're not hungry, then?"

He knew she suspected him the moment he walked through her front hall in to her living room. Datshlavers were trained to smell trouble and *treyfe*, especially *treyfe apikorsim*. But suddenly her grimace softened. He watched her smile for the first time since she had begun her questioning.

"*Ribonu shel Olam*. Is it possible that you are Baruch Berkovitch, the son of Judah Leib, the slaughterer, *olav-ha-shalom* and the good Rebeccah Leah?"

Baruch nervously stroked his moustache. "Yes," he said and hoped that would end it.

"I didn't recognize you," Rebbetzin said cooly. "Well, look at you… how could I?"

"I am an artist, Rebbetzin," he replied. For himself, his vocation provided sufficient explanation. He chose not to tell her about his teaching position at Columbia. Revealing that he taught art history at that secular institution would baffle her even more than if he told that in fifteen years since he had left Datschlav he had nurtured his art and neglected his religion. Obsessed with the thought of impressing her, he took out his mauve leather satchel from behind the rabbit fur bobbing back and forth on his jacket sleeve. "Would you care to see my creations?" he bravely asked.

Rebbetzin's face turned crimson and her voice grew tense and strained. "I can not look at your art, Baruch. You know it is forbidden."

Reb Lazare closed the commentary he had been studying and announced, "I'll wait in the front hall until the idolater leaves."

Meir Rabinovitch and Moishe Shatsky frantically nodded their heads in agreement. The three men marched out of the room, their hands shielding their eyes. In the vestibule, they stood facing the front door, Meir Rabinovitch engrossed in his recitation of Psalms, Moishe Shatsky re-checking his accounts, and Reb Lazare resuming his chanting of the Datschlaver commentary on the weekly Torah portion.

Baruch waited until they appeared settled before he continued. "I see custom has not altered in my absence. Art is still considered pagan. Come, Madam, surely if I tell you that I am a successful, highly acclaimed artist, I must stimulate your curiosity. We're alone now. You really ought to have a look."

Rebbetzin shrugged. "I suppose it wouldn't hurt if I were to take a peek." She had seen her husband, the grand rebbe, take plenty, closeting himself in the locked room where he had ordered Baruch to store his paintings and drawings when he lived in the community. He often told the rebbetzin that he had felt compelled to control Baruch, but an unusual look of satisfaction mixed with pleasure lurked behind his mask of concern. Once he had admitted to her that Baruch's art was shocking and unnatural. When she asked him to explain further, he provided the customary reply: "It is not for show!"

With trembling hands he wiped his perspiring forehead with his handkerchief before he removed his pictures from his satchel, carefully spreading them on the table. Pictures of Hasidim! Men and women, together!

In one picture nearly fifty gathered in a large circle around a Christmas tree. Each person, including the women, dressed in modern, fashionable clothing, carried a Torah. The women's kerchiefs covered only half their shorn heads. The rebbetzin shook her head in dismay, and he hastily began to pick up his portraits until she stopped him. "May I see another of your pictures, Baruch?"

Deliberately, he chose a painting in which there were just as many Hasidim, but this time they were naked, absolutely, except for the men's *striemels* trimmed with red fox and the women's multi-coloured head scarves. Baruch had drawn only the backs of the Hasidim, the men's bottoms slim, the women's fat and saggy. Rebbetzin screamed when she saw this picture. Her daughters came running from the hall where they had been eavesdropping.

"What is it, Mama?"

"Put those graven images away immediately," she yelled at Baruch. "Don't look," she hastened to warn her daughters.

"Don't look or the Evil Eye will take hold."

Baurch put his pictures back in his satchel. An uncomfortable silence filled the room until the rebbetzin chose to break it. "Look who has returned," she exclaimed, "Baruch Berkovitch, the son of the good Rebeccah Leah and the slaughterer, Judah Leib *olav-ha-shalom*!"

"Ah, Judah Leib!" the girls sang out, "it is good he is not here to see this shame. It would kill him!"

Baruch could not resist. "You did say *olav-ha-shalom*, Rebbetzin? My father is dead, is he not?"

His father was dead, but now he remembered that for these devout Datschlavers, his father was not really dead but merely on his journey to *The World To Come.*

He watched Rebbetzin stroke the hair on her chin before she confronted him. "Is it wise that your mother should see you? Look at the way you are dressed. And your hair, with no sidelocks, surely you will upset her?"

"With all due respect, Rebbetzin, I am her only son and isn't a son, even a rebellious one, a comfort to his mother?"

The rebbetzin sighed. "This is definitely a question for the rebbe."

"I would like to see the rebbe," Baruch assured her, "to ask permission to visit here today. Perhaps, for *shiva* too," he added.

Rebbetzin's daughters examined Baruch as if he were an intriguing, modern monster. They deluged him with questions while the men in the vestibule continued to ignore him. Frima, the eldest began: "Mister, why do you wear a dress?"

Baruch replied simply, "I wear whatever I feel like wearing."

"You choose your own clothes?" Frima asked in disbelief, turning to the rebbetzin. "Mama, how is it possible? *Ribonu shel Olam* will surely punish this Evil Doer?"

"Baruch is no longer one of us," the rebbetzin replied. "He is only a visitor."

"Yes, Mama," she acknowledged like an obedient child.

There was no open recognition of Baruch as her former betrothed. Only a bland, formal acceptance of her mother's explanation. Baruch attributed her apathy to her simple-mindedness as well as to the general apathy of Datshlaver women accustomed to accepting unconditionally all that was said to them by their superiors, usually men, but in this case, the rebbetzin.

Shaindel, Rifkeh, and Rachel raced to the kitchen, each returning with a plate of her own baking.

"Cinnamon buns with raisins. I baked them myself… try one, Mister," Shaindel said breathlessly. Rifkeh chimed in, "Wouldn't you like some of my honey cake baked just this morning?"

Baruch wanted to be courteous but he wasn't hungry. Once again he refused all food offered to him.

"You'll be weak if you don't eat. You should eat, Mister," urged Frima.

Rebbetzin hustled to Rebbe's office to tell him the news. She returned to announce, "The rebbe will see you first, Baruch Berkovitch." In the presence of the pious men, the beak of her head scarf cutting his cheek, she whispered, "It's good to have you home, my boy." Since her brief consultation with the rebbe, her attitude had changed. There were still some miracles, Baruch decided.

(1984)

M.A.C. Farrant

The Mirror

Each morning I wander outside in my white pajamas and dressing gown to squat among the cornstalks. Later I join the monks for coffee and doughnuts in the monastery lounge. The brothers sitting on the couch together worrying over me, their most difficult charge.

The trick I've played on them is to write to Father Abraham, who lives in the city monastery; I've asked Father Abraham to be the father of my yet-to-be-conceived child, placing the letter in the internal mail chute knowing the brothers here will find it and begin their fretful interception. Naturally the letter can't leave the monastery confines and what follows is the delicate questioning of me over morning coffee, the monks not letting on about the letter, of course, trying to keep their interception immaculate. But after details, hoping I'll reveal things under their seemingly innocent probes.

But I prefer to speak of my morning excursions. Squatting among the cornstalks is not always easy, I tell them, because workmen are often about, or transport trucks delivering frozen hamburger patties, chickens, and other foodstuffs to the monastery kitchen. (There Brother Abel wields his mighty cutting knife revealing forearms as thick as honeyed hams. Ah, Brother Abel!)

For the morning excursions I braid my hair and carry a hand mirror held firmly against my leg. From the monastery windows, the monks watch me in my solemn wanderings and shake their heads. It's a mystery to them why I don't walk with the mirror held before my face like the other young women do. But this is another strategy of mine to unsettle them—to appear both decorous and impure. I'm certain they whisper to one another in the pews before matins: "What will become of her?" I'm always on their minds. Oh, to be prayed over with such constancy and devotion!

But alone in the cornfield, free of the monks, I hold my mirror aloft and gaze at myself in admiration. What I see there: a cupid's face, rosy, full-lipped, blue-eyed. The monks think I go to the cornfield to relieve myself but the truth is I go there to gaze in the mirror, to revel in the seeming endlessness of my youth.

When the corn is not yet high enough to shield me in my gazing, I venture further, to the sea cliffs where the monastery hermit lives. Often I find him sitting on the large rock in front of his hut — a slow, sad hermit, slower than a mountain, slower than a tree; a breathing statue, an object of time. He doesn't have a proper name like Abraham or Abel; he's simply called Our Father Who Art. At the monastery it's said that if you stroll by the hermit at sunrise you may catch him stirring. Then you will hear the slow groaning of his mind forming thoughts — one wise thought a day for you to guess at.

When I hold my mirror before the hermit's ancient face he doesn't blink or seem to see what lies before him; his gaze is elsewhere — inward or to the sea beyond, it's impossible to tell.

Nor does he appear to notice me seated on the ground before him, my mirror held high, reflecting sun and sea and my gazing eyes, so clear and blue you'd think you'd found perfection.

And I have.

(1994)

I left my husband, children, and mother-in-law (who was living with us at the time) for two blissful weeks at St. Peter's Writer's Colony. From my notebook then I wrote:

> I'm loving the silence here, the exclusive focus on the self's small habits, the long stretches of writing and reading, the four-mile walks around fields of golden canola in the evenings, the seclusion and the remoteness. The things that so occupy me at home, that invade and dominate my mind, are no longer present: the children; the constant engaging with everyone; the worry if I can somehow grab a couple of hours to write; and what's in (or is not in) the mailbox, and have there been any calls, and who let the dog out, and what are we going to eat next Tuesday? All of these concerns have simply vanished — a miracle! There's just this small room and the page before me, the church bell tolling the hour, now and then a bird flitting by the window.

While I was at St. Peter's I completed one manuscript and began work on another. Both books were eventually published — in 1995 and 1996. There must be something exceedingly special in the air and soil around St. Peter's; I've yet to duplicate the outpouring of work that occurred during those two amazing weeks.

Dorothy Field

Jew in the Abbey

I have reason to believe we'll all be received ....
     ~ Paul Simon

These things I know how to receive: the golden-eyed
Peonies in the abbey garden, the long-tailed magpies chasing

A bone-thin mama cat, even the bloodsucker ticks waving come-on arms
From dry grass. And the voices. There is always song in the abbey. The
    monks

Face each other across two banks of desks, alternate verses, left side
Then right side, their voices resonating through the empty space of the
    silver girders.

The abbey welcomes us all. When I lose my place
In the songs a brother is there at my elbow, showing me the way.

Angels of all sorts in the abbey. In my room I contemplate the promise
Sung this morning at lauds, to protect Abraham and his Children

Forever. Outside a monk in a baseball cap and striped overalls rides his red
    mower,
Cutting grass already cut, sending up a wake of green shards. Like fireflies.
    A bell rings

And rings. Rings again. Calling monks to vespers. Calling
Me. They sing the cycle of Psalms, Old Testament words,

Father Son and Spirit tacked on the end. Is this welcome, this building
On the body of my people's book, as the conquistadors built churches

Over Inca temples they'd destroyed? The monks' song
Carries me. Can I receive as well the three

Kinds of bread from the abbey kitchen, the turning from the world to build
This world, an acceptance of a mystery that will never

Be mine, the glide past the monastery silo, the silence of owl flight?

(2001)

Being at St. Peter's was a tremendous stimulus to my writing. I was there for Conversation and Silence with Tim Lilburn and Don McKay. To the monks' amazement, our group chose to spend every other day in silence, a silence that made the abbey and the land even more eloquent. The details of that time and that silence became my companions — the morning shadows on the wall of the small room where we ate breakfast, the flamboyant peonies just opening, the straight dark lines of the pines holding us all in place. Most important for me was being at lauds and vespers, a drama and a stillness. I remember the welcome of the brothers helping me find my way in the prayer book when I was lost, and the grace of the women in the kitchen offering up the monastery's harvest. My time at St. Peter's sparked a series of poems about the ambiguity of being a Jew in a non-Jewish world, a series that is not always comfortable but that for me has been fertile and grounding.

Dorothy Field

HERE IN THE MONASTERY

                        we share words
but not tongues. Today's cantor sings soft, almost inaudible
leading the brothers through the antiphonies.

                        In *shul* the cantor
moves a small brass hand along black letters scribed on milky vellum
keens the cantillation. Forty-nine days after Passover we arrive at Shavuot
barley harvest, freshening ewes, Moses receiving the tablets, cheese blintzes
if we're lucky.

                        Pentecost here,
the descent of the Spirit forty-nine days past Easter, variations on epiphany
the counting in the first five books prefiguring the numbers of the four
    gospels.

                        Or that's what St. Benedict
would have said. As a child I asked for a gold Star of David on a fine gold
    chain
felt too shy to wear it. In Jerusalem my daughter chose another, blue stone
    from Eilat.
Don't wear it where it shows, we told her before she left for Poland.

(2001)

Dorothy Field

Hold Out

Over my bed Christ hangs, his small copper form on a tiny wooden cross
suspended from a picture hook, and I wonder

how I got here. Stretched below I sense Mary
in the fluorescent blue of my nylon blanket.
Where are the nuns who lived here when this was Saint Scholastica?

In my small cell
I am the Jew,
gristle
in the mouth of the Church, though this place is full of us —
in the words of the Psalms, stories of the Bible.
I am stranger
and guest
and more than stranger —
stiff-necked hold out
of the Chosen People
Still here.
Were we not, they could have been
the children of Abraham.

My last morning Brother Raymond reads from Jeremiah
stumbles on the Hebrew names, a text about Jews and Greeks
the ones who wouldn't listen.
You are so peaceful
says Brother Anthony as I leave
       hands me two saints cards
                     Mary & Jesus
for remembrance, for return.

I am all knot
hearing dissonance
in your harmony.

Listen
       I am listening now.

Dorothy Field

Ora et Labora

Double file pines, green-black ranks ring the abbey
planted one hundred years ago
                         in grids like the roads, an act of faith
                         green spires rising from prairie flat.
    More than windbreak, they are boundary.

                Inside the pines an open palm
                cultivated to feed the faithful.

Lunchtime. Abbey produce. Under their robes the monks,
just in from work in the fields, wear levis and work boots.
                        Brother Thomas takes the stairs two at a time
                           whistling *O Canada*, his stride fanning his black skirt.
This morning he sharpened hoes, oiled blades,
hung each tool back in its outline on the wall.

                  After lunch Brother Andrew will mow between stones
                  in the graveyard, tucked inside an evergreen circle
                  down an evergreen alley. Where they will lie.

Brother Basil will prune apple trees, water shoots that scrape the sky,
tame them into soft rounds. Until the bell for vespers.
                     Work and worship, a precise alternation.
                     A pulse.
In the abbey lawn a ragged prairie rose.
The monks clip the grass just up to it, leave the weeds.
          In the brush by the railroad tracks butter yellow ladyslippers.
          In the gully, tway-blade and at night

                  lightning bugs
                  a Las Vegas of blinking stars
                  handkerchiefs of fallow
                  holding the earth's wild heart.

Linda Frank

When Doves Cry

And all the faithful smile
and nod to me along
the discipled paths
crossing this catholic
splendour. And their icons
and their bells, and the beauty
of their paint and glass
terrify me

And the trees,
their trunks are monks
in black habit,
glory of god in the gold
they wear upon their heads
They have not yet shed
their benediction
And the yellow
the ecumenical scream of yellow
terrifies me

And the pale corn standing
stripped and naked in the fields,
holding on to the fallow
remains of truth
of what it means to be
over ripe and left to die
on the cob
I press my body
to their papery whispers
and I am terrified

When doves cry
out from empty
orchards, they are only
mediocre angels, terrible
divinity under a pious moon

(1998)

I doubt that any participant could extract the experience of living at St. Peter's from the experience of being a part of the Sage Hill Colloquium. I found myself, a non-practicing Jew, but a Jew nonetheless, a little overwhelmed at the prospect of living at St. Scholastica surrounded by Christian icons and a little daunted at the idea of spending three weeks in a working monastery. I believe I may have been the only participant the year I was there to leave the crucifix on the wall above my bed. It was somehow more comforting that way. It felt … right. There is a spirituality at St. Peter's that goes beyond religion. It affects your writing whether you want it to or not. I didn't want it to, but I can see from the poetry I produced when I got home just how profoundly I was influenced by my time there. It's a spirituality that somehow brings you back to why you want to write poetry, to what lies beneath, to where the poetry comes from.

Linda Frank

The Doorway of St. Scholastica

(for Erina)

You sit exiled
in this dank convent doorway
to chain-smoke your sorrow
alone, and stare out
at what will never
be framed this way again
except in memory

I take refuge beside you,
in the cold inhale
of how young you are
and how beautiful
There is comfort somehow
in the way we've become
these unexpected fixtures
in the convent doorway

We perch together
on upturned pails, two poets
in the thick haze of talk
and smoky perfume,
the symbolism of your growing
mountain of ash not lost
on either one of us

I find some inexplicable solace
in the way you call out
to everyone who walks past us,
in watching how you draw
each of them to tell their life story
to you, though you never give
anything away

How irresistible you are
to the soft-eyed women of Muenster
who hold their shadows
tight as they hurry to serve
the aging monks. And yet for you
they open, gauzy under a fickle prairie sun,
luminous under a full October moon

Even the Benedictines come
to talk to you. The plump,
cheerful brother who sings so high
and sweet, the Vietnamese with the Buddhist bow,
the gaunt ones, the haunted young
ones, still searching
Your red hair is like a beacon
to them. Even the old monks
can't help but look at you

In the doorway of St. Scholastica
we stay up every night
until you finally tell me
the story of your friend's death,
how she hanged her young daughter
before she hanged herself

Then you ask me to photograph you
naked and smiling bravely
among the abbey pumpkins

I too unfold my shadow
let it cover you
with the spread of dark wings
I wrap over your exposed shoulders

(1998)

Myrna Garanis

Roads Rise Up

roads rise up, huge as boulders,
gravel over, shovel under,
human figures all but disappear

road and rim of sky
so greedy for each other,
sick to death of east and east,
reach for perpendicular

a chickadee suggests the way,
    long fall, short rise,
        long fall, short rise,
simple rule to follow

come and meet halfway,
roads holler to the sky,
sky obliges, edges nearer,
stones sweat their slow route up,
ache clearly visible

(2002)

I plunged into a trinity of communities: first, the community of writers, come for nourishment; second, the Benedictine community hosts, swishing along the halls, voices rising from the chapel at vespers; third, the surrounding farms and town within walking distance by road or shortcut through fresh snow. My own forays into place and space are often underpinned by calendars, whether it be the Wheat Pool one, mapping the once-hundreds of elevator shipping points, or, at St. Peter's, the monastic daily prayers. February, the calendar month that sweeps land and heart bare, forces us to seek and dream of shelter. Of the many ways to come in from the cold, we are left on our own to choose. I chose to set down poems.

Myrna Garanis

Stay Among the Trees

good advice on a wind-chilled day
so soon after Ground Hog's

stay among the trees, there shelter dwells,
as long as you mimic winter birds,
crouch low among the deadfall,
snow will not disclose you,
nor passers-by wound tight
in camouflage, fur, and feathers

how long to linger feeding juncos
who guard Our Lady's shrine?
so long to miss the church bells,
lose sight of the last gliding train?

once you overstay your welcome
down among the trees,
there are penalties, there are mazes,
in may not lead out, distances deceive,
snow may cover every path,
only juncos give direction

(2002)

Myrna Garanis

A Day Very Much Like This

how February roads were never open
in the middle of Saskatchewan,
how my mother took the train
reliable in 1943, loading passengers
and troops

how the week before, she stayed in town
at her sister's one-room flat,
came home when nothing happened,
how time ran out,
she climbed aboard the midnight

how the family friend never came
to collect her at the station,
as steady as evening rain,
he'll be punctual in the army,
it was his time too, called to France,
place he'd never mention later

two AM, my mother rides a city bus
straight to hospital doors,
where I am born at four,
February sky still missing light,
war waging somewhere,
a day very much like this

(2002)

Connie Gault

THE FAT LADY WITH THE THIN FACE

ON HER TOUR OF THE ABBEY GROUNDS, Linda comes to the hen house door and finds herself confronted. It's a bit unsettling. First one chicken raises its head and sees her, then another looks up from jabbing the ground, then another. Soon they've all raised their heads with those limp slabs of red flesh wobbling any which way, and they've all stepped toward her. One chicken shrieks, another takes up the cry, then they all open their beaks and berate her. She supposes she shouldn't take it personally; this must be the welcome they give anyone who has nothing to give them.

She has nothing for the pigs either, but they don't care. Although their smell is aggressive, their house is calm. It's divided into pens, each pen dominated by a sow with her litter scattered around her. A few of the piglets watch Linda pass through. Others are sleeping or feeding or stumbling over one another. The sows ignore her. They are huge and confidently insouciant. She almost envies them. If she were more like them, she would not be here, or anywhere alone. She would travel with her husband, now her ex-husband, when she travelled, and a monastery would not be their destination.

On her way back to the guest lodge, she comes to the raspberry patch. She imagines the sun-warmed tang of the berries on her tongue and detours into the patch. She nearly steps on a monk. He is lying on his back in the raspberry patch. He smiles up at her.

"Yoga," he says. "Deep relaxation."

This story is not set at St. Peter's monastery. It's set in an imaginary place and filled with characters who lived in my head. But of course it was inspired by my visits to St. Peter's and by the environment and people there. The idea of cloister has always appealed to me and I first approached the monastery with an uneasy reverence at odds with my skepticism. I soon encountered the sophisticated brand of acceptance that welcomes visitors seemingly impartially to the grounds, the buildings and the life of the place. Still, I always felt like a trespasser there and that's a role that provokes a writer to explore, investigate and wonder. (1988)

Michele, on her way to visit the pigs, comes to the raspberry patch. It's a hot day and the raspberries smell as strong on the path as they would in the kitchen if her mother were making jam. Michele ambles. She is keeping her eyes open for her favourite monk, Brother Cory, who almost became a rock star. An extremely pretty woman is standing among the raspberries. She has fair hair. She is slender and poised and manages to be still gracefully. Michele's favourite monk, Brother Cory, stands up beside her. For a second, Michele imagines he has been on his knees proposing. The first time she saw him she thought he was too good-looking to waste himself being a monk. Now, while she watches, he throws back his handsome head, laughing at something the pretty woman has murmured. He stands head and shoulders above the canes, with his black hair and his black cowl and his knowledge of everything Michele doesn't know.

    She strides past beans and cabbages and onions. She could have known all he knows. By now she would have known, if she hadn't refused the closest thing to an offer she's ever had. She scowls at the rows of vegetables. The pretty woman talks to Brother Cory in the raspberries; if Michele was ever lucky enough to corner him for an intimate chat it would be in the turnips. But then she has one of those flashes from a book that come to her sometimes. This one is of Tess of the d'Urbervilles standing in a frozen field of turnips. Either Hardy put Tess there or Michele did, while reading. At any rate, it seems romantic now. "Fists of turnips punishing the ground," she remembers from somewhere. But it isn't turnips she's picturing, it's wheat, flat-topped fields of wheat, summer-green and not yet knee-high.

    "Hey, Beautiful!" they'd yelled. Beautiful. The gravel road had taken her through farmers' fields; she'd walked until she'd forgotten where she was. They drove up behind her. They were two guys about her age or a little younger, in a truck. "Hey, Beautiful!" they yelled. "How about a blow job?" She saw that they were smirking when they slowed down and had no real intention of stopping. "Wanna be our girlfriend?" the driver crooned. She walked alongside the truck and looked them over. A warm friendly wind pushed her from behind. The air smelled of stinkweed, wildly sweet. They were good-looking boys, squinting at her from the cab of their truck. They would have been surprised if she'd said, "Sure."

Hurrying from Vespers to supper, Brother Bernard rehearses his thoughts.

Each day slices open. Just as the Red Sea parted to let the Israelites through, each day slices open three times at the abbey.

He has recently returned after several months of study in the States. Now the abbey seems exotic to him.

And time is suspended and all the activities that keep us busy are suspended while we gather, not at the river, but at the dining hall and file through the food line rather than the miraculous river bed. We give thanks for our food as the Israelites did, no doubt, for their deliverance, and we have our earthly communion, eating together and sharing the events and complaints of the day which perhaps the Israelites dispensed with on that auspicious occasion. Each day and all our happenings are much the same; the provision for our needs is always miraculous when you regard it freshly.

He finds himself next to Michele in line. Oh humbug. He blushes to think she might have read his thoughts, to think that even the tone of his high-flying thoughts might have communicated itself to her, or that a pompous look on his face might have leaked his love of those rollicking syllables. He cannot think of a thing to say to her. Luckily she is scowling at the closed kitchen doors. He cannot think of a thing to think, either, now that he's afraid to think of his phrases, so he waits as he supposes a dog must wait, for six o'clock. But not as a dog waits, no, because a dog doesn't understand time's divisions, its constitution simply responds to its needs. Intriguing idea. He might write a paper comparing a dog with its tongue hanging out to himself standing in line with his tray in his hands.

He is always writing. When he has no pen in his hand, he rehearses lines for papers he might write so he won't forget them. Each line seems precious to him, but he's embarrassed by his habit. It's vain to think such lines would matter to anyone else, matter so much that he must get them down word perfect.

Even when he empties his mind — as he must — Brother Bernard feels the pressure of his thoughts, his vain thoughts dressed in bombast, piling up either side of the small space he's been able to hew, the small quiet space where the voice of God might be heard before the sound of his own voice floods back. He doesn't wait in line at all as a dog would wait. He waits rehearsing. The thoughts sneak back so he hardly notices, then tumble over one another in their eagerness.

At six exactly, as always happens, the doors open, giving us a flash view of the utilitarian kitchen (bare white and dull metal) and the sisters file out and lift the lids off the food that has been waiting, untouchable before this ritual, for the sisters must exert some small control. The sisters step back while the steam rises and the line presses forward eagerly, as if we haven't eaten this day and might not be fed on the morrow. The sisters watch our backs, pretending to find fault with our posture or the dirt on our shoes but really trying not to acknowledge our greed or show their own gratification. Three times a day, our weakness is abundantly visible. Their ability to fill us, to satisfy us only to see us here again a few hours later with our need in our hands, our plates held out, is cause for celebration among them.

The doors open. The sisters descend on the hot food bins. The steam rises, cumulonimbus.

At times their gloating is audible to us when we return our depleted trays to the kitchen window and catch them remarking how much Father So and So ate today and what a fondness Brother So and So has for this or that, and how quickly the desserts go; the men like their sweets.

With his tray laden, Brother Bernard follows Michele into the dining room and over to the table where several of the monks have settled into their regular spots. During the other meals this week, Michele has joined them at this table, but tonight Father Gregory, the guestmaster, takes her arm before she can set her tray down. Speaking in a low voice, he walks her across the room to a table where the pretty woman who arrived this afternoon is sitting alone. She and Michele are the only individual retreatants at the abbey. The other guests who occupy a third table are part of a group retreat studying spiritual graphology with Father Morris Abernaty, a noted Catholic graphologist from California. Michele does not look pleased to have been ousted from the monks' table and asked to sit with the pretty woman.

Brother Bernard digs into his meal without tasting anything, not even the tomatoes the guests always rave about that don't taste anything like the ones you buy in the grocery stores. He tries to visualize Michele without looking at her. Then he tries to find words to fit the shape she takes in his mind.

A roundness of cheek and eye, a cherubic quality. Or is she more a gargoyle? If you came across her at rest, if it ever happens that she rests, she would appear quite pretty in a pouty, pigeony way. But she is always on the alert and that means defensive. She has two modes, either chin in the air or shoulders hunched. Perhaps that's why she shrugs so often, to relieve the tension of those extremes. A nearly perpetual scowl. A little plump for today's standards, a little fuller in the chest than in other areas (which gives her the pigeony look), all of which combines to create a certain comicality out of her belligerence. Even he finds it impossible not to smile at times. Even he.

Brother Bernard has developed a habit of referring to himself, in his rehearsing, in the third person. This is because he watches himself as well as others. He is fated always to be aware of his own thoughts and actions and their folly.

Michele glares at Brother Bernard. She can feel his benevolence radiating in her direction. She hasn't spoken since Father Gregory introduced her to the woman whose name is Linda. She spoke very little during the introduction, for that matter, which had forced Father Gregory to make conversation. He'd remarked that she had no pork chops on her plate. "I visited the pigs this morning and grew to like them," she told him. She had the pleasure of watching Linda toy with the chunk of meat she'd just severed from her chop.

Doggedly she eats her meal.

"Please would you pass the salt?" Linda asks.

Michele acts as though Linda has interrupted her thoughts. It doesn't work. Any thoughts she might have had are similarly interrupted with little murmurs about tomatoes that taste so different from the ones you get in Safeway, and how odd it is to be offered three different kinds of pickles, and having two desserts to choose from, and how Linda is bound to go home ten pounds heavier. Of the many things I dislike about you, Michele thinks, the thing I dislike most is your murmuring. It isn't true. The thing she dislikes most is Linda's slenderness.

Proximity works wonders. In two days Michele and Linda are friends. They exchange information about themselves in a way Michele has only overheard other people do, in a way she has sneered at before, has rolled her eyes at before. In the hallways and the lunch room at high school she overheard these conversations, how I want and he wants and I say and she says, how I always wanted and I never wanted and I thought I said and I should have said. Now it's her turn. She says it all too; it's easy to say anything to Linda.

"I want to be a nun."

They have already discussed the fact that neither of them has religion. Michele is thrilled to find an adult who agrees with her.

"You want to try it on."

They are lolling on the grass in the shade of a crabapple tree. The crabapples are tinged with pink and give off a faint apple scent. Michele considers Linda's suggestion.

"Try it on. That's right. That's exactly what I want to do. I want to look like a nun and have nun-like fantasies."

A black ant is scuttling up her leg, between and over the bristles. She hasn't shaved for a week.

"I want black oxfords with heavy heels, black pantyhose, a straight navy skirt and a navy sweater and I want my hair cut short like a man's. I want a big cross to hang from a chain around my neck."

Her ankle tickles. Another ant.

"I want to act as much like a nun and think as much like a nun as possible."

"Is that why you're here?"

Linda is brushing them off too.

"I'm here because my parents started to wonder what I was going to do all summer before university starts. I couldn't find a job. Hardly anyone can. Obviously my parents thought it was going to be a long summer with me mooning around the house making them sad because I have no friends."

"You'd look cool dressed like a nun."

"Sure." She must say this with some disdain, must keep the hope out of her voice.

"Try it."

"Yeah?"

"If it's what you want."

Frail old Father Abbot drifts up to them. Usually they only see him when he wanders from table to table after meals with his little bucket of soapy water and a J-cloth, wiping off crumbs and milk. This time he has something concealed in his hand. He smiles at Linda and asks Michele a question.

"What kind of cookies do monks like?"

Michele shrugs.

"Hermits." He holds out his hand and leaves a cookie on each of their palms.

Brother Bernard, while hoeing between potato hills, is contemplating recording a series of conversations he hopes to have with Michele. Mentally recording. He wouldn't take notes or use a tape recorder. He'd record their conversation mentally then write it up for eventual publication under some title like *The Religious Life and the Imitative Impulse*. She turned up this morning for breakfast wearing a nun-like get up and with all her hair cut off. Ironically, she looks cute. The sweater is tight. Her hair is spiky. Brother Bernard fears the reaction of some of the brothers. Isn't the cross almost blasphemous?

The storekeeper looks up when the door opens. He's been thinking about the pretty woman who's staying at the abbey, idly thinking about her while doing the books. He looks up hoping it will be her. She walks into town every other day at least. She's getting bored at the abbey; it isn't only cigarettes and scotch she needs in town. Not that he's planning to supply much else. Just talk. A few smiles into the eyes. That's what she needs and they both enjoy that. But it isn't her; it's a weird-looking girl.
"What can I do for you?"
He hasn't seen this one before. Can't be a nun; they don't look like this.
"Nail polish?"
"You'll have to get that at the drug store."
The girl hesitates.
"Bet you don't know where that is."
"No."
"I'll walk you over."
He walked the pretty woman over to the hotel bar the week before. He gets razzed about this extra service he supplies to the women guests from the abbey. He says he's just being friendly and he sort of means it but he doesn't mind getting a laugh either.
"You're the first customer all day, you know that?"
"No."
"No, guess you couldn't know that. Come on then."
He holds the door for her and slips his arm along the small of her back, propelling her along but only for a few moments.

She's in love, she's in love. With a mature man. It's her secret; she isn't going to tell Linda. She's made six trips to the store in four days. Linda is talking about her childhood over tuna melts. It's Friday lunch time.
"When I was a kid I wanted to grow up to be really fat. I wanted to be a fat lady. That's because I tried it once and made everyone laugh. I'd never realized until then how much fun it is to make people laugh."
Michele is thinking how she likes him to look at her.

"It was for a circus my cousins and I put on one summer."

Michele is thinking how his look says — I like you.

"I was only four or five and had no talents, no tap dancing or singing like the others. I couldn't do cartwheels."

Just for a second Michele sees a tiny Linda with yellow hair tumbling head over heels but the image is replaced by his face, his lazy eyes on her. She knows he likes to look at her.

"I wanted to be the fat lady in the circus."

He makes her glad.

"My cousins said I couldn't be her; I was too thin. But I wouldn't be anything else. So to keep me quiet they put me into my aunt's dress and stuffed it with pillows."

She can't let him know how glad she is when he looks at her.

"My cousins stood me in front of a mirror to show me how dumb I looked, but I didn't care. I wasn't going to give up."

Can she?

"So they billed me as 'The Fat Lady with the Thin Face.' They made a sign and when it was my turn to go in front of the adults, they carried the sign out first, then I walked on. I stood in front of the audience and grinned, because I'd got my own way. They loved it. They laughed till they cried."

Brother Bernard sidles up to the table to say hello and stands shyly waiting to be acknowledged.

"You should always go for it, don't you think, Brother Bernard?"

Linda is kind as well as pretty. She wouldn't leave someone standing there for very long, waiting to be acknowledged.

"If there's something you really want?"

"Only those who will risk going too far can possibly know how far they can go," Brother Bernard says, quoting T.S. Eliot as accurately as he can remember, then blushing.

Later he worried that he should have come up with an 'on the other hand.' Should he have said something about temptation?

Unfortunately we don't always want what's best for us.

What a wonderful smile from Michele, though, as if he'd handed her a bouquet.

The storekeeper holds the door for his wife. They join two other couples in the corner behind the pool tables. Just about every Friday night they get together in the hotel bar. The hotel owner hauls himself off his chair and brings them their beer.

The girl from the abbey is sitting on the bench along the far wall. She's pretending to watch TV. You can tell she's pretending; her face is dazed. She's got a glass in front of her with coke in it and something else, by the look of her. She's probably under age. One of the women whispers to Geraldine.

"Get a load of Sister Charity."

Geraldine's too nice to reply in kind. She grins. "God, I worked hard today," she says, stretching her muscles.

The kid looks over once or twice and the storekeeper pretends not to notice. It's kinder not to notice, he feels, especially when he's with his wife.

The storekeeper's wife and one of the other women are playing pool. Michele knows he is looking at her. She can tell. Inside she hums — her whole body hums. In her centre there is the sweetest ache. The humming, the vibration that started when he walked in the door, rocks the ache, swings it back and forth and keeps it alive. He's looking at her while his wife plays pool.

The bench she sits on faces the window that overlooks the train tracks and elevators. When she first arrived the sun had almost set but was still burning too brilliantly to allow her to look out the window for more than a second at a time. Now the window is black and she has the feeling only this room exists in all the world. He's looking again. He ignored her for a while so his wife wouldn't be alerted, but now he can't stop looking at her. He likes to look at her so much.

She turns and catches his eye. He gives her one of those slow smiles. She smiles into her drink. This is fine. To think she was wasting her time mooning over Brother Cory. And what a contrast to those kids in the truck. She never did have much in common with other kids; now she knows why.

It's warm still, the moon is out and she can see far over the fields, though not all the way down the road to the abbey. The town is quiet, the street deserted except for his truck angle-parked at the corner in front of the store. She gave him ten minutes to drop off his wife and come back for her. How she knows this is the way it works she doesn't know. He's sitting in the truck, watching her.

She walks over slowly. She has no idea what she's going to say or do when she gets there.

He says hello so she says hello.

"Nice night," he says.

He turns and faces forward, looking out the windshield at nothing. She thinks: he's going to let me make my own decision, no interference from him. She walks around the truck to the passenger's side, opens the door and climbs in beside him. She shuts the door softly and joins him in looking out the windshield. His windows are down and a breeze blows through so soft and sweet she feels it's inside her.

His wife comes out of the store. She locks the door then walks up to the passenger's side of the truck and smiles at Michele.

The storekeeper says, "Geraldine, I've offered this young lady a lift back to the abbey."

Geraldine says hi. She climbs in beside Michele.

They drive to the abbey with the strange girl between them. Geraldine is kind to her. She asks how long she's been at the abbey, how long she's staying, whether she's been to visit their little cathedral with its famous German paintings. She should go at sunset, Geraldine tells her, she should walk in and leave the doors open because the doors face west and the paintings look very beautiful in that light.

They drop her off at the dormitory and turn around in the parking lot.

"You bastard," Geraldine says. It's the last thing she says to him for two days.

Brother Bernard cycles up and down the side roads with his skirts bunched at the knees and an old fishing hat jammed on his head to keep the rain out of his eyes. Around every corner, over every little rise, he expects he'll see Michele.

Michele is walking in the rain. It's a warm rain and in the woods not much of it reaches her. She's done just the kind of thing in front of everyone at breakfast that makes people say there's something wrong with her. And it's Linda's last day. She wanders along the path in the woods. It doesn't matter where she goes; she always fucks things up.

Brother Bernard tries the little cathedral. A person might go there for solace. He checks inside the confessionals, rehearsing as he goes.

All true confessions are made at night, to another human if one has no God.

If he could talk to Michele some evening, she might unburden her soul. From her defensiveness it's easy to see she expects to be criticized, she expects to be asked for explanations. She was shocked when that wasn't the response she got this morning. Father Gregory, the guestmaster, who wasn't there at the time, was the only one who asked for an explanation, and he asked Brother Bernard. Michele had already gone by then. No, everyone was concerned for her, Linda most of all. No one saw her anger building or knew where it came from. As he explained to Father Gregory, Michele and Linda were sitting opposite one another as usual when Michele yelled something (it was not really incomprehensible but Brother Bernard saw no reason to repeat her language and lower her in Father's eyes) and dumped her breakfast on Linda's lap. The brothers came running. Father Abbot brought his J-cloth and started cleaning up. Everyone was solicitous of them both. Michele went out crying and now no one can find her.

A hummingbird hangs in the air like a miniature helicopter. She steps toward it. The hummingbird flies off but then it returns. It's as green as the leaves; it disappears into the leaves and a few seconds later reappears. All along the path it keeps ahead of her, flying in fits and starts. Like a kid, stopping at everything bright. She decides to pretend it's leading her somewhere.

Our destination is pre-ordained by our nature, but only in the widest sense. If our nature is open to God, we will find him. Dear God ....

Brother Bernard is praying for Michele, in the way he prayed as a child, as if writing a letter. It's the only resource left him. She's been gone all day, she's missed lunch and supper. Linda has put off her departure. She wanted to talk to Michele before she leaves, but now she's lugging her suitcases to her car. She's packing her trunk.

The hummingbird takes Michele to Mary's shrine in the woods. "Hail Mary, Queen of Peace," she reads inscribed above the plaster figure of Mary. The hummingbird dips its miniscule beak into the snapdragons that bloom in jam jars at her feet. They were its real destination.

"Mary, Mother of God," Michele says. "You look too young for the job." Those were the words of the one employer who interviewed her for a summer job.

"In the end my immaculate heart will triumph." Those are the words at Mary's feet.

"Lucky you," Michele says.

The rain has stopped. The clouds have cleared. The sun is sliding down and the trees are letting only streaks of light through to the path. Michele, in her damp clothes, feels chilly. It's time to go back and find some way to apologize.

The pond is a surprise. No one told her about it. It isn't on the abbey map. It's like a secret pond, in an unknown clearing, a pretty little pond, brushed with the gold of the low sun, with rushes at the edges.

It's warmer in the clearing. She stands for several minutes looking at the pond then she takes off her clothes, hangs them on a branch, and wades in. This isn't something she really wants to do and at first it's disgusting. The soft mud sucks at her toes and her feet sink almost to the ankles. But she is doing this as she would climb up on another horse. That's how she thinks of it. She believes what Linda and Brother Bernard told her; she'll never know how far she can go if she won't take risks. Her entire body shudders as her foot sinks once again on its way to the bottom.

Linda has gone to the guest lounge for a coffee before she departs. Brother Bernard says he'll have a last look in the woods behind the gymnasium. Linda says she thinks Michele doesn't want to be found, but Brother Bernard thinks she will want to atone, or at least that she'll be sorry later if she misses the chance.

She is up to her neck and the water settles around her in layers, warmest at her neck, cool down to her legs, cold at her knees and warm again at her feet. She turns this way and that. The water tugs at the hair between her legs. The water is golden-streaked and strange long-legged insects skate across it. She turns and turns.

Brother Bernard hurries past the statue of Mary.

Wading out of the pond, she feels the water falling off her.

Halfway between the statue and the pond, he halts. Though his inclination is to forge ahead, Brother Bernard goes back to pay his respects to Mary, to say a short prayer for Michele and another for himself, for the doubt that has slipped in and mingled with his good intentions. A hummingbird is drinking from a snapdragon close to his knee. He sees how fast its wings have to beat to keep its body in the air and he thinks that's how fast a person has to pray to keep believing.

She is cool again and dresses quickly. She should find Linda and apologize.

Hurrying past the pond to the path that leads out of the woods, Brother Bernard comes on Michele. She is sitting on her haunches.

"Look what I've found," she says.

Wild strawberries.

She hands him a few and stands. She thinks, finally I've got a man in the berries and look who it is.

Brother Bernard thinks she's almost beautiful but he's much too shy to tell her so. She is giving him a very peculiar look. For a second he thinks it's lascivious but it's not that. It's the absence of something that is peculiar. The darts are gone from her eyes. He's been calling them darts because he's seen that she has a liveliness (you might even call it mischief at times) inside her that she tries to hide behind averted eyes or belligerent stares, and this liveliness darts out at others quite often in spite of her desire to hide it.

A person, finding himself the recipient of these darts, may feel they are in response to him, to a humanity, a kinship she recognizes in him, perhaps. He may feel that he has stimulated her in some way so that she must let the darts fly and fall as they may.

Brother Bernard supposes he calls them darts, too, because they sometimes mysteriously hurt.

There are no darts in this look. It is simply Michele, looking at him. No mischief. No defences. No expectations. He is looking into her face, into her eyes, and she is letting him see her.

Here is what excites him most: there are no words.

Of course by the time he's thinking all this, it's over and she is asking whether Linda has left yet and he's telling her if they move quickly they may catch her before she goes.

Follow me, he says, and tears off.

Hiking up his skirts to facilitate his progress over the odd fallen twig on the path out of the woods....

Michele is behind him. His thoughts race ahead.

He has made a great discovery. He has witnessed a soul bared, and there were no words. No words needed.

He's heard of this before, of course.

Words must be eschewed; the communication can only be non-verbal.

But he hasn't experienced it before. Surely it can't be a common experience. He must write something on it. He might work it into his paper on *The Religious Life and the Imitative Impulse*. It won't be a series of conversations, as he'd first planned. He and Michele haven't had any — a series of non-conversations, he might call it. A highly experimental piece, perhaps breaking new ground.

Linda's trunk is packed. Father Gregory walks her back to her car which sits in the lot facing the road home. This was her first visit to the abbey and it will be her last. She hasn't found any peace. She has only been bored and restless and a spoiler. Father Gregory is telling her about the newspaper they publish at the abbey and she is murmuring responses. She's good at small talk and doesn't need to think to keep it up.

She can think her own thoughts, which are troubled. She thought she was just what the girl needed, a sympathetic adult, someone to encourage her to open up, to face the world without defences. She should not have given advice to a kid who is obviously confused. Whatever upset Michele, if it had something to do with those stupid conversations about going all out for what you want, she's responsible. It's bad advice, Linda thinks, remembering her own humiliation. She blushes to think of it. She pretty much offered herself to the village storekeeper and got turned down. Standing by her car door, listening to Father Gregory talk about the problems of editing some of the more enthusiastic submissions he receives, she blushes all over her face and down her neck.

Brother Bernard dashes out of the woods with Michele behind him. They startle several of Father Abernathy's graphologists who are walking into town for a beer. Brother Bernard spares an instant's pity for them.

If words are nearly useless in matters of the spirit, how hollowly trivial is the handwriting in which the words are recorded?

He might work up a paper on that subject as well, when Father Abernathy has returned to California.

Father Gregory, still talking to the charming pretty woman, has noticed Brother Bernard hastening out of the woods towards them. He has seen Michele running behind him. Her cross bouncing on her chest. Father Gregory grins. She looks as cute as a button, he thinks. It's a phrase his mother used to use. He wonders where it comes from. Michele is waving and calling to Linda. He's very pleased to see it.

When Brother Bernard and Michele reach them, Father Gregory says goodbye to give Michele and Linda a chance to talk.

"Brother Bernard," he says, "just the man I was looking for." He leads Brother Bernard off toward the buildings. "Good work, Brother Bernard," he says, once they're out of earshot.

He is listening to Father Gregory but thoughts come to him.

Is the idea of the love of God a fantasy of the religious? Could the same idea be phrased by the secular as a feeling of belonging in nature? Had he come upon Michele in a secular prayer?

Intuitively he rejects the equivalence. Even with his mind half on what Father is saying, when he thinks of God's love he thinks of an area around his head, and when he thinks of belonging to nature, he envisions his feet. Not at all the same thing. Although of course this sort of concrete thinking would be unacceptable in academic circles, it will form the basis of every argument he makes in this regard for the rest of his life. He knows this. Furthermore, he believes it's the same for everyone, even if only the naive would admit it. He is very happy suddenly.

He is as a child, and for some things, that is good.

Linda's face is red. Michele thinks she must be very angry with her. Usually when people get angry with her, Michele gets angry back, but not this time. It makes her feel really nervous and almost strangles her, but she says she's sorry.

Behind the parking lot is a corn field and behind that a dozen or so pine trees make a row of dark spikes. They remind Linda of the monks. If the monks put their cowls up when they filed to mass or whatever ritual it is that takes them three or four times a day to chant in the chapel, they would look like that. Around the pine trees and around the monks she sees wavy lines of motion. A Van Gogh painting. Swirling. She can't bear to be here another second. She can't wait to get into her car and drive away from here. It's pity, pity swirling around her, for people who will never, never learn.

As soon as she's on the road, she jabs at the radio buttons until she finds music no one in this part of the world would listen to, music that belongs in a smoky basement dive, to people whose eyes have seen it all. She turns the volume up, buzzes down her windows, passes every vehicle in her path.

Sue Goyette

On Building a Nest

You've hooked up fish line and a sinker
to your light switch so you don't have to leave
your bed. One pull and
darkness. Pull it. And now
think of the broken mirror
words, the ones that hold seven years'
bad luck and shards of light
that cut. You must swallow

these words. Here's a tip:
some birds eat gravel along with seed:
the process of grinding. Here's another:
if you need to know more about luck,
study bones, the clavicle, also known as
wishbone, and its muscles that unfurl the wings.
Stop here if you already think you can fly.

Those kinds of thoughts are stones
and you'll end up going nowhere with them.
But if you've ever been walking a road and realized
roads are just another species
of longing, we should meet, outside,
at midnight: I'll be the one wearing blue. I can't promise
miracles; these things take time. Turn the light
back on. I forgot to say
you have to spend at least one week with cows. Notice how they perch
on the very edge of land
and sky. There are many birds who over the years
have lost their wings. This has nothing to do with luck
but with need, you'll see that in their eyes. And then you must crawl
into the word *extinction*. This word is a small cave shaped like an egg.
Your knees will be under your chin, your arms around them;

you'll have only yourself to hold onto. Here's another tip: bring something
to think about; you'll be there for a while. And this is important
to remember: a sparrow can sing as many as twenty variations
of the same song and a morning can have a wingspread
as wide as a week. Trees migrate from season to season
using cloud patterns and stars as guideposts. You'll have to
improvise. I'm only telling you because I'm lonely.
I've made you a shelter of twigs and this, I hope, is bright
and shiny enough to lure you in. I've been measuring
rainfall, the light of day; we're running out of time. Tomorrow
I'll sing another variation of this. Already I know it'll have something to do
with the word *pelican*
and with *glide*.

(1999)

If you walk from the main building of St. Peter's towards town and cut through the field and narrow band of woods, you come to a meadow. In June, this meadow is awash with prairie fire and at dusk, fireflies. There is a small bridge crossing a stream. Lie down. Though the water is shallow, it is still a true mirror. The clouds are doubled in it; each small stone is possessed with a secret. At the end of some thoughts, bells will ring out. You are not alone. The field is populated with leftover prayer. Crows lift from the pines like ideas. Brilliant, brilliant then: watch me. In Muenster, there is a grocery store with a freezer full of Popsicles. There is a bar with a great jukebox and a collection of poetry books. There is a dance floor and a bartender who likes to talk. There are railroad tracks and cows between here and there. The monks are generous with their bicycles and their tour of bees. The desserts can bring you to your knees. The land is flat. The dirt roads, smooth. If you are so inclined, you can ride one of their bikes for a great distance "no hands." The windows are open. The silence is several gospels deep, the sound of bird song, a winged mass. Here, all of it is holy; here all of it is a poem.

Sue Goyette

Meadow

A tree is a love letter, a tall pine,
slender and unopened, waiting
to be read. It is whisper, it's all ears
and it's moonlight
dressed up in wood
and needles and cloud. Roads stretch
all the way to morning
or all the way to night. All of darkness
may be behind you or just ahead,
all of light.
And this foot bridge, small and necessary,
is a hand reaching back, a lover
on her way home from his house, the placing of each plank,
her desire.
And the meadow is mirror and nest. The genealogy
of grass. Distant cousins. Great, great aunts. I am
surrounded. Beneath, above, they all move
through me and I lie on this bridge, each plank
a vow, each bird a wish, and I respond leaf
to leaf: *yes, I am yours* and *yes,*
yes, you are mine.

(1999)

Heidi Greco

No Wallflowers Permitted
First Time at Danceland: The Poets Take a Break from Sage Hill

(for my grandma)

1.
Saturday night   the girls are out
    good thing it seems
tonight at least   the brothers
should be safe
    back at the abbey
probably praying hard on their knees
whirring through extra rosaries
asking that we won't come back that way
    again

2.
we preen up all goofy and hop in the van
rowdies clambering back to the farthest of the seats
you'd think we were smoking up some fatties here tonight
we are all so high on each other

down the road beyond the town the sunlight finally hits us
suddenly the moon could come out   we're singin' out loud again
eight days a week echoes different in a van
consternating harmonies in motion

leaving behind the coolness of those hallways
the grace of the convent where we've lived these twelve days
looking down the highway we keep curving our way down
humming toward a different kind of graceland

old-fashioned dance hall like something from *The Shining*
a place to find a guy who wears his hair all pasted-backed
can even tie a bowtie or lead a decent two-step
someone new to listen to our stories

3.
what must the brothers have wondered
when they looked outside their windows

scratch marks on winter glass granting
moonlight invitations
transubstantial visions   offers
of holy ecstasy

seeing all our lights still on
nearly half past two
knowing we were making love
nothing but words in our hands

4.
northern lights above our heads
unfurl a shuddering banner
not such a sky since angels have walked
these legends are older than God's

        exploding bears and wolverines
        open wide their jaws
        howl a silent war cry
        trample cross the night

5.
sitting together at a table here tonight   elbows sticking a bit to the
plasticized cloth   such a good position to see all that happens
here   surveying realms we have seen somewhere before   looking for
places we know we'll see again

this table one of many that are fanned around the room   each with its
own waxy rose in a vase   stiffly pink determined enough to wait for
forever   stubby candle burning in a red coloured glass

we form a kind of island near the steady wave of dancers   they are an
ocean swirling past us   constant and in motion   mouthing words as they
pass by   the songs a chant that holds them in step with the beat of the
clarinetty band

we watch the circling dance parade   faces reflecting the light   look how
careful he holds her hand up high as they glide by   his other wrist how it
rides so light on the flat at the small of her back   you know that they are
still twenty when it comes to being in love

I'm half expecting trails of colour to stream out from behind them   follow
them like dry ice leaving its breath around the room

6.
I can't help think of Mayme
who was my mother's mother
think about a reason why I gave her that name
know she would have loved it here tonight

(1999)

Having never been part of anything so committed-sounding as a poetry "colloquium," I headed to St. Pete's full of doubt and misgivings. Still, all the squirming proved to be worth it, as I'm still reaping the benefits of my time at the abbey. While I was there, I accomplished a feat that had stymied me for several years — sorting through and revising a ridiculously large number of poems. The miracle was, by the end of the three weeks, I'd not only pulled the assorted bits of paper into a manageable manuscript, I'd somehow even found a title for the thing, *Rattlesnake Plantain*. And yes, I owe that title to my time at St. Pete's — it came to me from one of the many books the angels delivered to me. All right, maybe it wasn't angels, but someone must have been guiding the selection of books that seemed to keep falling into my hands while I was living in that wonderful room in the corner at St. Scholastica.

Frances Greenslade

SKELLIG MICHAEL *from*
A Pilgrim in Ireland: A Quest for Home

A hedge of trees surrounds me, a blackbird's lay sings to me,
praise I shall not conceal,
Above my lined book the trilling of the birds sings to me.
A clear-voiced cuckoo sings to me in a gray cloak from the tops of the bushes
May the Lord save me from Judgment; well do I write under the greenwood.
~ WRITTEN BY A NINTH-CENTURY IRISH MONK IN THE MARGIN OF A MANUSCRIPT, The Scribe in the Woods

I HAD FOLLOWED most of the place-names pencilled in on my mother's chart, worried that I would run out of time. With about a week left, I decided to take a detour down to County Kerry to see the Skelligs Denise had told me about back in Clare. She had also raved about a good hostel in Cahirciveen and since the weather had taken a rare summery turn, I was in a holiday mood.

On the west coast, it was surreally sunny and very hot — the hottest, I was told, in seven years. My room in the hostel had only two beds, no roommate and a window that opened out onto a view of dark blue mountain with a white church below it, and hundreds of white birds wheeling in the sky. Travellers gathered to chat in the kitchen, thanks mostly to the efforts of a sociable young American named Jeff who was spending his summer working as a jack of all trades in the hostel. He introduced all the guests to each other, with a few notes of interest like where we were from or the kind of work we did. Jeff was eighteen with a new Celtic tattoo he'd had done in Ireland. He was working on his Irish accent, and had incorporated a few Irish-isms into his speech, like "brilliant," "half-six" (instead of six-thirty) and "cracking." His enthusiasm for things Irish was infectious.

On my first evening I met Akiko, a Japanese woman, compact and ready for anything in an oversized T-shirt, walking shorts and bright new running shoes. Akiko radiated independence and a sneaky sense of humour. We discovered we were living parallel lives on opposite sides of the world. We were the same age, both writers, and both had younger partners named David. Our mothers had both died of cancer. As Akiko poured some tea for me on the balcony at the hostel, she leaned over my shoulder to look at the book I was reading: Yeats's *Writing on Irish Folklore, Legend and Myth*. She showed me hers: the same book, in Japanese.

Under the influence of the unusual heat, Akiko, Jeff and I fell into a lazy holiday routine. We ate a leisurely breakfast on the hostel balcony, sharing stories of our lives back home, then Akiko and I did some shopping and walking while Jeff looked after his hostel duties. Then we met up with Jeff's friend Max, an older man from the village, and drove out to the beach, a place as idyllic as its name, which was something like the Blue Strand. The water was breathtakingly cold. Jeff swam anyway, the only person at the beach fully submerged, while Akiko and I waded and Max stood fully clothed, smoking.

One warm evening, I asked Akiko if she'd like to go for a walk to look for some ruins and stone forts. We set out, her in her bright white running shoes and I in my scuffed boots. When I had led us into a bog of black mud that squeezed up through the seams of our shoes, within sight of the ruins but still a swamp-crossing away, Akiko confessed that she'd misunderstood my English and thought we were going to look in the stores. But she good-naturedly rinsed her white runners in the river and we went on. When we reached the ruins, we sat beneath the crumbling stone walls, with the sun turning orange.

"My David does the sweat lodge in Belgium," Akiko said, as she scraped mud off her shoes with a stone. (We had taken to calling our partners "my" and "your" David).

"Oh!" I exclaimed.

"The Indian sweat lodge," she explained. "Do you know it?"

"Yes," I said. "They have sweat lodges in Belgium?"

"Many people practice it there. It's very popular. I have been in it two times. And your David and you?"

"Yes," I said. More was required of me, but I wasn't sure what else to say.

I thought of Helmut Walking Eagle, the blonde-haired, braided German from Emma Lee Warrior's story "Compatriots." He had walked back into history and taken a chunk of Plains Indian tradition for his own, living in a teepee resplendent with Indian art and sacred paraphernalia. I also knew that jokes ran among some Plains people about the popularity of teepees and sweat lodges and drumming circles in Germany. But here was Akiko, a woman I respected immediately, on a search parallel to mine.

What had been so easy to laugh at before, the New Agers who played with religions like Birkenstock styles, swerved head-on into my own doubt about my right to take part in a culture that wasn't mine. I had the feeling that I had met the collective unconscious, here in a swampy field surrounding Irish ruins. What Jung called "modern man in search of a soul" was Akiko and me.

Searches like ours have been responsible for stirring a spicy mix of Celtic symbols, runes, feathers, power-stones and talking sticks into an appealing stew of nature-reverence and navel-gazing. It seems that the flood of interest in holistic and earth-centred religions springs from some gaping chasm that yawns dangerously through the lives of Judeo-Christians. But I wondered about Akiko and me and her David, sincere as we saw ourselves. What business did we have, now that we'd lost the meaning in our own ceremonies, to appropriate bits from other cultures? And would it even work?

"I wonder why the sweat lodge is so popular in Europe," I said to Akiko.

"People are looking for something," she said. "Do you think so?"

"Yes, I do think so."

We had both come to Cahirciveen to use it as a launching place for the visit to Skellig Michael. We had both been putting it off.

"There's got to be something there," Akiko said. "Six centuries of monks. We must be able to feel something on that island."

That's what I was thinking. We were on a quest, though we couldn't name the object of our search exactly. Something. Something we had once had, or our ancestors had had, in Canada, in Ireland, in Japan. Something we had lost and knew it.

The day planned for our trip was another perfect beach day. Jeff tried to talk Akiko and me out of Skellig Michael and into the beach instead. The temptation to collapse into the hot lull of white sand and the bright holiday ease of the present was strong, a siren song luring us to forget our quest and to stay, "eating the Lotos day by day, [and watching] the crisping ripples on the beach." But we had already arranged for a fisherman named Patrick to pick us up at the hostel door. On our way to the harbour, Patrick had to make several stops. He was trying to find someone to turn peat for him, a job that has to be done to ensure a good supply of dry peat bricks for heating fuel. But it was clear that at twenty pounds a head, ferrying tourists to Skellig Michael was too lucrative an opportunity to pass up. Everyone wants to go there, it seems, except Jeff.

Skellig Michael is a pyramid of jagged black rock that juts 650 feet out of the foaming ocean seven miles off the southwest coast of Ireland. Scruffy bits of vegetation and some tenacious wildflowers cling to the craggy rock. On a calm, sunny day, like the day we approached it, the rock (you can't really call it an island) rears suddenly up out of the ocean like a threat, forbidding and dangerous, the kind of place they might exile criminals to. In stormy weather, wind and breakers slam into the rock, sweeping away anything that can't keep its clutch on the slippery stone; sea spume fizzes right over the peak. But over one thousand years ago, a few ascetic Christian monks decided that this would be a good place to found a monastery.

They were looking for a landscape that would sculpt them into diamond-hard Christians, like the hermit monks who crawled into caves in the North African desert, fasted and scrubbed themselves of bodily desires till they were smooth, clean shells ready to be filled by God. The Irish monks who sailed into the Atlantic looking for an environment that would test them as much as the desert, must have felt a thrill of challenge when Skellig Michael cast its pointed shadow over them. Here was an impossible place, inhabited only by puffins and gannets which took shelter in the tiny caves made when chunks of rock overlapped. No trees grew here; no animals, except the occasional seal, could be hunted for meat. The only building material was rock. The monks would build a monument to God, far from the comfort of other men's routines and the clutter of soft opinion. They would start with nothing at all.

They scrambled up to the saddle of rock five hundred feet above sea level, turned their faces to the battering salt-wind and exalted in the adventure this place would offer their faith. They named the island after Michael, the archangel of high places. God confirmed their choice with a miracle: the lonely crag, surrounded only by ocean, held fresh water, cradled in small pockets of rock. (Rational minds, bothered by miracles, figured out that the fresh water is actually rainwater, filtered down through the rock.)

Today, the pilgrims who visit Skellig Michael are tourists like Akiko and me. Patrick loaded fifteen of us, mostly Germans, onto his boat in Portmagee and we made the gentle trip out into the ocean, with the jutting peaks of the islands looming not far off. We didn't know that we were lucky to have picked this super-calm day. Though the trip is short, the swell of waves on an unsettled day can make the journey a white-knuckler or too dangerous altogether. Already the sun had chased the hatless into the small shade of the boat's canvas awning. They fiddled with cameras and squinted out at the looming triangle islands slicing up the horizon.

We first approached Little Skellig. Patrick cut the engine and we heard a weird, unearthly din — anguished cries, warning shrieks that made my mind go blank. We glided beneath the shadow to have a look. The rock was painted white with birdshit and birds, teetering on ledges and lifting their wings menacingly. The acid stench was overpowering. There was something absolutely desolate and foreign about the scene. No human could ever live here. I was glad when the motor started up again and we got back out into the sun.

Skellig Michael has been tamed to accommodate tourists with a dock and a concrete ramp, protected by chain link fence, that leads to the beginning of the path up the rock face. But there were no chip stands or drinking fountains here, only lots of tourists trying to escape the unexpectedly relentless sun in all manner of makeshift hats: newspaper cones, T-shirt turbans, maps. Still, the easy landing and the anthill line of pilgrims and sightseers winding up the rock face took some of the spiritual sting out of the place.

Our group had a long climb ahead of us to reach the cluster of stone huts, sunk into the swoop of rock between peaks, that made up the tiny monastic settlement. The path climbed steeply, and was made dangerous by loose, jagged rock. We picked our way carefully; sweat sprang up and soaked my shirt. The sun was almost directly overhead now. More men took off their shirts and wrapped them around their heads and necks. Jokes and complaints buzzed up and down the line of climbers. The smokers had to stop for a rest.

Looking down was dizzying, and I thought of the German woman I'd heard about in Clare who'd lost her life here. She was climbing this rock on a rain-slick day, her legs probably unsteady in the driving wind. She had gone off the path, Denise had told me, when everyone knew it was reckless to leave the trodden rock. Maybe she'd been trying to get away from the chatter of other tourists; maybe she'd been trying to hear the spirit of the place, off alone, perilously close to the edge. Denise said she watched her drop over the side. A Swiss woman had scrambled down after her and given her heart massage, but it was too late.

Near the top, Akiko and I crouched in the skinny shade of a rock outcrop to wait for the bottleneck of people to clear. Akiko kept us entertained by sweetly telling winded, heart-attack-red Germans, "You're halfway there!" Below us, a strange-shaped slab of rock about nine feet high seemed to face out to the sea, looking like an armless stone goddess with wide curved hips. An elderly couple in golf hats and shorts sunned themselves beside it.

At the top, the site swarmed with Americans, Italians, Germans. Two overheated student guides tried hard not to lose their patience, shooing people and their lunches off the ancient stone structures. The stone beehive cells and small oratories were built from pieces of rock found on the island and fitted together so tightly into a beehive shape using dry stone construction (no mortar), that they remain impervious to water even today. On the hottest day in seven years, I had a hard time fixing on an image of the twelve monks, tapping their tools on stone in the raw wind and bursts of cold rain, painstakingly trying to shape a rock the perfect size for the next hole. The shelters made of this sharp rock are so perfect and smooth and symmetrical, they seemed to me to be something built by insects, ants or bees — by something genetically programmed to knit the raw materials of its environment into a viable community.

The interior of the largest cell is about thirteen by sixteen feet. I had to crouch to enter through the small doorway, which could have either acted as a constant reminder of humility or could have just been a practical way to let in less wind and rain. Standing alone in one cell, I looked up and saw a small opening in the roof. I sat in there for a couple of minutes in the semi-darkness, trying to picture the monks who had squeezed their lives into the limits of this scoop of rock. Somehow, they made a terraced vegetable garden. They buried their dead here, under the thin soil and stones, and erected rough stone crucifixes over the graves, perching their humble little cemetery on ground that overlooks the expanse of sea blending into sky. The arched window in the chapel frames a view of the mysterious Little Skellig.

In spite of their commitment to pare down their lives to spirit alone, picked clean of sensual pleasure, the place they chose hummed with a terrible beauty and they couldn't help themselves. As the small group of monks worked day after day scrambling up and down the rock face, heaving stone into place, shaping the skellig with their bare hands, they would have to fight back rising vanity, one of the eight capital sins laid out in the rules for monks in the Penitential of Cummean: "One who boasts of his own good deeds shall humble himself; otherwise any good he has done he has lost on account of human glory." Harder still would have been the hyper-awareness of their bodies, which ached with the burning fire of stretched, hard muscle. Alone with the smooth, curved muscle of their shoulders, their taut stomachs, the beauty of their sinewy forearms as the tight muscle turned and stretched beneath skin, they had thirty-three variations on fornication and thoughts of fornication to resist. For sodomy, seven years penance would be exacted. The mere desire to commit fornication, without the means to carry it out, carried a one-year penance. If a monk was "polluted by the violent assault of a thought" of fornication, he had to do seven days penance. Even in sleep, he had to be vigilant. If he was "willingly polluted during sleep," or even "unintentionally polluted," he had to sing Psalms, on his knees, and fast on bread and water. But the land that could kindle their passion and vanity could also be the means of their punishment: lashings of winter wind, razors of cold rain, slices of sharp rock to mortify the flesh.

Like their pagan relatives, who found the sacred in places like springs, lakes, and oak woods, the Christian Celts intertwined their faith with place, like organisms clinging to the rock, suffering the environment, and adapting. The land became a part of their spirituality; it helped them to express it. Somewhere in making the move to Christianity, my ancestors gradually left behind this spiritual connection to places. There were no Catholic holy wells on the Niagara Peninsula, no pilgrimages to rocky places. The priests and government were busy erasing the animism from Indigenous religions, and they certainly weren't going to encourage it in the settlers. It was this connection that I, and maybe Akiko and some of the other tourists, had lost. And we were reminded of it here, in this painstaking monument to wonder and to mystery.

A ghost of that mystery brushed against me briefly in the cool, cave-like cell. Then human voices chased it away as other tourists appeared in the square of sunlight in the doorway. When I peered into the other structures, I saw other people standing quietly, listening for something just out of hearing.

On Skellig Michael, a place pared down to unadorned holiness, I thought of things that seemed holy to me: the pure desire of the monks who had walked away from the safety of the world; the sudden splash of my healthy body cracking the still surface of a northern lake; a mother absorbed in scrubbing jam off her baby's cheeks. I wondered if I was too far gone altogether.

Last time I'd been to Mass, on Lough Derg, I had been bothered by the dryness of the church — the dry pages of the Book of Worship; the hard wooden pews; the thin, papery voices warbling uncertainly through an uninspiring hymn. The words of the prayers seemed lacking in any sense of vibrancy or gratitude. The Church had gone through a lot of changes over the years I'd been part of it. There was the move from Latin to English. Then the priest turned around to face the congregation instead of turning his back on them. In the sixties, I had a catechism that had a hip-talking Jesus who said things to the disciples like, "What are you getting so uptight about? It's just me, man." But all those changes had really made such a small difference. I read somewhere that Christians are stuck on the idea that all the major revelations have happened already; they're written in stone. We're left like children who have inherited their parents' house, but aren't allowed to take any of the plastic off the lampshades, let alone buy new ones.

But Skellig Michael seemed to hold out some kind of hope. On the rock that day, I dreamed that like the Celtic monks, I could weave my religion into the place I lived. I could be touched by something truly holy thundering through my everyday life. I dreamed that like the monks, I could find a pure, rock-hard core.

On the boat ride back to Portmagee our group was subdued. We had collectively snapped several rolls of film. We had considered the impossibility of the place, marvelled at the thousand-year-old primitive yet ingenious architecture. We had had our lunches in the sun, looking back across the heat-hazed Atlantic to the island of Ireland, and had nearly lost our footing on the treacherous path down, sending showers of stone to ping off the backs of other tourists' sunburned legs. Akiko and I had each pocketed a sharp black stone, hoping that we might feel the power of the place in the stone someday. We had been drawn to the rock by some common desire to learn the secret to the monks' purpose-drenched lives. But an unmistakable feeling of disappointment hung over our little boat. Was it worth the twenty pounds? Should we have gone to the beach instead? Karen Armstrong, in her book *A History of God* says, "The famous tag *post coitum omne animal tristis est* still expresses a common experience: after an intense and eagerly anticipated moment, we often feel that we have missed something greater that remains just beyond our grasp."

(2001)

I had three chapters of my book, *A Pilgrim in Ireland*, left to rework when I decided to go to St. Peter's Abbey for a week. At home, I had been trying to write about homesickness and monks and longing. But it was mid-April, on the verge of real spring, and the spin of daily life and the illusion of indispensability kept drawing me away from the writing. I had exams to mark, meals to cook, books to read, laundry to fold, a garden to plan. In between, I tried to imagine the life of a ninth-century Irish monk. All I could imagine was escape, the seduction of an ordered life guided by indisputable rules. My room was a robin's-egg-blue concrete rectangle with a large window, a bookshelf, dresser, single bed and a nice big desk. A simple wooden cross hung over the bed. I sat in front of the desk and arranged my yellow writing pad, books and a pen. Stillness. I sat there for about half an hour when the three o'clock bell chimed. Then silence rushed back in. The next day I walked through the fir trees where a thick blanket of cones covered the ground, baking sweetly in the spring sun. I sat in the long brown grass on the sunny bank of a pond alive with frogs and smelled the maple-syrup scent of new pussy willow buds opening. In among the trees a shrine to Mary chattered with birds. Afterwards, I went back to my desk and with the April breeze coming in the window, I wrote. The robin's-egg-blue walls brought back my childhood bedroom, the scent of my mother, the longing for home. Every day, I walked under the fir trees with my notebook in my pocket. Every day the winter disappeared a little more as I sat by the pond and wrote. I wrote into the night, and when my head still buzzed with the story and I couldn't sleep, I put on sweat pants and walked the dark halls of the sleeping abbey and watched the white moonlight-cast shadows in the courtyard. It was in the quiet of this routine, sinking into the story, putting one word after another, that I saw the courage involved in a monk's life. It was not escape, but commitment: trimming a hedge, canning fruit, tuning up a tractor, every day the simple routine of work a prayer.

Catherine Greenwood

Monk Love Blues

I got a little thing
I call the Monk Love Blues.
Remember Heloise and Abelard?
Well, this kind of thing ain't new.
See, when I say *monk*
I ain't talking Thelonius.
The monk love I'm feeling
done verge on felonius.

Yeah, I got those old Monk Love Blues.

I begin to quake and quiver,
I shiver and I pant
when I don't get my hit
of sweet Gregorian chant.
I'm jonesin' for a fix
of my Brother man-in-black
(he ain't heavy, honey,
he's just the Monkey on my back).

Got chased by the abbot
for courting a habit.
I'm hooked on those Monk Love Blues.

I need an injection
of Holy Spirit,
but no matter how I try,
I can't get near it.
I flirt my man in chapel
but he won't look my way,
if I walked up to him naked,
he'd just bow his head to pray.

I got me the Monk Love Blues.

So I tried a little witchcraft
to make him mine,
slipped a dose of number-nine potion
in the communion wine.
Well, I stirred up a commotion
with the rest of the Brethren,
but my monk was immune,
didn't even need confession.
I feed him raw oyster?
He heads for the cloister.
I'm stewing with the Monk Love Blues.

So I'll tell it to ya straight, Bro,
I ain't making any bones,
the Spirit's moving in me
like the Devil in Miss Jones.
Sometimes, you know, Baby,
we all have that urge.
How's about you lay it on me,
let me feel your scourge.

Come on Baby, let me ring your bell.
Let me light your candle,
I'll even vacuum your cell.
Let me polish your cross,
I'd do anything for you,
I'd wait till hell freezes over
just to warm your pew.

Cause I got me the soul-selling, bible-thumping
sweet, crazy Monk Love Blues.

O, Brother!

(2001)

Maureen Scott Harris

Ghazal for the Evening Games

The intoxication of naming: western red lily, merlin,
musquash (*Ondatra zibethica*), sweet red raspberry.

Thomas, Basil, Demetrius, Gerald, Anthony, Peter.
Lorna, Barbara, Jane, Joanne, Carol, Catherine, Liz.

I have never bought a dress in Swift Current.
What belongs and what doesn't is a constant worry.

"The subject of the traditional ghazal was usually love."
Warthog, Grasshopper, Traditional — then there's gin.

The clandestine order of words and laughter.
In the rough circle do we choose or find our places?

(1997)

Coming to St. Peter's for the Sage Hill Fall Poetry Colloquium in October 1995 changed my life. Those three weeks devoted to poetry, in a setting that I remember as filled with golden light (late fall sun, elm trees with yellow leaves, stubble fields, sloughs banked with dried grasses and reeds), offered me something that I have trouble putting into words — a deepening into both my work and myself is as close as I can get to it. By the time I left for Toronto I knew I had to come back. I believe the deepening I experience every time I come to St. Peter's is a gift of the place itself. Details of its landscape and weather lead me toward themselves and writing both. I've learned much about attentiveness, the close listening and looking that seem to me more and more essential to both poetry and my life.

Maureen Scott Harris

THE NEXT MORNING, ST. PETER'S

Rain falling and a tumult of dreams —
all those men with intentions, with
places to get to, and in a hurry —

Outside my window: grey sky and its
steady rain, the tender beginnings of
gardens, the wet fields beyond.

Rain and the birds still sing
though the magpies and crows are distant.

What is it I want anyway?

Let me be here, waiting for breakfast
and watching the dappled puddles
on the sand road. Let me listen
without knowing what I'm listening for
or to, the sounds sinking in
like dreams which surface and sink
and surface again, knitting the night
into the light.

The constant heave of the wind through
the elms washes into my room,
reminding me where I am:
where I want to be.

(1999)

Maureen Scott Harris

Walking in Saskatchewan with Rilke

All summer I've been walking with Rilke, the two of us
kicking up the dust. "Rainer" I'd say, "Look at that!"
my finger straight out, pointing at the sky burgeoning
over the flowing field or the spruce trees swimming
beyond the dugout. Mostly he didn't answer,
except for a slow nod, his own glance sweeping
along the arcing grasses — those dusty ones
which sway and dance at the verge's gravelled edge —
his mind caught in the brooding chamber. Our walking's
been companionable and he's a patient man, perhaps,
silent in spite of my garrulousness, and as for me,
I guess I wasn't waiting for any particular
answer, no marks given for poetic sensibility and
certainly no rose handed to me or letter inked
on scented paper, only some days
                              — the way
things surge into being, *here*, claim eyes, claim
mind, claim my very heart, beating and beating,
bird in the breast, this longing for sound —
                                       his silence
pulsing makes me want to throw back my head
and yap like any old dog, yellow fur rough with dust,
skin flaking, and a flea in my ear driving me
crazy, so I'll run for miles, nose down on prairie
scents, heart wild with sky and wind.

(1997)

Maureen Scott Harris

A Walk by the Dugout

Any place on the circumference is
an entrance. The field behind
the dugout, for instance.

In the field the flowers are
riotous, a toss and tangle, a fling
of scent poured out by the sun's
heated touch.

Above the field three crows
raucous a hawk, banging, clanging,
their black calls relentless
teetering its steady flight.

But turn from digression, even
from the world's sweet presence and
ask your hard question.
What remains?

What remains but the hard
block in my chest my hands full
of breaking and my own
loneliness?

> *The field also remains.*
> *Your hands will empty.*

(1996)

Julia Herperger

St. Peter's Abbey

At the end of summer, I stand in a field
of wild grass and purple clover. Here I can see
everything for what it is: the falling sun,
the abbey bells ringing out
into the still and clear air.

(1999)

Julia Herperger

Brother Basil

My last evening at the monastery, Brother Basil
offers me a ride into town tomorrow.

In the monk's garden, among the white mimosa
and blue air, he smiles as he looks down

at his feet, and it's not hard to imagine
he was the shy farm boy who left saucers of milk

for the barn kittens. Tomorrow we'll drive
past barley fields and sage, but just now

we are still, held silent
between blue air and earth.

(2001)

Trevor Herriot

On Mount Carmel

THE LAND FALLS AWAY from us here in a theatre of grass not quite as ancient as the sand and clay beneath it. The sun is aloft, but we're waiting. Karen, who walked up here with me an hour ago, sits quiet in the refuge of her thoughts on a flat boulder just downslope. My thoughts are ranging away from here too far to embrace the peace that I have felt before on this hillside. A trip that was supposed to be a spiritual retreat now feels like a flight into bewilderment.

We made our arrangements weeks ago, knowing Karen would need a respite from the work it takes to get four children pointed in the right direction at the end of summer. Music and dance lessons, basketball registration, school supplies and clothes to buy. One child starting high school, one in elementary school, one still homeschooling, and one just weaned — sometimes Karen feels like she's packed fourteen years of child-rearing into thirty days.

August rolled on by with me lost in my own projects, oblivious to the bedlam downstairs. I've been preparing a submission on the birds and plants that would be affected by a dam proposed for one of the continent's last great stretches of wild prairie river. Six days ago I was on the river with a good friend, Rob, his son, Orion, and my son Jon. We had some weather so the boys learned the rough side of canoeing in a long day of trudging the shoreline, rope over shoulder, head down, hauling a loaded canoe into driving rain and a headwind too stiff to paddle against. Things cleared the next morning and the wind shifted, came round. We lashed the canoes together and hoisted a sail made of tarp roped to cottonwood staves. We ruddered our way down the river through five-hundred-foot-high cliffs

---

This piece is the introduction to the second part of a book I am writing on the subject of religion and wildness. *Jacob's Wound,* to be published by McClelland & Stewart in the fall of 2004, includes several passages set in and around St. Peter's Abbey. I had intended to write a different book, but somewhere in the summer of 2000 when I first began visiting the abbey and attending the writers' colonies, the manuscript headed off on its own uncharted path.

and badlands, sagebrush flats, cottonwood groves. We found a bullsnake that day, prairie falcons, and several eagles, both golden and bald. As evening drew on and we neared our campsite, a pair of golden eagles flushed some geese from the river right in front of us. The larger eagle, the female, rose into the air and then swooped on the panicked geese, knocking a single bird down to the shore. We drifted by in silence, watching her wrestle the goose into submission while her mate waited nearby. A foot on the goose's breast, she ripped at its breast tossing feathers into the wind and checking now and then on her audience. A piece of down landed in Jon's hair without his noticing.

That night we camped on a large sandy island with cottonwood forest at our backs. With supper over and the boys in the tent, Rob and I reclined by the fire to drink tea and watch the night sky. A strange glow that was not lightning throbbed on and off a couple of times to the west. It might have been artillery exercises at the military range twenty miles away and I said something about almost having forgotten the world beyond the valley. That was enough to shift our talk to the second most popular topic for discussion around the campfire on canoe trips (the first being bears). Anyone who has lived by canoe and river for a few days will recognize this kind of palaver: what a great day it was… you know, I could live like this all the time…. I guess this is what it was like for the Indians before we buggered things up…. Rob had just followed through with the next sentiment — *we deserve to live like this more of the time* — when a plough wind blew in from nowhere, extinguished our fire in a single stroke, and flattened the tent with the boys inside.

As we ran to the tent to rescue our sons, I heard a strange sound coming from the water's edge, a hollow *ka-dunk, ka-dunk, ka-dunk*, rhythmic but getting quieter with each iteration, as though receding from us. A canoe might make that kind of sound, it dawned on me, if it were tumbling along a beach and off into the darkness of a storm. I ran blindly in the direction of the river, chasing the sound through utter blackness. I reached the river just as the sound stopped. It had to be somewhere in front of me in the water. Rob arrived with his lantern, swung the beam across the churning surface of the river and there it was, a few feet offshore half-submerged and floating away in the shallows.

After we had hauled the canoe out of the river and beaten a path into the shelter of the cottonwoods, where we were able to anchor the tent with lines, the message settled into my thoughts: *this too was part of the old life in such a place.*

It was a kind of rude grace, that storm in the midst of utter tranquillity and comfort, a small comeuppance that has lingered in my thoughts this week when we are all of us wondering about the messages borne in a sudden moment of violence. The day after we got off the river and returned to city life, the calendar flipped over to Tuesday, September 11, 2001. Now on this hilltop, five days later, there is a tranquillity again, but it feels wrong, dishonest. Waiting at home there are facts I can't retreat from: in particular, four children I am rearing in a culture that is beginning to harvest the fruits of its long fear of the pagan and the wild.

Disasters abound. I heard an ecologist say recently that we will lose fifty per cent of the continent's biodiversity in this century. A farmer whose sons have given up their dreams of ever living on the land told me last month that he thinks the seed and chemical companies will have complete control of prairie agriculture within twenty-five years. And now political and religious leaders are trying out old words like "crusade" hoping they might stimulate the righteous hatred that fuels vengeance.

Escape bears its own despair. At dusk the earth will look like a good place to rest, as it has to others on this hilltop. Now, while the sun still shines and the wind blows over this upland, I am having trouble recalling what it is in our faith in God and heaven that cannot be taken, owned or earned. A sound floats by on the breeze, a rolling *groa-oa-oa-oa-oo-oo*, the edges softened by distance, the rhythm like a thumbnail drawn across the teeth of a comb. Hearing this, the call of migrating cranes so far overhead I cannot see them, I believe in their journey miraculous and wild from northern marshes to southern ones a thousand miles away, and I can at least imagine the possibility of such unfettered truth in the human longing for spirit.

Grace, as tent-flattening storm, the cry of cranes, or the still voice whispered in the prophet's ear, is a kind of sympathy expressed between Creator and creature. St. Paul used the Greek *charism*, meaning a gratuitous gift, something that can never be taken or appropriated. Church doctrine says that grace belongs to the "supernatural order" of things. That may be, but it spills over into the natural order and touches us from somewhere within the fierce heart of wildness.

A few feet behind Karen and me on the top of the hill there is a statue of the one who is "full of grace." Here she is known as "Our Lady of Carmel." This is the Mount Carmel in my corner of the Americas, a hill of remnant grassland perched atop the watershed I think of as my home range. Christians have been busy renaming heights of land "Mount

Carmel" since they first jumped off the boats and walked uphill. This Mount Carmel, a graceful rise of mixed-grass prairie 1987 feet above sea level, is a mountain only in our fondest imaginings. From the top, though, a pilgrim gains the view that made its namers think of alpine. Four hundred miles of skyline encircle us here, all of it arcing around farmland that, before a colony of German settlers arrived with their ploughshares, was one small cove on the northern coast line of this continent's inland sea of grass. Only the crests, this one and its outliers, have kept their pelt. The native grass in small tatters now, I can make out in the middle distance grey remnants, two or three acres here and there, where the slope was too steep, the soil too stony, for the plough.

Mary wasn't the first virgin to honour this prominence with her spirit. A girl named Hatty McKay died here 130 years ago — before anyone claimed the hill for Our Lady of Carmel. In Hatty's time, the generation that preceded the ones who turned the sod wrong side up, this hill had other names. An early map calls it "Keespitanow Hill," a story calls it "Big Butte," a local history says "Round Hill." Sir William Butler, romancing his way across the Great Lone Land with an eye out for anything that might make a good chapter in his memoir, conceived the hill's name in phonetics that would roll off the tongue of a Victorian reader:

> The hill of the Wolverine and the lonely Spathanaw Watchi have witnessed many a deed of Indian daring and Indian perfidy…. Alone in a vast waste the Spathanaw Watchi lifts his head, thickets and lakes are at its base, a lonely grave at its top, around four hundred miles of horizon; a view so vast that endless space seems for once to find embodiment, and at a single glance the eye is satisfied with immensity. There is no mountain range to come up across the sky-line, no river to lay its glittering folds along the middle distance, no dark forest to give shade to foreground or to fringe perspective, no speck of life, no track of men. Nothing but the wilderness. Reduced to its nakedness, space stands forth with almost terrible grandeur.

Butler published his florid travelogue [*The Wild North Land*] in 1873, a year after Hatty died, but the hilltop grave he mentions could not have been hers. An old Métis plainsmen, Isador Dumas, interviewed in 1928, recalled the day in 1872 when he built a coffin for Hatty. Isador and a friend, Alexander Ablais, dug a grave and buried her at the base of Mount Carmel. Hatty, or Henrietta McKay, was a Catholic — "Irish," says one of the accounts, which is the word that local histories will sometimes use to avoid the less appealing term, "half-breed." There were no Irishmen in this region before 1890, not full-blooded ones anyway; McKay is a common

Métis name, and Fish Creek was a Métis settlement just up the river from Batoche. The story goes that she refused to marry an "Englishman," the euphemism for Protestant. Her parents were insistent for some unspecified reason. She may well have carried his baby, though the gloss of local legend carries no hint of that. Whatever its cause, her fear of life in his hands grew until she lit out for the hills one morning.

The first discalced Carmelite, first unshod Christian hermit in these parts, Hatty took refuge in the wild anchorage offered by a height of land her native flesh knew to be blessed and holy. Hers was the same half-wild impulse that sends us out to the country beyond our scribed and sheltered lives, looking to be saved but not safe, gone to thunder, bewildered by wind, hobbling on stones as old as starlight. But the Word had already diminished the oral tradition of her ancestors, suspending her somewhere between the old truth carried in narratives known and remembered in the heart's love of stories and the new sorcery of scripted truth. None of it bore the warnings she needed, the injunction against eating water hemlock or camas bulb. Or had her Kookum taught her the dangers of such plants and she sought them out at the foot of Keespitanaw, choosing to return to earth rather than surrender like settled territory signed away in treaties? Either way, the death-from-life distilled within roots and leaves bore her down to the wet, rebirthing greenery that skirts this hill in spring.

Where are you now, Hatty McKay? They've searched this hillside over and your small bones are gone away. Did you whisper prayers to the one who is filled with grace, the patroness of all virgins who'd rather die than fall into the grasp of the unholy? Hail Mary, full of grace . . . . words that spring to the lips of every Catholic in times of fear and bewilderment.

"This is the first Sorrowful Mystery — The Agony in the Garden," my mother would announce before we launched into the first ten Hail Marys as my father drove the Dodge at five miles per hour into the oblivion of a January blizzard. To this day I associate Mary with bad prairie weather. We'd pray the rosary until a light from a farmhouse appeared and then my father would get out of the car and vanish into the white swirl while we chanted another decate from the backseat. Too many moments later he'd re-emerge, open the door and shout above the howl, "Okay, they can take us in. Let's go," and we'd follow him across the snow toward the yellow light that meant sanctuary from the storm.

Fear marks most of my early memories of the Virgin Mary. I remember hearing adults talk about her appearing to children at a "grotto." Steering clear of grottoes was easy in a prairie town, but the plastic figurine on my mother's dresser vexed me. As a small child given to nightmares, I'd often end up in my parents' bed before daybreak. One morning I woke to find myself alone in the room — just me and the figurine, which seemed to be shimmering on the dresser. I stared at it, frozen in dread, and then the damn thing moved, just a little, a trick of the half-light and my imagination. I threw off the covers and bolted from the room, never to sleep there again.

I was terrified, in the way only a child can be, that I would be chosen for a visitation. Right now, on this hill named for Elijah's mountain, I wouldn't mind a sign of some sort. A little reassurance would be appreciated. I settle in next to Karen on her boulder and wrap an arm around her small form. We've decided to wait for the sun to set. There's dust in the air from harvest so it should be a good show. Holding onto the woman who long ago decided she can put up with my ways, I am thinking of all that has fled embrace: Hatty and her people, the surviving wildness, the spirit of rural life. Most remote of all, though, are the mystical forces of redemption and prophecy carried forward in our traditions of Mary and Elijah. This has not been a week for hope. You wonder if we have a prayer. Maybe that's all we have.

(2002)

Gerry Hill

North Central Baseball League Semi-Final, Muenster Red Sox vs. Melfort Brewers, July 23, 2001

Prologue

Late in the game, the Red Sox give up the tying runs,
the last with two outs and two strikes on
McCard, the Brewers shortstop, who bloops a game-
tying single. The umpires confer, glance at the dark
skies beyond left field and consult Article Nine of the
Official Rules of Baseball. In a moment the home plate
umpire, Mr. Todd Hunker, rules as follows:

Two things hit me bright and early this morning. One:
Mom's birthday, she's 86 today, and the other:
the ballgame. Happy Birthday, Mom. She's
the best. I had a card to Mom in the mail by 9
and my shirt and pants and gear laid out by ten thirty,
then nothing else to do but wait
the 7 ° hours till game time.

And now we've got trouble. It's known as sundown.
And the Rules are clear: in lieu of daylight, it's dark.
In lieu of daylight, there is none. Game called
on account of no light.

In the moment of raw silence that follows, the players wonder. *What "no light?"* The sweat still glistens on Rauchman's goatee. *I got half a bag of seeds left. What's a little darkness when a ball game's on?* As they spit on their hands, hoist a couple of bats or windmill their arms to loosen up, preparing for extra innings, each member of the Red Sox starting line-up steps forward to speak.

#11, Garret Korte, left field

*My dad would keep playing. Uncle Joe, Grandpa —
they'd keep playing. Hell, grandma'd still be out there,
taking ground balls, chattering a mile a minute. They know
what it means to go all the way at a time
like this. We'll catch hell from all of them if we don't
keep playing. The history of baseball doesn't end
in a tie, so don't give me any of that guff
about light, ok?*

#22, Jason Blechinger, shortstop

*See that tater I hit in the second? Off the roof of the Lutheran
church in deep right field, I mean* deep *right field. What's
deeper than a Lutheran church? And for the sake of you folks who believe
in miracles, that's my fourteenth miracle this season. I plan to hit
another just like it. Tonight. With Elaine here (he kisses
his bat). Me and Elaine — POW. Don't make me put her away,
mister umpire. I promised I'd hold her all night long and it ain't
all night yet.*

#47, Daniel "Rock" Rauckman, third base

*I ripped my pants diving for a ball in the top
of the first, ripped 'em worse in the second, damn near
ripped right through 'em in the sixth. Going to keep
playing till I'm naked, I guess. Then you'll see
some loose balls (just kidding). But we gotta
keep playing. I just took a look, we're miles
from sundown. Who cares about sundown anyway?*

#4, Jeff Loehr, right field

*You might have noticed every inning I run a quarter mile
out to right, a quarter mile back at the end of the inning, not to mention
chasing fly balls, or backing up first base. I'm a race-
horse, man — a regular Whirlaway. You don't run me then say
I can't run no more, just like that. Any more than you'd get a horse
lathered, tell it to walk the rest of the way. No sir, watch me
suck down a cool one, run back out there.*

#19, Chad Hoffmann, first base

*I'm the kind of guy takes a couple of innings to open
my eyes, a couple more to warm up. I usually
kick in about the fifth inning in time to crank one out when
it counts, know what I'm saying? Picture this: the potential
winning run's in scoring position and the crowd's going crazy and
my sweetheart's jumping up and down and I'm at the dish, working
the count in my favour, about to light up this place
for good. That's when I'm alive, man. Screw
sunlight. Extra innings is* my
time to shine.

#9, Brent Loehr, catcher

*Make you a deal. I admit I'm a tad worn out from
squatting and standing up and squatting again every
five seconds — plus from legging out that double to the base
of the center field fence in the fifth, see that? And I admit
it's tough being the guy the ball comes to on every play. But you
admit I got a fire in me that don't go out, especially
in the dark. All darkness does is stoke me up. Hell, I'm
praying for the dark.*

#20, Jesse "James" Korte, second base

*Everything my brother said — ditto
for me. And here's something else. Those are my kids
chasing foul balls for a quarter a ball. That's Tom
over there, age 8, and Lucy in the blue, she's 6. Wouldn't
be right to take them home to bed before the game
ends. Just wouldn't be right. Might spoil
their dreams. I say keep going till they see
their old man win. They'll sleep good enough
after that.*

#17, Derek "White Tail" Blanch, center field

*I don't know, they say I'm fast like a deer, must have been born
half deer the way I cut off line drives heading for the gap. I'll leap
against the fence to keep a fly-ball in the park if I have to. It's my
country out there, my wild land where I run free and no one
can hear me. As for tonight, I'm best when it's cool anyway. You might
not see me till I jump out in front of you, but I'll be there, leaping
out of nowhere when it counts.*

#18, Brent "Sookie" Suchan, pitcher

*I could chuck ball all night. I'm just as strong as
I ever was. Got a rubber arm, man, and a jug of Absorbine
Junior and a bag of ice to take care of the arm later. It's
standing around that tires me out. I left a couple
of fastballs over the plate in the sixth, and McCard
was lucky to get his bat on my sinker in
the seventh or I'd have fanned him. Give me
the ball, quit yacking, let's go.*

#8, Jim "The General" Korte, Manager

It's all about mental preparation. You spend 48
hours getting ready, winding your clock,
so to speak. You settle your affairs, make sure your
loved ones are taken care of, say goodbye to mom
and dad, tie off loose ends at work — it's a little like
the last supper, really. That's what we're up against. Let me
put it this way: We don't give in to darkness, tonight
or any other night. The way I see it, when a man stands up
for a game of ball, he don't sit down till it's over, right?

Mr. Todd Hunker, umpire

I still say the sun's too far
gone for the boys to finish this game, but I sense
a greater power at work here.
All right,
you folks in the bleachers, go park your cars around
the outfield, turn your headlights on. Harv, send me down
two or three more balls. And Mom, wherever you are, I hope
you're having one great birthday. Play ball!

Epilogue

The following night in Melfort, it was Brewers
12, Red Sox 6. Now it's on to Marysburg.

The writers colonies at St. Peter's Abbey let me be where I belong: at the edge of the dugout, or watching the crows fill their black bellies out by the burn barrel, or back and forth along the CN main line or the grid roads. I'm at home near what for decades has been third base on the ball field. I'm drawn to the routes of silence and observation through the cornfield, the berry patches, the rink, the burial ground, and any number of other field stations at the beginning or end of some path. All the time I'm facing the wild blue yonder as much as my notebook, one becoming an alternate version of the other. Over and over again.

Gerry Hill

Prayer for the Sun

Not that my teapot is full of rain or that it
runs from the corners of my mouth and Brother Anthony
when he carries trash to the burn barrel wears a peaked cap
and the spark in the cylinders of my Olds must bore
through dampness to fire,

                                          or that the morning
drags at my ankles and we've all worn
the same colour for days and puddles lie like
minefields and even skunks smell of
water, or that my left shoulder is three
months older than my right,
or that bells
shiver where they chime or millions of
creatures a week old don't believe you ever were or
that the berries look wan and even the spruce
pine for you,

                      or that the junkyard is a ferocious
green from the grass up, the crows
don't trust each other, the press
prints tracts of pain and you are neither here
nor there,   you, page one in the book
of stars and planets, you for whom Crayola
invented yellow, you the nearest hot
spot, give it up for the writers of Toronto and the others
who huddle in a cave of rain, eyes dull with water.

(2001)

Kitty Hoffman

Ghosts

*Only after many years would I be able to write what I then imagined…
when I knew that if I did not write, death would not do it for me. You start
by writing to live. You end by writing so as not to die. Love is the
marriage of this desire and this fear.*
    ~ Carlos Fuentes, *How I Started to Write*

Wherever I go, these particular ghosts have come with me. I don't know their names, or what they look like. I only feel their presence, male, stern, demanding yet loving. They are all the fathers, back through a line stretching from Warsaw and the Ukraine, through some unknown place of detour in Germany, back through southern France and perhaps even Spain (I know this from a family name on my mother's side, linked to Sagi-NaHar, the great Kabbalist Isaac the Blind), back to the beginning, Jerusalem before the expulsion, the holy place that was our special link to the Source. It took me decades to piece together this line, to learn where it started and how it meandered through the Mediterranean and northern European worlds of exile.

    Throughout my childhood, I felt their presence, but mistakenly thought they were all from my parents' time, merely the ghosts of all the grandfathers and uncles murdered in the last round of killings. This was crowded enough, a cloud of male presence that accompanied me wherever I went, claiming me for their own unfinished purpose, requiring me to remember their unspoken teachings, surrounding me with their stifled yet powerful love. I felt their presence as a burden, their silent demands weighing me down with the mystery of obligation. They needed me for some purpose, but I had no idea how to find out what that purpose was, let alone how to fulfill it. And yet they held me captive, hovered around me with the constant reminder that my life was not mine alone.

I felt them strongly this morning, as I took my first walk in the grounds of St. Peter's Abbey. I am here on a writers retreat, in the middle of the prairie, an urbanite unfamiliar with this flat, open landscape. I arrived last night in time to follow my curiosity to a choir concert in the monks' chapel. The ubiquitous crucifixes and constant references to the shelter of the Christian saviour were disorienting. It was Friday night, the beginning of the Jewish Sabbath; I was acutely aware of the irony of coming to such a place for my internal exploration of my Jewish identity. While Jews around the world, even my own little *shul* community back home in Victoria, were lighting Sabbath candles to welcome the *Shechinah*, the female aspect of God who hovers close on *erev Shabbat*, I was listening to Christian hymns under the sign of the cross. I'd felt the ghosts with me last night; I had expected that they would be critical, wagging their fingers in patriarchal judgment. But as I sat in the chapel, I felt instead their sheltering protection, and a bemused ironic acceptance. As I prepared for my first night in the sparse room that had once housed nuns, I realised that I had to remove the crucifix from over the bed, but there was no need for me to customize this place beyond that act. My ghosts were here with me.

The irony intensified this morning, as I came upon the cemetery, small and tidy, encircled by a neat hedge. Reading the tombstones, I remembered reading that this abbey had been founded by Benedictines who had come north from Minnesota, and as enterprising founding fathers had bought up all the surrounding land and made it hospitable for their flock. This is Germanic country: German Catholics settled here from south of the border, and from their place of origin in Bavaria, where Hitler had started out; Germans, kinsmen to those people who had created the entire state apparatus for the murder of the Jews. These graves marked the remains of spiritual men, contemplatives who had devoted their lives to a holy purpose. Yet they were branches of the same cultural tree as those who had created the conditions for the destruction of my people. The names on the tombstones were all Germanic; through the Christian Latin renderings of their birth, novitiate, ordination, death, their spiritual names as monks, rang the Germanic syllables of their last names of origin. Like my own last name, Hoffman, a reminder of the Jews' thousand-year sojourn in *Ashkenaz*, the Hebrew name for Germany, the name by which we European Jews call ourselves. I sat on my stone bench in this abbey cemetery, and was transported to another cemetery that I had visited over twenty years earlier.

It is midday under the scorching holy sun of Israel, and I am sweating as I sit on a hillside dotted with gnarled olive trees. Like most hills in this place, vegetation is sparse, scrubby and tough, matching the people and their ideas. This holy land, this holy space, is harsh and demanding. The sun is blinding in its light, like the other Light that reveals itself most intensely here. I am twenty, visiting the land of my ancestors for the first time, the land promised to us chosen people, and I am thinking of my particular family history, wondering why so many were chosen for death, wishing like the old joke says that some others could be chosen for a while so we could get a break to just be, just live. While all hills in Israel are special, holding stones that speak of struggles for light and struggles in darkness over millennia, this hill that I am on is extra special. Somehow, following the tourist trail, without really knowing where I was going or what the significance of the place might be, I have found myself in the holy graveyard of Safed, called *Tzfat* in the original Hebrew, a medieval town in the hills above *Kinneret*, the Sea of Galilee. I am sitting among the tombs of the holy rabbis of *Tzfat*, not even knowing how privileged I am to be there, for soon these tombs will be closed to women, accessible only to men.

I know nothing of these holy rabbis; even their names are meaningless to me. I sit on this hilltop filled with a Holy Land awareness built up by my four precocious years of university literary studies, filled with the Christian interpretation of this landscape. Earlier, in Jerusalem, I walked the Stations of the Cross, visited the Garden of Gethsemani, made pilgrimage to the Churches of the Ascension and the Assumption, encountered this sacred city of my ancestors as the Holy City, through the overlay of interpretation of those who took my great-great-grandfathers' stories and retold them for their own purposes.

In that era, the cemetery is still somewhat obscure; Kabbalah has not yet become trendy, the shrines of its great mystics have not yet achieved wide prominence; the great all-night vigils on holy days are still to come. But as I sit there, twenty years old and ignorant of the spiritual teachings of my own tradition, I feel something. I am aware of a power, some essence that I cannot name or even describe, something that fills me with what I can only call a blue light. I am aware of certain presences around me, certain other consciousnesses that are in this space with me. They feel somehow male, although I cannot really say what that means or why I feel this. They are connected to me in some way, although this too is unclear and I cannot say what I really mean by it. Unlike the male ghosts who have been with me all my life, these presences have a power I have never felt before. All I know is that I am not fully alone on that hillside, among these graves. I am with others, although I have no idea who or what these others might be, and cannot even say what I mean by this.

Oddly for me, taught by my mother's traumas to be fearful of just about everything, I am completely calm and peaceful.

As I sat in the abbey graveyard this morning, and felt my familiar ghosts joined by the spirits of the Germanic monks who had brought the teachings of Benedict from sixth-century Italy to nineteenth-century prairie wilderness, I remembered that graveyard in *Tzfat*, remembered the blue light. And I thought how strange it was to be in this Christian place on this *Shabbat* morning.

    Years after my brief time in the *Tzfat* graveyard, I would learn that I had in fact visited the graves of the four holy rabbis of *Tzfat*, the great mystics who had expanded on the *Zohar*, the primary text of Kabbalah, or Jewish mysticism. I would learn that the presence I'd felt, the blue light I'd dimly sensed, had been at the grave of the great sixteenth-century rabbi, Isaac Luria, the holy Ari, the one who taught that what is below is also above, who explicated the correspondences among the four levels of reality. I would learn Kabbalistic teachings about the various souls within us, how the lowest level of soul is inextricably linked to the physical body and dies with it, but other levels of souls correspond to the various other levels of reality and are linked to these worlds beyond physical life and death. I would learn how one level of soul can speak to our consciousness even after the physical person has died, can return to visit us as an invisible *ibbur*, a dimly felt presence who guides or helps us. These *ibburim*, the Kabbalists teach, are the souls of those who no longer live with us in this physical realm, but come to us when we need their help, providing assistance even when we are not aware of their presence. These *ibburim* find it easier to come near the site of the graves of their physical bodies, or in the presence of the *yahrzeit* candles lit on the anniversary of the death of their physical body. And I would learn that another grave on that same *Tzfat* hillside was the last home of the great mystic and poet Elkabetz, who had composed the lyrical love poem "*Lecha Dodi*," "Come My Beloved," sung by the Kabbalists of *Tzfat* every Friday night in their mystical welcome of the Sabbath Queen, their anticipation of the weekly consummation of the cosmic union of the people Israel with their beloved *Shechinah*.

    I sat in the graveyard of St. Peter's Abbey imagining a monk's life, given over to holy service, dedicated to a reality that cannot be seen. I tried to imagine the life of one of these old monks establishing his saviour's dominion, a dominion of black robes and plain chant, in the wilderness of the New World. And I remembered the hillside in *Tzfat*, a town that was built on the model of Toledo by the Jews expelled from Spain after the Inquisition.

I sat under the prairie sun, and remembered the scorching sun of the blue light of *Tzfat*. It was Saturday morning, *Shabbat*, and as my own extended family around the world was in *shul* hearing the ancient chanting of Torah, I was sitting in a monastery graveyard. I was filled with the enormity of it, the strange combination of historical and cultural forces that had come together to culminate in me sitting in that place. I felt the deep contradictions within myself, contradictions that had fractured my spirit. "Be brave," my family ghosts had told me since I was a child, "go out into that wider world and make something of yourself among the nations." But whenever I got close, whenever a moment of integration and purpose seemed imminent, whenever I seemed about to enter the flow around me, the ghosts would issue their warnings: "Be careful, don't lose your wariness." I had to enter the world around me; my life was among the others; but I was never allowed to forget, was surrounded by the ghosts who always reminded me that this alien world could never really be my home. "*Lecha Dodi*," these ghosts now invited, "Come My Beloved, let us greet the Sabbath Queen, who is coming to meet her bridegroom Israel." Not for me the sheltering arms of the saviour, not for me the cleansing blood of the lamb. I could sing the songs, feel the spirit; but never partake of that salvation. My ghosts would always remind me of who I really was.

I could stay in this graveyard no longer. The crosses were no longer merely markers of others' faith, but an irrefutable reminder of my own divided soul, my own incessant alienation. I longed for my own family cadences, the oriental pitch of the *Shabbat* morning prayer. I rose from the bench, turned and left the quiet circle. The sun continued to shine, and I realised what I needed to do. I had no *shul*, no *minyan*, the ten Jews required for a Torah service. I had no *tallit*, no prayer shawl; I had no *siddur*, no prayer book. I had no *mizrach*, no prayer guide to point me in the direction of the holy Jerusalem. But I had the original *mizrach*, the sun in the east; and I knew that I had to offer my *Shabbat* morning prayer.

I stood in the road leading to the monks' cemetery, stood on the grounds of St. Peter's Abbey amid the prairie grasses and, like my dispersed and exiled family members over the millennia, I faced the sun in the east and remembered Jerusalem. I swayed gently back and forth in my private version of Chassidic *shockelling*, the jerky bobbing and swaying that marks the pious Jew's intensity and wards off the evil impulse. I silently repeated the *Shema* over and over: "Hear O Israel." I performed the subtle bow and dip of the blessings of the *Amidah*, the required prayer: "Blessed are you, O God...." and I added my own improvised ending, words that appeared out of nowhere and escaped before I had time to consider them: "Blessed are you... who brought me to this place...."

And they came to me again, my ghosts, my *ibburim*, also men dressed in black. Not the black of the monks' robe and cowl, but the black *shtreimel* and *kapote*, the hat and frock coat, of the *Hasid* of eighteenth-century Europe, the black garb of my great-great-grandfathers. I felt their love, I felt their protection. But even more, something new and wonderful, I felt their approval. "Yes, *Kitkele*" they addressed me by the Yiddish diminutive of my name, "It's alright. It's good you're here. This is where you should be. They're good men, these brothers, and they've made a place that is good for you."

For the first time, I felt and believed the truth of the words I always utter when confronted with others' spiritual traditions, the words I always speak to the Catholics and the Hindus and the Buddhists I encounter: "Aren't we all just on different paths to the same place? Isn't it just different cultural styles, different ways of saying the same thing?" I say these words, trying to diminish my otherness, trying to deflect what I have been taught to expect at any moment, lurking just under the surface of the civilized veneer.

Other things that I knew, that I had been told, fell into place as if for the first time. I remembered my mother's story of how, after she had witnessed the shooting of her entire family in her village square, after she herself had been shot and lost consciousness, she revived and, feigning death, heard two Ukrainian Gestapo talking about her: "That one's still alive, I think I saw that dirty Jew move; I'd better shoot her again to make sure." And the other voice, possibly the voice of a young Ukrainian neighbour, now enlisted in the local Gestapo "No, don't waste your ammunition; I'm sure she's dead." Saving her life. I remembered her many stories of the various Ukrainian Evangelical farmers who'd harboured her, hidden her behind stoves and under beds, transferred her from hiding place to hiding place, risked their own lives and all their family to shelter a hunted Jew. Saving her life.

"It's okay, *Kitkele*," my ghosts said to me. "This is where you should be." I had often wondered why my birthplace should be Norway, why my home should be Canada. For many years I longed for the Jewish homeland, or even for the Jewish New York of legendary immigrant life. My mind turned to these Germanic monks, with their last names just like mine. Building something new in a new place. I imagined my family ghosts, in their black *shtreimels* and *kapotes*. I imagined the ghosts of these monks, in their black robes and cowls. I imagined they saw each other, nodded, exchanged brief smiles.

(2002)

Maureen Hynes

Clang

Quick, throw on your coat and run outside because all the bells are
ringing — this is war's end, happy marriages for all and a plentiful harvest
fused into sound —; ringing as if the despot had been dethroned, the lost
recipes for kindness found, earthquakes and calamities dispelled
from the land. All of them, all at once, seem to peal from everywhere! Run

to the bellcot, never mind the hard westward slants of grey rain — lift your face
up into the chimes glancing off every aspen leaf, fencepost and vole. Watch
    the bells tilt
and scatter buckets of O's in every direction, they are birds' mouths, opening, filling,
opening again. If you want to ring like a bell, you must ring from your core
to your fingertips, scalp, your hardened soles: wholehearted — it's dangerous
to rattle just the clapper from within, you will crack like early ice on a lake,
a huge piece missing thereafter like the five-ton Russian bell.

Stay for the fade, the one long note again, again, again — its ache and
residue; joy is still in our repertoire, and we,
perversely, wish it gone.

When I went to the Fall Poetry Colloquium in 1997, my father had died about ten days before, and it was an extraordinary gift to be able to spend time with my grief and write about it. With gratitude, I remember all the help and support that the other participants and Tim Lilburn gave me. I hope that the appreciation for that awareness and support comes through in the poem "Dance Pavilion," about our wonderful trip to Danceland. The three weeks at St. Peter's were extremely productive for me. Though in my teens I had made a big deal of severing my relationship with Catholicism, the monastery seemed so perfect an environment to begin to heal from the long ordeal of my parents' illnesses and deaths. As the fall at St Peter's deepened, and fewer and fewer aspen leaves remained, I kept up my morning walks to all my cherished spots – inside the two hedges around the graves, to the sloughs, to the various grottos and to the apiaries. And suddenly one Sunday morning, awoken by the church bells ringing for several minutes, I had a kind of revelation that I tried to put into the poem "Clang." I realized that "joy was in my repertoire," it was a choice I could make. And that seemed like a wonderful gift from St. Peter's.

Maureen Hynes

Dance Pavilion

Manitou Lake, Saskatchewan

Inside the van, they consider the approach
of sunset; quiet laughter
as the road, straight-pinned onto the prairie,
pegs its way forward like a curtain seam
spilling out of an old sewing machine. Overhead,
muted calls and the sharp angle of the geese's flight
widens, splinters, tightens. Then the van

turns the only bend of the trip,
the bend that hugs the sudden
low hills still etched with tipi rings, the bend
that rims and crosses the salt water lake
in the middle of this province of pelicans
and grid roads, arches and softens the evening,
releases it with the bounce, bounce, bounce

of a let-go ball of yarn. Under
the dancehall's rounded roof,
greyed and graceful couples
move in circles on the sprung floor,
the O's of the saxophones
surround them, *My Blue Heaven*,
the vocabulary of nostalgia
  — console radio, they think, sunset and the quarter moon;
dance us back to Casa Loma, the hotel suite
at war's end, that return and the stories
sealed for decades. O, the fidelity
of the pavilion, and the old bandleader's skill.
At the edge of the polished maple dance floor,
two young women in thin dresses and Doc Martens hold
each other gingerly, we'll learn this here,
try out our affection. Is this, then, how injuries
are healed?

Barbara Klar

Three Weeks

There is a hole in the year
where, a year ago, we gathered.
I will call the place *goldenness*.
We were the leaves
of nine related species on one tree
taking light from the fields
that would not stop shining.
But the precious fell.
The wind blew east and west,
us to our cloudy basements.

In the dream of not parting
we won't all fit in my truck
and no one gets to the airport.
That is not how it happened.
There was harvest. Fields
went out. I will call
these weeks a hole in the year
where we shone before parting.

Don, Hilary, Marlene, Maury, Pam, Ruth, Sara, Trish: this poem's for you. "Three Weeks" is a small attempt to describe our good-byes to St. Peter's Abbey on October 21, 1996 — the last day of our Sage Hill fall poetry colloquium. For three autumn weeks, we lived poetry, read, spoke, breathed, and drank it, even sang it to the pigs, danced it at Danceland. And *wrote* it in the small rooms of old St. Scholastica. In front of the convent, a big old tree had just begun to lose its leaves when we'd arrived, insecure strangers with our manuscripts of doubt. Great winds blew, full of discovery, clarity, and connection. By our twenty-first day, the tree was stripped bare, as were our poems, their branches uncovered by the caring eye of McKay, by our courage, by our acceptance that summer is not endless and not all our words are golden. Leaving, too, was full of light and loss; all of us a little dazed that morning, afraid of winter and the tearing away. Ruth gave up the vest that no longer fit in her suitcase, Maury's son decided to be born, Sara lost her hat, and she and I drove west in my yellow truck toward our homes and what the autumn had become.

Myrna Kostash

Demetrius: A Saint in Progress

"It was the nineteenth year of Diocletian's reign and the month Dystrus, called March by the Romans, and the festival of the Saviour's Passion was approaching, when an imperial decree was published everywhere, ordering the churches to be razed to the ground and the Scriptures destroyed by fire, and giving notice that those in places of honour would lose their places, and domestic staff, if they continued to profess Christianity, would be deprived of their liberty. Such was the first edict against us."
~ Eusebius, *History of the Church*

For months after that edict, and through several others, the priest, deacons and bishops of the Christian communities of Thessalonica as everywhere in the Empire had lived with the imperial command to sacrifice to the emperor, and prevaricated or bribed or just waited. The unlucky — or the zealous volunteers — had been seized, tortured, sometimes barbarously executed, then went straight to heaven. The repressions petered out, flared again, there was panic and flight, then the incumbent authorities fell afoul of palace or army intrigues or the Persians burst over the borders again or the emperor died…. But on this April day 304 the situation had become much more dangerous: every citizen of the Empire was under order to sacrifice.

Ever since I first discovered the writers' colony at St. Peter's (when I was writer in residence in Regina 1996-97), I have thought of it as my "beloved" Benedictine monastery, all the more since I no longer own the quarter-section of aspen meadow in Alberta where I used to retreat prayerfully to write. St. Peter's is no meadow, although it shares borders with farms and ravines and the brothers do grow flowers and their bees do buzz around making honey. St. Peter's is an intentional community of contemplatives and farmers, choristers and theologians, where, over the years, winters and summers, as I have become obsessed by my Byzantine memoirs [of which this work in progress is a part] I have found a calm centre of men going about their soulful business while I spend long days and nights of writerly struggle. Somehow it soothes me, to get up from my desk at the abbey and go down to the dining room, to look for Father Demetrius by the coffee urns, and tug him on the sleeve.

I.

At first, I thought Demetrius must have been a young nobleman of Thessalonica, say twenty-five years old in the year of his death. I thought a nobleman and Thessalonian because this is how he was eventually described in the Byzantine hagiographies. And youthful, because this is always how he is represented in his icons. He was martyred two hundred and fifty years after St. Paul's foundation of a Christian church in Thessalonica, and so I believed my Demetrius was a Thessalonian born into the faith, of pious parents who made sure all their children, girls and boys, were instructed in Christian dogma and rituals.

The hagiographies all said he was arrested for preaching the faith, and so I began to imagine him on the last day of his life, that April day of the martyrs of 304 — going out to preach.

I imagined that Demetrius walked through a doorway and down the street from his house, his parents' house, which I think of as surrounded by cypresses and tall, ochre-coloured walls, toward the centre of the city, to the forum. But then I read that little is known of how houses related to the streets on which they stood at this period of the Late Roman Empire:

> We do not know how many windows there were, what size they may have been, or where they were located; in most cases we do not even know how they were closed. Nor do we know how windows were used. Were they kept open or closed? Did people stand at the window or on a balcony?
> *[History of Private Life]*

Even the ochre-coloured walls are wrong (perhaps these are Byzantine or Turkish?) for it was by porticoes not doorways that people came and went between house and street.

Demetrius walked down a marble pavement, feet slapping it with thin leather sandals. This was still the age of the draped not sewn garment, white, embroidered folds of linen that swayed to the stride of his legs; there was a jewel clasp at his shoulder. It was a hot morning. Some dogs gave a perfunctory bark as he passed. There was no wind. I imagined the soft thud of oranges falling off trees in the gardens but perhaps April is too early for falling oranges. Down the slope to his left lay the sea lacquered by a silver sheen. To his right, up the slope, loomed the defensive walls patrolled by archers. He knew there were soldiers at the gates. But the troubles lay within the city, not without. Ahead of him rose the elegant columns white as chalk of the temple and the arcades of the forum. It was so hot and airless that sweat beaded then dribbled down the back of his neck, across his forehead, along his arms. He glistened, he shimmered. As he left the shadows of the houses on the marble pavements and crossed to the forum, he walked shimmering in the glare of the sun.

Demetrius is now sometimes afraid. His priest has already been dragged off to the prison cells. The homes of the deacons and subdeacons have been searched and scriptures seized. But Demetrius enters the Forum to preach, as usual. Heat, clattering noise, the stench of rotting food and animal blood and excrement, hawkers' shouts and lewdness. His listeners cannot save him — they don't even know how to pray! He teaches them what he has been taught but he himself is imperfect in his understanding. He knows he is not alone — the martyrs have preceded him — but what was it they knew that vouchsafed their joyful passage through death?

From a letter to a friend: The priest here at the abbey to whom I take my questions and dilemmas as they arise is Fr. Demetrius (!), raised a Ukrainian Catholic on a Saskatchewan farm. But we've "bonded" around our shared Patron, although I have the impression that Fr. D doesn't really think too much about St. D, just kind of takes him for granted. But we have talked quite a bit about the idea of "sacrifice" in the Scriptures, as I've been trying to understand from St. Paul's letters to the young churches, what exactly lay at the heart of the Christians' refusal to make sacrifice to the Emperor. I have assumed that it had to do with the prohibited eating of a burnt offering (Pliny the Younger, for example, way back in the second century, was already complaining about the Christian boycott of meat markets in Bithynia) but I find St. Paul completely confusing on the subject. As it happened (I'm no longer surprised by this kind of coincidence), 1 COR 10:23-33 was the text of the reading from the Epistles at last Sunday's service, all about to eat or not to eat "whatever is sold in the meat market." When I asked Fr. Demetrius to explain to me why St. Paul would say it is really not a matter for Christian conscience whether to eat meat "offered in sacrifice," he explained that Paul was underlining the relative unimportance of what a Christian consumes, that "the real defilement lies not in the sacrificial meat but in the spirit of the individual." The point of the Christians' refusal to make the offerings to the Emperors was that, after the Resurrection of Christ, there are no more sacrifices; Jesus died once and for all, and so it was unthinkable that a Christian could participate in a (cyclical) pagan sacrifice.

I joined the community here at Mass on Sunday — a shock after all these months of going to Ukrainian Orthodox church services: these are so stripped of visual and acoustic "glory" (except for the joyful peals of organ music by Brother Gerald) and so plain in their language. Fr. Demetrius officiated, and gave a quite wonderful little homily on the text MATT 8:2-3, *about how we, like Christ, can "choose" to pour out healing to the "lepers" of our own communities. This was fine, but as I listened to him I realized that I was identifying with the leper; I cornered him later, by the coffee pots near the kitchen, and asked him to say something about who we are as "lepers," and he said, "We are asking to be healed - we are* choosing *to ask for healing."*

II.

There, under the brick arches of the market stalls, surrounded by his audience of townsfolk — the old woman with her fistfuls of mint to sell, her grandson the basket-weaver, the widow with her begging bowl, the blind poet with his, the sailor and fisherman and seamstress — he preaches what he himself has heard preached. He has a growing reputation as an inspired *rhetor*.

He is a virgin. His betrothed is his sister in Christ. Their flesh burns away in the Divine Service. Only their bodies remain, God's handiwork and a temple for the Holy Spirit.

But today the crowd is smaller than usual and even most of these slip away as the soldiers of Caesar Galerius approach.

They've come to arrest him. They know him. He has already once, twice ignored the edicts to perform the ritual sacrifice to the Emperor. Others he knew had been brought before the authorities and questioned. It was just a question of time, but he was steadfast and would not sacrifice. It was unthinkable.

The soldiers seize him and drag him off, only a few of his followers brave enough to shout *Help!* in the Forum as others slip away into the shadows. Then these brave ones too fall silent.

He was thrown alone into a cell of the baths. From that moment until his death, Demetrius lived in total silence. Even the vermin made no noise. A little light seeped through chinks in the brick wall. Even his prayers were silent.

Outside, some friends stood sentinel in the shadows, anxiously waiting for a sign of his fate.

He was speared to death in the cell. He was one man against half a dozen soldiers. For all his prayerful meditation on the glory of the martyrs, his own life was still so fresh and muscular in him, leaping through his blood, that he cried out in disbelief. The soldiers of Galerius left him to bleed to death on the bare earth where his friends, creeping in from the night, made him a shallow grave, then slipped away, cupping bloodied soil in their hands as though they bore the Eucharistic wine and bread.

Eight years later Christianity became officially tolerated in the Roman Empire; within a generation it became the faith of the emperors. Demetrius's story — if indeed there ever was a Demetrius who died in Thessalonika a martyr in 304 — was forgotten and his grave unknown.

(2003)

Judith Krause

Retreat

Late afternoon and the bees are still busy
in the dark half-closed mouths of the lupines
I am picking to colour my convent room,
my refuge for one short week from home.

So much noise from such small wings
as they move up and down the stalks,
not missing a single sweet spot, not missing
one fervent inch in the prior's flower plot.

Ah, little engines of selfless love
with their work already laid out in tended rows,
right at home in this private place,
the hedge-green walls and high blue ceiling

where there's no room for doubt, no confusion
about the worldly dance that sends them
straight to the honey, that blessed gold,
their pollen scrapers sharp and ready to obey.

No room either for vanity and pride in the dining hall
where one young monk offers to model
the straw gardening hats a visitor brought
and two of his brethren leap forward

in their cotton robes — the exact brown
of freshly tilled earth, the fullness
hiding their sharp male angles the way
a woman's housecoat hides her curves and folds.

Here then are three stalwart sons of God in hats,
arms looped to ward off wayward spirits —
three, a holy number for the camera,

which holds the wide bloom of their faces.
Its quick flash of light captures
these duty bound men in such a rare moment of play

that I must bow my head in wonder at their lives
spent in chores and prayers and a silence
loud as bees who never stop moving in the garden.

(1995)

Going to a colony at St. Pete's is much like slipping into a favourite pair of jeans — I feel comfortable and ready to work almost from the moment I pull into the parking lot. The business of settling in — to my room, to the group, to the rhythms of work and play, happens so quickly that, within an hour of arrival, I can hardly remember my life in the outside world. This is the magic of the place. A place where reflection and quiet are part of the daily routine. Monks and writers have a lot in common, though you might not know it from the clothes they wear.

Judith Krause

DEVOTIONS

To pray is to work, to work is to pray
  ~ ANONYMOUS LATIN SAYING

After touching a woman
whose skin is smooth as vellum
the artist can't wait
to get back to his studio tonight.
Can't wait to stretch
his paper, soak each sheet,
then tape it flat.
The more water he uses now,
the less cockle and pucker later.
Losing himself in the process,
hands moving over the rough, over
the pressed papers,
he milks this simple pleasure
the way a mother might
suddenly lean down and rub her nose
over the top of her baby's head,
creating a noseprint
the mind cannot forget.

The mind cannot forget
the writer sighs,
looking for her next word,
head bowed over an open book,
inhaling the odour of ink —
relishing its comfort, this mouthing
of vowels and consonants, alone
in her room, fingers held
lightly over her larynx
to feel the press of air,
a silence so urgent
even the moon

coming up behind the honeysuckle hedge
outside her window seems to hurry
to throw more light
without understanding how
something this quiet could be louder than
even the birds in the garden.

Even the birds in the garden
underestimate the signs,
raspberries *that* ready to be picked
they simply fall, grateful
to be chosen, into palms,
their deep red juice staining
fingers and mouths,
as visitors move up and down the rows, looking
for the fruit others have missed.
Behind the sweet peas, their perfume strongest
in this heat of late day,
the soil still moist
from a morning rain, a monk
scoops a handful of dark earth,
then holds it under his nose,
breathes deeply and smiles,
the way a man might smell love on his hands
after touching a woman.

(1999)

Judith Krause

Wolverine Creek

(for Shelley)

Carpet of snow, of crocus, of grass,
of golden beans, mushrooms, leaves —
the year spread out, season to season,

here in this room. These plots,
these small squares of earth
make it hard to look up,

laid out, as they are,
edge to edge. Each one,
an image of what was once

under your foot, and is now
a path through time
the man who watches

over your work tells me
I can walk on, if I slip on
a pair of felt slippers.

How disappointed he looks
when I decline, as if
I wouldn't share

my secret resting spot,
which is, by the way, just over there,
to the left, perhaps late August,

in the run of mushrooms,
that place on the trail
where their mottled flesh

pokes through the underbrush
and the air behind me
holds forever their wet smell.

Katherine Lawrence

Please And

Thank you for the flutter of feathers at my shoulder,
a brown nuthatch, its heart bold as my stare.

My gratitude is great, you are too kind,
but let's face it; you could be kinder. I want

my path filled with the winged and four-footed,
endangered, domestic, plain wild. I'll take

the finned if you're willing, so please —
lay your creatures on thick as butter, yes, *thank you*

for food. Bread restores the hiker as she walks
along grass trails, snowy footpaths, ledges of sand,

watchful, attentive, ready to kneel and whisper
thank you into the velvet ear of the kingdom.

(2000)

Peace and quiet, warm blankets, hot running water, fresh bread, strong tea, and when I can't possibly stand the life inside my head another living minute, I take to the forest outside my door. I wander, watching for birds, until I am either refreshed or exhausted. The mantra is always the same: thank you thank you thank you. I am grateful for the wooden desk and sturdy chair that wait in my room.

Ross Leckie

DANCELAND

It won't work if you do it that way,
squeezing the rough can-opener
onto the metallic sky,
hoping to spill its mackerel.

The farmers clambered up the vault
with their hoes and tilled
the rows of their potato crop,
raking the puff of weeds.

The rose is a button
on a blue chemise,
white as the heart
of a piece of cottonwood fluff.

Upside down you tack
across the pearling waves and the blue
swell of a lake, the rippling
luff, into a wind like this.

Or a rippling sleeve and a white cuff,
the invisible hand of the wind,
a pair of cufflinks,
two luminous gulls.

The open mouth and the body's huff,
the tug of the earth,
the shivering blue,
the sashay of the ruffled cloud.

(2001)

Ross Leckie

Lady's Slipper

A dollop of margarine scooped from a plastic tub,
the yellow too garish to be good for you. For the stem,
take a piece of wire wrapped in green baggy ties and bend
it at the neck. But how to construct the glow that pools
beneath the long grass, the way a night light shimmers
under the mirror that reflects the sallow scar of your face?
Could porcelain be fired to just that livid yellow that
hovers above the sandy ground beside the railway
tracks? The flower is not livid, though, in its
contemplative dangle toward the skittering life
of the insect glued to the blossom's insole where
the juices are sucked right out of it. It is as if the billow
of the sky were a giant blossom pouch and the fuzz
of the prairie grass the sticky filaments and tendrils;
as if we were glued to this belly, this gummy confabulation
of feral stuff, its density in the wood and its luminescence
at the edges of the leaves, this powdery fluff of confectioner's
sugar, this green, green figment of profound belief.
What does the fly know? In its dollop of pleasure
and terror that is the buzz of the body straining
against the world's teguments, does it desire
to follow the ontology of the flower's forgiveness?
In its hour of relapse, does it hum a graceless tune?
Across the field behind the abbey the conifers praise
the infinitude of needles and their medicinal injections.
I look and look at a little yellow shoe and the print
it makes in the impressionable gravel of the mind.
Its dipper is made of the matter of star fields.
It is a globule of the sun itself, spun of the filaments
of solar flares. Growing along the embankments,
it is a rare thing. It clings to your eyeball and keeps
you glued to its articulate totality, to its ember
of nothingness, to its return, its return, its return.

Tim Lilburn

I Bow to It

      Earth, earth, earth, stone lobed, blue, earnest,
blundering Godward with lummoxing barn fever, the dead's reliquary, the dead
bunched as flowers in its arms, the stone-sung-to
dead, the lovely, horse-sensed,
devout earth, jewelleried with the dead, earth,
      earth, dog-adored, wise and ambitious sleep, anti-fire, intelligenced
    with diva-fat, cadenced purpley as the long Book of Isaiah, the slow
exhalation of itself, earth, wasp-pasture, dragging a shadow
        of water, singing trampoline of winds, moving, bee-brocaded bosom
     first, bright in the dark ray of its tonnage, bright in the dark
   ray of its tonnage, potato-ganglioned,
bright-dark, unfolding.

(1988)

Tim Lilburn

Touching an Elephant in a Dark Room

Poplars know everything about sleep,
their glossolalia saying even more than the *New Catholic Encyclopedia*,
speaking sleep's endless hexameters as a child syllables til her mouth blurs,
so I'll ask them, rosarying there in the wind, Saskatoons ripe-dopey under them,
if they think there's a true world next to ours
that sleep, the animal, visits often because it feels more at home there.
And I'll ask them if they think this shadow-place, sleep's nook in the country,
is not a shadow place at all, but the place where the grass elopes to,
or water keeps its money,
or at least where those nostalgic shadows in long grass in July that make us
wish we were born grass come from.
I'll ask if this world which is not a shadow-place but seems to be perhaps isn't
the true, flat lap where we sit, asleep or awake, when we hear that well-known voice
rushing past us, pure force,
expertly thrown, that ventriloquizes our lives into place and some kind of order.
Ah, telos.
All the lovely darknesses in the world growing out from there.
Rain engorged over cut hay, bees fattening over roses.
Where the shadows of light are truth itself.
This is what I want to know.   Is what we are really doing, *really* doing
with our lives whether we think of it or not,
a beast, or one of those forces that terrified Newton changed into an animal
galloping along in the dark afternoon of that other place, the one, lovely home
place, intuiting its way through the grassy savannahs they have there,
thinking out from between its shoulder blades?
If so, then we're completely at home in the real world.

All the lovely darknesses.
I have no doubt the poplars, masters and mandarins of sleep, could give
    them to us
chapter and verse, and tell us of all this together, the world, the whole
seen and unseen, how it's
ingeniously physical, and how it makes sense, not by doing anything, not
    by using
some bloody verb, but just by growing fatter each day with variety
as when magpies pass a song through the trees at 6:00 AM like a basketball
at a Harlem Globetrotters warm-up,
until the world gets into that happy numb state where judgements become
    even more
gorgeously impossible and love gets fluid and doubletake-sleek
as showboat acts fluked off in dream.

(1988)

Tim Lilburn

Hawk

He takes
the Greatest Hits of Fabian,
Teilhard de Chardin's pensées,
and Bernini's *Ecstasy of St. Teresa,*
plots it all out aerodynamically
into kill-paths and exact head twists for sizing distances
and, like that, it's him gliding
over to me
barking in falsetto   *Ya stupid shit*   *Bozo*   *Hike off*
He's done something brilliant
with the sky, correcting it into himself.
Ah, Concupiscence, I love the way your circling
holds murder at slow, steady boil.
Laughter, crying, shouting show out from his feathers.
The belly is calf-curve of a beauty pageant leg.
He turns his head in tight machinery jerks
to take in me beneath him.
He doesn't know me from St. Thomas' third proof
for the existance of God, a pound of hammers, from a night club
act paying tribute to, Wayne Newton.
                    He doesn't believe the colour blue exists.
                    He hears the wind scrape over the Rocky Mountains
                    four hundred kilometers to the West.
                    He thinks the world is red like the small drop
                        of oil in his eye.
Linebacker-souled, Sharp-shinned or Cooper's,
he warlords the hot pine rows, eyeing
two and a half times more than what is there, spiffy
in his fastidious rage.

What keeps him over the trees half a day
fussing and rocking, nest or corpse, I haven't found yet.
Maybe he's just staked the plantation's northwest edge
as ego's homebase the way we'd draw a line in the playground dust
and say cross this and you're dead.
I want to take him on, hormone to hormone.
That's why I come out and stand inside the flexing circles.
Kreeee   Kreeeeeee   Kreeeeeee   I am rabbit-punched.
His open wings look like love itself.
Here is loving into the very center of the earth.
White, blond, black.

Satellites tip and yaw high overhead in a daylight
that makes them absent.
They are full of souvenirs of us, the loneliness
            of instruments, breath pause in a countdown series, 1969.
Later I go to weekday Mass in the monastery chapel,
the room shadowy, dense,
and eat the host and suddenly
I'm what the hawk is.

(1988)

Jeanette Lynes

SILENCE AT ST. PETER'S ABBEY — MORNING

9 AM / Wearing your panic shell, reach for cell
phone (no one needs to know, keep voice
low). You've always been a cheater. Make an honest
woman of yourself, for a change. Press *end*.
Shut your trap. Change your life.

9:30 AM / The day seems to continue without
your platitudes. Ticks along in highly lyrical manner.
They didn't say no gazing out window. Wind,
laundry days for aspens. Loads of green hankies
pitch in their tall Vs. Cottonwoods limn lane to the steeple
release a slow, exquisite snow. Cleanliness next to...

10:00 AM / Godliness. Walk among the dead
Benedictine brothers, five rows of dove-toned stones, whole lives pared
down to prayer, dates. Look at this soul: born, inducted, died
all on the eleventh. A rare symmetry.

10:30 AM / This lane, the pull of it. Wind listens, needs
no answer. Barn cat skitters past, shy of quiet
giant, you. *Why did you cram your life with junk*, its eyes, sudden
small searchlights, ask.

11:00 AM / Hoary Puccoons. Grass thick with them, *Guide to Western Wild
Flowers* says so. It's a trick, laugh at their funny names, break your vow.
Don't fall for it, do one
                        pure thing, for once.

11:30 AM / In this lush
        thicket of hush, it behooves
you to behave. You've clawed back words all morning, you're better
for it. You heard birds chip away for the first time. Another day, say
   silence is about relatives.

12:00 / Dining hall, others. Shock of cutlery
plinking, a fine stew brewing. How you'd like to bray
you did it, kept your trap shut, didn't make one call. You heard wind,
birds you could not name. Sometimes you were afraid. Should be noted,
   too
you rose above botany's drollery. (Open your trap. Chew)

(2001)

When I arrived at St. Pete's to participate in the Silence and Conversation workshop, the first thing I noticed was someone hoeing potatoes. For me, someone hoeing potatoes is the farming landscape of my past, now lost. I'd drifted far from those fields, so St. Pete's was a homecoming of sorts. Same goes for the barn cats, the blue delphiniums craning the sky, the beef stew. Perhaps this is merely nostalgia, but I think there's more to it. Writing at St. Pete's was a rare moment of grounding, of return to a home I hadn't been to for a long time, "home" in the sense of a rural place. The conversations at St. Pete's catapulted me into a whole new line of thinking and reading I'm still pursuing. The days of silence I first saw as a constraint. The panic silence can breed is reflected in the "Morning" poem. On the days of silence at St. Pete's, I listened to the world much more closely than I had for long time. Time is different at St. Pete's. Each minute composts away, slowly, in a manner that allows you to pay attention. The journal-notation format of "Morning" tries to suggest this allowing, this opportunity. The discovery is, of course, that silence isn't really silence. "Night" celebrates the edge where silence mingles with community. "Day in Town" is just a little map of pleasure and discovery — another, more comedic journey back in time to a blissful era of hippie euphoria. The pleasure of discovering the beat-up, twenty-five-cent paperback in the bin. There's not enough pleasure anymore. St. Pete's is the only place where I can go out with rollers in my hair. It's important for a woman writer to have that kind of place. St. Pete's is really meaningful for me. I felt less homesick there. I wrote lots. I listened, for a change. And now, amid the big blue funks, I know someone's there, hoeing potatoes. Pulling their bright sticks along the earth.

Jeanette Lynes

Silence at St. Peter's Abbey — Night

We are the stunt ravens.
All swoop & good intentions. Not without
our devious joys, our
undercurrents. One of the silent ones, one of us, in the laneway at dusk,
I saw her. Her sneakers barely skimmed the gravel, she
has learned well. Voice will get through. Drum fetch
what it can — not the stale vocal
chords that thrum
distant and strange across the postcard
scrawled with all the requisite lies — but new, nuanced caws
tuned to the attenuations between. Humble in the face of no words
for having flown. Good night, sweet birds, may you
dream polylinguistic dreams. In a few hours we'll break the sound barrier.
We will have many things to speak about.

(2001)

Jeanette Lynes

Day in Town: Humboldt

Summer. I take my big hair
walking in Humboldt. Like
wow: a hunter in coonskins
is painted on the bank, his
rifle cocked roofward (fills
whole Royal wall, this
Crockett). My hair & I dash
into the thrift shop, heaven
of macrame, ball caps, swag
lamps, books. I'm drawn
to one: pink waves on cover,
the word *Alone*, a contemplative
man beating his way along
the sand, white shirt billowing
in breeze. *Best of Rod McKuen*.
After the hunter, why
resist Rod? He's having
a tie-dyed day. His ducks
are in a row. He promises
he'll take me where the big
boys play. He's cool,
only fifty cents, I'm there.
Reading him while strolling
past old Ford Torinos, swan
plastic planters (beauty is
you *can* read Ron McKuen
while strolling alone with
curlers in your hair at height
of summer in Humboldt
Saskatchewan) I am (hardly
ever does this happen)
happy beyond my wildest
iambic dreams.

Hannah J. Main-van der Kamp

Why Prairie Barns Are Red

Potatoes, cod cakes, cauliflower.
Guests in the abbey dining room mutter.
Blandness tastes like a personal slight,
a reduction in sophistication status.
They crave exotic condiments
to mask wholesomeness as thrilling
as the corn stubble horizon.

Maelstrom of gulls churns over calcareous fields
just turned. Grey mantles, black wing tips reeling.
Their lower mandibles, red-spotted.

Red as counterweight.

Do you want all of that red at once? Now?
Pour it down your discriminating throat?
Panic Red, Passion Red, Pope Red, Choke-
on-it Red.

Don't forget what the abased in Spirit get.

Circle of white-faced cattle, rattled by a juicy jackrabbit
that corrals them. The cows bellow off; the rabbit
sits down like a hummock
and disappears. A surfeit of grey counterpointed
by dots of barns
like low bush cranberries in pemmican.

When you're in Rome,
eat as the Romans eat…
honeyed turnip, braised onions,
Slowly your eyes learn to savour what is set before them.
That way, Feast Days will practically blind you.

Today, Thanksgiving! Chokecherry wine and mead.
Sarsaparilla laces pumpkin pie the way
barns strut at dusk.

October 1997, my first visit to the Prairies, and St. Peter's, as part of the Sage Hill Poetry Colloquium. I'd walk to the chapel before dawn for Eucharist, chant psalms interwoven with dreams, poems and the stained glass in the chapel. In the afternoons, I'd walk for hours in any direction, stunned while musing on Tim Lilburn's amazing utterances. His "torque it up" became a mantra. It was a spiritual retreat masquerading as an unforgettable experience in poetry the way Lilburn gave spiritual direction masked as poetics.

Dave Margoshes

Triumph of the Light

St. Peter's Cathedral, Muenster, Saskatchewan, decorated with eighty life-sized figures and dozens of smaller paintings by Berthold Imhoff (1868-1939)

When Imhoff saw God what he saw was
light, circles of luminescence around the heads
of monks standing in as humble models
for even more pious men, an incandescent triangle
around the head of his vision of God
Himself, for whom no model dared sit, not even
Abbot Bruno, whose German profile inspired
the Roman nose of St. Paul.
                                    Imhoff took
a final look at the deep Saskatchewan sky and set
to work, his eyes closed the way he imagined
Michelangelo working, on his back, sweat
obscuring his vision. Paint flew from his brush
with divine direction, the faces and hands
of saints and angels taking shape without effort
or design. All of this is recorded
in his journal, the count's handwriting elegant
but cramped, his German unaffected by the years
in America, Canada, so far from the home
that oppressed him. *Feb. 26, 1921: today, the image
of Jesus that has eluded me revealed itself,
a stigmata in my hands. March 16: the darkness
overwhelms me. April 9: The lamb calls out
to me, praise to the lamb. May 4: I am blind,
the brilliance has won. June 12: Today we
finished, cleaned our brushes, stood back; tonight
word came that Bruno has died. God turns in ways
we cannot understand.*

                              What is left
is the light, infusing the thinning paint as if the walls
were eggshell, onionskin, tears, the sky pulsing
with aurora borealis, the ceiling not a depiction
of heaven but heaven itself, heaven on earth, earth
filling itself up
with light.

(1998)

Dave Margoshes

The Photographer's Eye

To the photographer's eye there are
few certainties, the only blacks
in the monks' cassocks, the only whites
a bleached sky, all else infinite shades of grey
and shadow. The verdant abbey garden struck
dumb in its bath of grey as if transmogrified
to fungus, graceful limbs of trees suspended
in time as they are in space. Only the artifacts
spring to life, the chalice and aspergillum breathing
in artificial light. His is an overcast world, as free
of moral compass as it is of sun, of colour,
the sensual curve of Brother Michael's leg
a temptation, Brother Anthony's seeming glance
off the frame an alluring diversion. Follow
me, Anthony seems to be saying, the print
bleeding out of itself as if to suggest
the impossible possibility.

(2001)

Mary Maxwell

A Wise Heart

*Teach us to number our days that we may
apply our hearts unto wisdom*
    ~ Psalms 90

We grew from peasant stock
dirt poor farmers who carved a living
implement blades dull as poverty
but even in this forsaken place they called home
our grandfather loved to dance, his boots tapping
a tune on battleship linoleum,
blunt fingers tweaking his violin.
Once a year taking a drink, Canadian Club,
bitter comfort in his despairing dark.

What caused you to forget, my brother, that your legacy was land
  — plain Saskatchewan dirt, soil both your grandfathers knew —
what made you believe your place was north
sentenced to wander, searching for salvation, for home
in the shadow of Yukon mountains,
your young memory clouded by drink,
alone in a squatter's cabin at Clinton Creek
dying on a gravel road that first Sunday in spring
far from the line of our grain.

Today I wander among men I call brothers
break bread and sing —
The cantor's sweet tenor leads vespers
his young voice lifting psalms across the chapel, into the hallway and out
over the fields, the garden and orchard, heavy with fruit.

His monk's face, from where I sit, could be yours, my lost brother
deep set eyes, hands rivered with motor oil
about your age, had you lived.

You could have found refuge here too
among these farmers and sons of farmers
men who lift their voices in praise four times daily.

Monks and brothers singing across the chapel
in the garden weeding, pruning the orchard
souls for the final harvest.

Brothers who have learned to love God
earning their place of rest in the plain wise heart of the prairie.

(1997)

My first experience at St Peter's Abbey was an afternoon in high summer, my mother, father and six siblings peeling ourselves off the sticky car seats after pulling in from the dusty road that leads to the abbey. Irritable from the heat, the younger ones whining for a drink of water. I remember being one of the first to reach the door, stretching up to pull it open — it was so heavy. The cool, dark hallway lay in front of us as we walked quietly on the smooth polished floors; in the distance men's voices lifted in song, afternoon lauds from the chapel. The sweet chant carried through the halls, quenching something like thirst. When I returned thirty years later, the monastery had changed, but again I found spiritual nourishment in this place. The summer garden, heavy with fruit and abundant vegetables; the winter orchard where deer lay down to rest; the winding path through the woods to a shrine; the cedar-lined walk around the cemetery where chickadees keep company with monks who have long gone. The hallways echo with the same song, monks' voices lifted in praise. Even some of the faces are the same, although like my own, are lined and seasoned, the endurance of many days on the wide prairie. It's no wonder I've returned to the abbey for rest and refreshment. Here is where I found my voice, my inspiration and courage to write what I have been given.

Don McKay

Vespers

In the abbey wood as the vesper bell begins to toll, waiting for a red-breasted nuthatch to decide whether it wants to come to my hand for a peanut or fly off. Bold empty headlines from the mineral world, each note trembling with echo, trying to stir itself into the air like its iron supplement. The nuthatch still uncertain, still perched on the jack pine waving its needle-beak in my direction as though reading the situation with a wand.

I'm not so certain myself, suspended between the nasal air-within-air voice of the nuthatch and great floated world-weight of the bell with its stony musical groans. All those forces that shaped the original rock — pressure, stress, heat — were actually slumbering ogres who've been tamed, and trained to sing. I think it is a simple song about time; or it may be that time is the singer. Something about translating its infinity into eternity so we can hear it without bleeding from the ears. Something about night falling.

With my arm held out this way, I might be asking the trees for alms; I might be hitchhiking. As so often, I have entered the condition of waiting and forgotten to watch, so the arrival of the nuthatch is a familiar lurch of the heart. A tiny black fire for an eye; a smudged red chest; feet on my finger like intelligent twigs. It takes the peanut with a sideways scoop and flies back to the pine it came from.

The bell's last gongs disintegrate. Their flakes fall to the earth and begin to burrow back into it. Head down, the nuthatch is hiding its peanut under a flap of bark.

(2002)

We say we're going on a "retreat," I suspect, because it's easier in the difficult life of writing to say what we're departing from than where we think we're heading. Safer, too. I'm one of those superstitious people who say he's leaving for a walk when he's secretly hoping to see harlequin ducks. (Even better is to go with Dave Carpenter, announcing to the world that you're scouting for trout, while sneakily watching for ducks out of the corner of your eye.) We say "retreat" because we really want to approach, or be approached — as, for example, by the famously friendly chickadees and nuthatches of the abbey — and do not wish to jinx ourselves by naming the hope. We want to be acutely ready but not locked into expectation. And the abbey, with all that it isn't (luxurious, chic, handy to shopping malls, cybernetic, revved) and all that it is (affable, agrarian, plain, marginal, hospitable, copiously chickadeed and owled, Benedictine) enables us to sustain that difficult creative posture, alert to whatever might, in whatever surprising guise, approach. St. Peter's will be remembered as one of the most important places on our literary map, not just because of the fine work actually accomplished there, but because of the imaginative space it naturally, and generously, helped us to inhabit. Listening, as the Rule of St. Benedict puts it, with the ear of the heart.

Don McKay

Northern Lights

(October: Muenster, Saskatchewan)

We had outwalked the abbey's modest halo,
the under-hum of ritual, the monks like sleeping bees,
to face north with its cold
neurological laughter. Underfoot the frost
crisp in the grass, overhead
shafts and scarves that rippled and
unrippled in faint glacial aqua, something dangerous,
radioactive, light that has strayed so far it's
lost touch with its first
catastrophe, light with no reference to heat,
no family tie with reason.
I thought of moonlight,
doling out illusion like a medicine
month after month, how there are other madnesses
immune to myth, jokes we don't get.
We might as well be insects
walking to our final metamorphosis, old
and fresh at once, unable to tell which selves are the moths,
which the chimerae,
                    which the ghosts.
It would not have surprised me then to meet
some member of the dead, perhaps the one
who ran off with the dog, or the one who still lives
as a wounded bird under the porch — to meet
and mingle, one cloud of charged particles
passing through another,
and passing on.

(1996)

Arlene Metrick

February in Saskatchewan

Light. It's the light, you say,
as we walk, not touching, afraid
we might crack the cold. Each edge
of grey, blue, violet hue off the snow,
clear line of barn breaking
the dry air, crisp
beyond knowing. I try to see

the knife that made that first cut
of roof, its edge tipped back,
it bright white leaning
against deep mauve shadow, steep
angle of grain auger bent low, hiding
its cruel nature.

We stand quite still, palms out,
peanuts for the chickadees, their black
heads, anxious eyes search
for food in our ungloved hands
until the frost bites our fingers
and the streams of water
from our noses freeze
on our faces.

"How can anything live here?" you ask,
meaning "I hope I survive this
winter on the prairie, wind
blowing the temperature well
below zero, where the snow holds
all things secret."

(2001)

Erin Michie

St. Peter's Ghazal

*kitchens, women and fire: can you
do without these, your blood in your mouth?*
    ~ John Thompson

Even dreams of home — these days they rarely go all the way.
    ~ Po Chu-I

A landscape you've never seen before, an arranged marriage.
The birds are at it again. Soup in the belly.

The amen corner needs addressing.
One earring, damnit. All that wool.

After frost, cosmos lean. Every assumption, fuel.
Cattle corn. To serve the emperor of emptiness.

Pee, dry, October leaves, fresh air bidet, northern lights.
Burn the backdrop. No roof!

My neck, a highway of heat.
The first thing about missionaries.

The freedom of the ghazal reflects the expansion I felt attending the Fall 2000 Sage Hill Poetry Colloquium. This latitude was supported by the particular rhythm and order of life at St. Peter's — including the meals, the Benedictine schedule of worship, the progression of the moon above its grounds under the rural prairie sky. I had the good fortune to stay in one of the hermitages for three weeks. Every morning, I practiced yoga beside a space heater on the cold floor, and then wrote, watching the changing light across the fields. I'd emerge for the noon meal, noting the transformation of a row of Swiss chard from the October frost, the colour of the elm leaves. If I was out in the evening, I'd walk back to my hermitage through the dark without a flashlight, senses enlivened, grateful for the sanctuary provided by St. Peter's.

Jane Southwell Munro

Great Horned Owl

Looking for the owl
a bit early — the sky still lucid blue
with a few downy cirrus
around the base of wind's quill — as usual, hoping
for magic — a textbook
silhouette on a tree branch
at the edge of the field: *whooo*
would you be, walking my way?
its ears perked up
grooming from its nimbus
a key to unlock these days
of not expecting much, having greyed
like the driest summer on record
to colours in the owl's range
not that it would speak to me
I'd just overhear it
like the radio — driving into town, a voice
reading a story's first line: *some things don't change* —
oh yeah? I say, tell me what, feeling pissed-off
by mutability, glaciers retreating up peaks,
smog like a yellowing bruise above the city —
why so irritated these days? get out of the car
on with the errands — God, it's as if there's
no refuge — nothing lined
with breast feathers — you watch a man age
the way wood weathers: cracks deepening
surface slivering — each brush with death
polishing memories: as a child
it was one of the spooky questions — where's space?
when you're outside of everyplace, is there
an address? The owl
wasn't there — hearing wind's traffic in silence

along a tractor trail
between ploughed field and poplar bush — noticing
the first pale tuft tangled in grass
bending for it — so, I was, after all, in the right place —
downy fluff from a fledgling owl
then larger vanes rippled in umber and pearl —
collecting a bouquet of feathers —
a marvel sufficient to the night

(2001)

If St. Pete's were a medieval abbey with quirky columns capped by carvings of local beings, surely among them you'd find a crow, a frog, a great horned owl and an apparition. They're creatures of that place — part of its spirit — not the whole story, but emblematic of what you may discover on its grounds. These poems each started some July while I was a colonist at St. Pete's. They come from different years: "Great Horned Owl" is the most recent. In my mind, they act like snapshots. I could show you the reedy margin where frogs leap, point out the field planted with canola that rainy morning I woke to crows, and take you to the spruce grove where the owls nested. No matter how frazzled I've been on arrival, after two weeks at the colony I've gone home with drafts of new work, itchy mosquito bites, refreshed energy, and an abundance of gratitude — for the time to pay attention to poetry, and follow whatever moves me.

Jane Southwell Munro

Crows

The crows this morning yell
like angry old men. Who am I hearing
as their voices shout down my dream?
The one where I cry *help*
but can't make a peep.

A magpie wing of cloud trails long feathers of rain.
Crows strut on the melting chocolate
of a newly wetted field. Mud
cakes the soles of my sneakers.
Canola behind them — a dimpled lemon layer
on lime jelly — bright as penny candy.
Even when I find the day hard going, the land is sweet.

Dug up from a night's midden of thunder, I come
into daylight feeling a bit garish.
We're left to guess what passes from one creature
into another. Perhaps I harbour
a pelican's white glow, a merganser's float.
If I cracked the dream, what might hatch in my throat?

(2000)

Jane Southwell Munro

Frog

Sheets of lightning stretched
from west to east like a line of laundry
snapping in the wind.

A tempest to the south, but overhead
the big dipper slowly stirs the constellations,
keeping them from sticking.

Who can sleep? I'm blown tree to tree,
silk pajamas flapping from my knees,
a frog's skin across my breast.

I remember twenty years ago sliding out of bed
to walk naked through starlight
across a granite bluff — my bare feet

picking up the rock's stored heat —
squatting to pee and staring overhead
at the egg-masses of galaxies in their milky gel.

No end to promise then. Now midlife
this midnight — high pressure, low pressure —
I've lost the courage for wishing.

A friend screamed each time I said, *I'm sorry.*
A friend sent me a gold cup.
A friend washed her father's bones.

Where has my compassion gone?

I need to put my finger on
a frog hidden in my heart,
feel it, restless, in my palm.

Brenda Niskala

from STAGLINE

(a story in progress)

THE VESPERS BELLS RING. Kathy can hear them from the safety of St. Scholastica convent. Vesper service, the singing of the monks, side to side, answer to answer, was designed to soothe, inspire, but there are no questions. The songs consist of only answers.

The church windows illuminate the faces of the men, grace their dark robes with a patchwork of colour. At vespers, monks intone answers, and in her head, only questions. Kathy walks towards the snowy gardens, the steamy barns, and the cemetery instead.

Snow blows in from the south, the last cold blast of the winter, bitter, invigorating. Spruce sentinels line the road to the monastery graveyard. They sway with lodged frost. Between the rows, the chickadees flit demurely. Kathy digs into her jacket pocket, finds, among the clumps of dried tobacco, a few sunflower seeds.

"Come here, my chirpy ones, come on." The birds swoop by, one by one. Then, as if they'd made a decision by committee, three vie for the privilege of perching their achingly delicate feet on the edge of her palm. At first they seize one seed quickly, then flee to the safety of the upper branches. Each eager landing and clicking as seeds are opened create puffy blizzards, weatherfronts in miniature. The chickadees elect now as a group to take turns pausing on her fingers, examining her with one bright eye, then the other, heads cocked thoughtfully. They dare to pick up two seeds. "Ah, you're getting greedy." She keeps her voice smooth and low, the voice she uses for all birds and animals. They don't startle, would have made less than a handful of grey feathers had she decided to close, to capture. Less than a mouthful for her cat, who, like her daughter, did not accompany her on this retreat, but would not have hesitated a moment in betraying their trust.

Would she have been able to forgive him? For only doing what was in his nature?

When there is nothing natural about chickadees coming to roost on a human hand. Nothing natural about the way these trees grow, little soldiers. Nothing natural about thirty men living in close quarters, peacefully, and without a woman's touch.

As if to argue the point, the branches nearby part, and one by one, a train of deer cross the road, trooping to the cattle barns, where a scoop of grain and bundle of hay is spread for them. Nothing natural about a herd of deer being fed, either.

The answer to her question — she hasn't completely framed it as a question yet — a lovely stag, pauses to study her, as if she were another tree, a large bird, a possible food source. She regards him as if he were a talisman, a message from the gods, a possible trophy. "Shoo, go on, don't you know people are dangerous?" Definitely unnatural.

In nature, the stags battle for ascendancy. One wins. The rest go off and hang out, practice fighting, look for new herds to conquer. Some go to monasteries.

Kathy is hungry. As part of the herd, after a short rutting season, the females must nurture themselves, deliver fawns, nurture them, do all the laundry. Then, when they're totally worn out, they can lie down in the snow of the season's last blizzard, a grey cloud on the horizon; they can lie there and just not get up again. Or find someplace where they're fed. Where they're given a warm place to stay and not expected to talk to anyone.

Kathy tells Joy, her daughter, how wild she was in her youth, naturally crazy and impulsive. Of course that's not really how it was. It couldn't be; wildness was not allowed. Her favourite question, "Why not?" was most often answered by "Because we said so." Now Kathy is at the other end of that tunnel, with just this one final window before Joy flies away. Every instinct in Kathy's body prompts her to tie that kid up in a sheltered place so she doesn't have to get hurt.

(1998)

St. Peter's is the kind of place I thought I would tolerate, at best. The concept of organized religion of any sort gets my back up. The community of St. Pete's, though, accepts the writers and artists with open arms, is not judgmental or overtly critical or even demanding or rule-bound. All my expectations shattered, I was able to enjoy my writing time that February, interspersed with walks through the grounds and visits to the barns. I felt completely at home, completely safe. And welcome.

Jacqueline Osherow

Saskatchewan Sonnets

I.

Why so prostrate, prairies? What do you see?
and to whom are you offering this incense?
It can't be for that puny scrap of tree,
though it *does* cut quite a figure from this distance.
So, I suppose, from where *it* stands, do I....
Is that why I love it here, because I'm tall
for once? My only competition is the sky
and even that is much lower than usual....
What a boon to this exhausted heaven:
someplace it can finally lie down
and in green pastures, just like the psalm!
Is that rain or is its cup just running over?
But David never mentioned this perfume....
Who needs frankincense where there's sweet clover?

III.

Maybe I'll learn something from these prairies:
so determined to extend themselves,
they can't take time from rolling up their sleeves
to bother with the usual trappings of grandeur
(not — look around — that they're in any danger).
They have mouths to feed, they're getting old
and a load of equally persistent worries:
this perfect growing weather; will it hold?
But, as if against their will, the grandeur's happened.
Watch the staggered curtsy of that barley in the field,
how a single breeze unlocks its treasuries.
Low to the ground or not, these no-nonsense prairies
are still comprised of filaments of gold
and nothing earthly moves like gold in wind.

IV.

Look how well this landscape does without us:
no middle distance, just earth and sky…
as if to make completely unambiguous
that there isn't room for us. We're temporary —
astonishingly blunt, if nothing new.
We're lucky to be tolerated at all.
But how long can such a pinched good will —
in this expanse of harshness — continue?
Remember the enormous cache of dinosaur bones
unearthed nearby; that tyrannosaurus
had no option but to disappear.
Such bullies, these prairies, going on forever —
or is this their one lesson in endurance:
Just keep your heads down.   Follow us.

(2000)

Miranda Pearson

A Week in an Abbey in Saskatchewan in the Middle of February

Everyone said *"you'll love it"*. But I am, apparently, unable to love. Yes,
the room is full of snow-light, generous mauve shadows
ribbon the fields outside. But this place smells
of celibacy, of sweat, of old lunch.

When I was fourteen in Tunbridge Wells, *"frigid"* was the word we most
 feared. So much
was daring myself otherwise (floppy schoolgirl hair shadowed eyes
 squinting into the sun,
desire always for the wrong woman, the wrong man).

When I walk these corridors I am again that frightened girl, tripping
over my long feet, late for class, sanitary towels and cigarettes in my bag,
inkstained, ashamed.

This place shrinks me. The smell of unwashed hair, un-made beds, floor
 polish.
I turn a corner and expect a towering school-mistress, her rebuke.
Portraits of the glaring dead in their pie-crust bonnets, their purple
 dresses, breasts
risen smooth and solid as moors.

Between that time and now: Years. Miles. Seas of snow. Surely I
have come too far to find again these polished corridors, this red-faced
 brick, these
startled prison-windows? I cannot pray for forgiveness. I do not
believe in sin.

(2002)

Miranda Pearson

THAW

the soft
of water   rushing far away
the hush   of ash

there is a word
for the single flaw
that makes the elegant whole

but look around, furrows
of dark earth emerge from snow
like the first lands   cracking a white sea

there is sun on the thaw

the small
neat slippers of animals tracks
thread their necklace off
into the woods

a fence
throws sharp purple lines
and the softer lattice of trees,
vague-er
more blue

and hush   stand still
Nuthatch

will flit down and feed
from your outstretched hand.

(2002)

Elizabeth Philips

Below

The white-winged crossbills, in waves of frenzy
        and calm, come to feed on the tawny
                cones of the spruce. The snow

feeds on wind, the wind on the barely suspiring
        conifers. The storm makes the birds'
                red more vivid,

like a sudden visitation of sorrow
        or joy. Joy lies in the woman
                walking below, her listening

as the birds work the cones, their quarry
        summer's sweetness. I do not know if you have
                failed, but I have often

mistaken the wild for another kind
        of hunger. And now, in this first
                month of expanding light

I want to eat with such fierce intent
        the day's offering. To find the one
                source, and fall

on it, nothing in mind but that. Satiation
        as close to hand as the tree, the fruit, the low-
                flying sky.

The few females, inconspicuous, an uncertain
        grey, display on their crowns the imprint
                of sun.

I do not know if it is a blessing
        or a stain.
                Who walks below?

Looked down upon from above, from the tree's
    peak, her uplifted, human gaze
        shimmers in an oval of exposed

flesh — of all the species, hers is the animal
    that bears through each living hour
        such a tender

face. She yearns, even in winter to touch
    with her palms the supple,
        overburdened branches,

and hear how clearly the birdsong
    moves inside
        silence, not

breaking, but parting it, as the wind
    does, harrowing
        the snow.

I've attended colonies at St. Peter's Abbey since about 1986. At least one third of my work was written there, or had its genesis there. I find the grounds — the aspen bush, the regiments of spruce, the pine and tamarack, and the understory of wild plants — conducive to writing. As an obsessive with a fascination for all things botanical, access to undisturbed prairie has been a godsend. The poem "Wild Mint" was written after a particularly ecstatic walk through the swampy sections of the aspen. The poem "Below" resulted after another, very different walk in a winter storm, in February 2003. I came upon the frenzied feeding of a flock of white-winged crossbills as they systematically dined on the yellow cones of a mature spruce near the graveyard. I have to say I have been influenced more by my own pagan devotion to nature than by the presence of the good men in black and their daily rituals. But perhaps I have felt compelled to complement their Christian preoccupations with a return to earlier forms of worship. Although these two paths do converge — most notably at the shrine to Mary in the spruce grove north of the abbey and south of railway tracks. I have been influenced in other ways, too. I took up the sport of badminton out of deep longing to learn to outfox Abbot Peter at the net. St. Peter's has had a profound influence on my life, enriching my work, strengthening my cardiovascular system and wearing out the cartilage in both my knees (making it difficult, if not impossible, to kneel for any length of time).

Elizabeth Philips

Wild Mint

And then a door opens at the end of a tunnel of leaf-heavy
trees and you're back on the path
through aspen, the understory
glistening beneath the lenses of yesterday's rain
and you find false dragonhead, self-heal and giant
hyssop, one after the other. And they're all mint
when it comes down to it, as if the world's decided
on freshness over

decay, everything radiating an uncluttered, clean
fragrance, and for the moment you've recovered your old
clarity, eyes keen and blossoming over each

green quill, each arrow

separate yet tangled in the grasses, all the lavender
flowerheads, tangled, knotted, frayed and
pointing at you. *But*

was there a door? You whirl to face the trail curving away behind you.
No door. Just a quickening, an
astringency, the place
you slough off the grey of habitual

inattention. This is where the mint comes in, the thinnest knife-
blade peeling back the layers to reveal the thirst
inside each stem, stems like straws
siphoning the alkali goodness of soaked

clay, and everywhere you look, careening from green
to green, the world exhales

mint, entreating you
to taste it.

Alison Pick

Wildflowers

We walked through the prairie and you named them
for me, *columbine, aster, Saskatchewan lily,*
and the one that loses petals each night —
I forget what it's called.

All that week they opened between us
in the gravel at the edge of the road,
three kinds of raspberries, themes
on desire: *stemless, arctic, wild red.*

Does *chamomile* stand for the feel of the sky,
its hot sweet smell at night?
Or *buttercup*, dissolving on the tongue,
lighting up a face from underneath?

Or maybe *train*, the word roaring past us
leaving spikes loose in the ground.
You gave me one; I called it a peg
as in *tent peg* or *pegging you down.*

Which may be what I was trying to do
when you kissed me and backed down the drive,
repeating them silently under my breath,
lady's slipper, clover, blue flax.

I committed them to memory, all except
the flower with a name that escapes me still,
petals falling on the cracked dry dirt
like a heart letting go of what it loves.

In 2000, I stayed at St. Pete's for several months. I loved the silence, the deep listening, and the routine. I lived in the red hermitage and rarely went in for breakfast, waking up and writing instead. I worked on the farm in exchange for room and board. The guest wing was empty — every day after work and before vespers I'd go there to have a bath. "Washing Meditation" comes out of that time.

Alison Pick

Washing Meditation

Late afternoon, monastery lights
gone out, I bathe in the darkness.
Snow out the window: a ghost of
what never was there. The scrape of a ladder
along the hall floor. For every monk praying
another one fixes the wiring, the fuse,
kneels at the sink reverently coaxing a torrent
of worship from pipes. The sound of

this service, of bathwater rising,
a slow soapy washing of skin to the tempo
of psalms. The dirt itself perfect,
the towel, the plumber, the sheen of things
broken, things mended. An old Chinese poet
bent over the desk of his breath. The run of his pen
across paper turns into the washcloth
across my bare arm, the arc of gonging
from the gold bell that signals a coming

of light. It slips through the window
and takes up the book, poems wide-eyed,
blinking so slowly, so still in the nursery
of tears. I read them out loud. My voice in
the bathroom the same as this silence
with shadow to give the words

back. Stand in the tub, dripping dry.
Snow like a memory of heat.
Weeks since I've seen a woman's body,
I open a circle of steam to myself
in the glass. Wonder who
I am seeing and what prayer could mean.

Ruth Roach Pierson

Below "Imponderable," A Yellowed Iris

1.   (The Abbey in Fall)
Out over the rows of cornstalks stirring
like skins poled to dry in the wind, the bell
tower tolls the hours. Between the cornfields,
sunflowers stand in defeated lines, heads hanging,
or headless, their dead-green leaves curled.
A mound of poppies slumps, the orange bloom bruised
but still vivid after the frost. Raspberry canes,
tattered, fruitless. And under cloud-creased sky,
concentrically hedged by blue spruce and cedar: the brothers'
graveyard — white granite headstones in ordered
rows to the rear of their founder's monument.

5.
Brother Basil leads us out a scullery door,
early Christians entering the catacombs,
down a corridor tunnelled deep beneath the abbey
into an underground chamber braced with shelves
on every wall — a library of preserves
newly massed after the fall harvest, stocked
in the past by nuns for love of God, now
by women from the town for pay, but either way
with arms up to their elbows in brilliant juices,
then standing the jars of stewed tomatoes,
chokecherry jelly, small white pears
on their heads to check the sealers
for telltale bubbles before righting them
to store in row stacked on row, glowing
dimly from within like a saint's countenance.

7.   (Saying Goodbye to the Abbey)
Brown leaves under a scrim of frost. Groaning
an auger sucks up wheat from a truck,
spirals it into a silo. Elevators already full
though no one's been able to combine all week
because of the wet. Deep furrows
score the earth at the base of the oaks.
On the crest of the path to Muenster,
a stand of sapling aspen, stripped bare:
silver broom straws scraping grey sky.
A chill wind rasps the last of the cornstalks.
Re-entering St. Scholastica I hear
everyone packing, Pam
crying in an upstairs room, Marlene,
next door, humming ballad shards.

9.   (Return)
Sloughs brim with the crackle of frogs
we never heard last fall,
and ducks we rarely saw in the woods
flap up this spring, squawking,
from every jack pine and cedar.
There's only the skeleton
of oaks over the cemetery road,
arched umbrella ribs stripped
bare. I follow the path
to the cabin, peer
through a window's film
at the table covered now
with oilcloth, no
clutter of pens, pencils, poems,
the hut's air as still
as the sky. Sun
warms my skin and the wind
is your breath on the back of my neck,
but I know if I turn round, you
can't be there. The chickadees
have returned, though — look, one lands,
picks at seeds I hold in my outstretched palm.

Joanna A. Piucci

Communion

*I tasted, and I hunger and thirst; you touched me,
and I burned for your peace.*
    ~ St. Augustine

Your lips pressed the back of my hand,
lingered and stopped. I saw your eyes
grow distant, studying some inner mechanism.
I watched your face, saw you contemplate
my sapor, in an act of rumination, tasting,
pausing, tasting, pausing, learning me cell by cell
into your own body. You turned my hand over,
kissed the palm. I tasted you with my skin,
drawing in the soft sweetness of your mouth
through my pores, knowing it like
the palm of my hand, from the inside out.
For some moments we consumed each other so,
slowly breathing, an exchange too delicate to speak of,
in silence: the lexicon of desire, with its secret word for peace.

I arrived at St. Peter's Abbey in the summer of 2000 after two days' travel, somewhat disoriented. St. Pete's was an oasis on the undulant, treeless landscape of Saskatchewan, under vast skies, with far-off weather patterns that formed and dissolved on the horizon. The extended hours of northern summer daylight, the subtle fragrance of the prairie grasses, the brash strutting magpies, all were proof to this New Yorker that I had left the familiar behind and entered a world apart. Equally extraordinary was the abbey itself — the serene, ordered daily lives of the monks, many of them far advanced in age, faithfully keeping the canonical hours. Days were long here. Though I stuck to my original work plan, I had plenty of time to wander the grounds, explore the abbey library, make friends with — and learn about Canada from — my colony-mates. I was a writer living with writers, not a monk or a retreatant, and yet I never lost awareness of being in a sacred place. This awareness informed my own days and hours, as well as my writing, even at its most urban and secular.

Marion Quednau

Osmosis

The distribution of water in living organisms is dependent to a large extent on osmosis, water entering the cells through their membranes ... there is a tendency for separated solutions to become equal, the water (or other solutions) flowing from the weaker to the stronger ... osmosis will stop when this balance is reached ....
~ The Oxford Science Dictionary

slant sun, aching cold
and a monk who sees to the spuds
in October, sets himself a purpose
against a cold ruse of rain,
or early snow,
opens the trap doors wide —
raking and turning
the pale harvest in the large cellars
below ground, keeps watch
through the propped-open   portholes
to a bright pewter sky
hears a last gleaning in the fields —
idling tractor, and spare, raised voices

he knows how this works;
everything weak and strong
and flowing
his absurd prayers
for a returning plenty
making him ashamed, this yearning
on his tongue for salt
and salvation and a winter's worth
of preserves, these bins and bins of overweening
potatoes, soon roasted, mashed, pan-fried
may the Lord make us truly
(with a mulling butter, fresh basil,
sharp black pepper)   *thankful*

it's a delicate osmosis:
silent brothers sharing mealtimes
with poets always hungry
and huge with sound,
sprung from their lonely cells
still floating in chant, where well-seeded
nuns were once in danger
of dissolving, being rinsed away
toward a sweetness
from resolve

the poets, thinking themselves
bold, play cards, smoke and drink gin,
fasten coats over their nightdresses
and recite their small conceits, coy petitions
while pacing round the nuns' graves
bid the spirit world goodnight
by bending over
the unblinking root cellars
at midnight,
risk a falling sensation
in receiving what they need
the deep-set eyes of the potatoes
                            staring back
from one darkness to another;

the weaker
flowing to the stronger
like the leaching of prairie into sky
the pouring of heaven
into prayer
a slow, stubborn thing the sisters perfected
so it could happen over and over
a cool human harvest
pale and uncertain as potatoes
of making any difference
beyond this hard season, or the next;

slim belief
only bound to grow more obdurate,
and transparent truth less plain
all our solutions found equal
in the end

This poem evolved out of our joint experience — eight women poets gathered together in the autumn of 1998 at St. Pete's — taking in the enormous root cellars below ground, shelves of copious preserves, as well as the bins of that year's potato harvest. We were reminded of the huge job it once was for every prairie household with a long Canadian winter in view, to grow and harvest and make preparation for that cooped-up time of contemplation. It's a food-for-thought kind of season, a time I call in one of my poems "the great big indoors of winter." The osmosis theme evolved through my remembering an experiment in school in which we observed "the weaker solution flowing toward the stronger." So, I suppose, in staring so hard at those heaped up potatoes, I saw a metaphor present itself for a balancing act of spiritual and seasonal renewal.

William Robertson

Sainthood

Let's all be saints in this morning
light as the days on days of dull sky
turn to sun and we walk from snowy meadow
to snowy spruce, the paths kicked up
before us by the deer, each of us stopping
stock still, palms outstretched and full
of seed for the little balls of chickadee-
dee-dee who take forty seconds to get to know us
then drop from the branches to clutch for
seconds a finger, lift a seed, and go.

Let's be St. Francises all, lover
of birds and the sky, your form
an angel's silhouette against the sun
where the path leads out of the trees
your hand high, feathered ball of trust in your palm
and the little laugh in your throat,
what God saved for you when you grew
impatient with being a child.

I first attended a writers' and artists' colony at St. Peter's Abbey in 1986. I wasn't sure what to expect, but what I found I liked immediately. I think it was the pace I liked best. We writers were left to ourselves and could work if we wanted — of course, most of us did. But we could also go for walks around the grounds, step into the chapel for some quiet, watch the birds, or wander around the working farm. I loved the cavernous kitchen and pantry. The supplies of food, most of it grown and preserved right there, impressed me no end. This was self-sufficiency, and yet the people there reached out to travellers, to its religious and spiritual community, and to the Saskatchewan Writers Guild and other organizations for visitors, offering the welcome of St. Benedict. That combination of sanctuary and workplace on a busy road told me a lot about how I could set my own pace. I opened up there and the writing happened.

William Robertson

Hunting Truffles

The poets can't stay away
from the pig barns.
Every day in their short pants
and sandals
they stare in awe
at the size of the boar
and his sows
at the pigs' look of concentration
as they piss and shit
in each other's path

the poets murmur their fascination
and between pens
joke about pig imagery in poems
pig symbolism
sausage.

In the next pens more sows
and their day-old farrow
scrabbling for the tits
one runt that gets nothing
and one dead/ rolled on
by its mother

the poets ask probing questions
of the pig keeper:
how many are crushed? why?
and what about those two
lying like death
but still panting?

The poets nod knowingly
at all his answers,
the matter-of-factness of life
and death
this contact with such primitive passages
that beneath their ready assent
appalls them
so used to euphemisms
hospitals and funeral homes.

Two weeks of every year
those who talk of life, death
and the elemental
stream out of the city
to be thrilled by pigs
and the bluntness of their keeper
whose earthiness they will celebrate
in song.

(1986)

Mari-Lou Rowley

1ST CONFESSION

"The house of my soul is narrow for your entry."

Insignificant birds perched on mizzen
hitching a ride to sea
their thin songs muffled by flapping rags
of the lowest tattered sail
waiting for wind.

Somewhere in an alley they squat with needles
shooting for calm amidst fury
rain pools with blood with urine
they wait for sun as the fix fades.

The house of my soul is narrow for your entry
the doorway thin as a mitre's crack
step through sideways
onto the cracked, parched earth
sit, and wait for rain.

(2002)

To get into the "zone" of writing a poem is to enter a mystical place, a place of reckoning and redemption. In earlier work, I coined the term "relevation," to refer to an elevating revelation — and to entering into the zone of poetry. My experience at St. Pete's was a relevation in every sense of the word. I found inspiration in the silence, the companionship, the landscape. And I found St. Augustine in the monastery's excellent reference library. Among the many editions, the 1983 translation by E.M. Blaiklock was truly a relevation in its brevity and beauty of language. The epigraphs used in the poems are from *Confessions* I.v., I.iv., II.iv., and IV.x. respectively.

Mari-Lou Rowley

2ND CONFESSION

*"You love but without disturbance,
are jealous but without care."*

daffodil sun and running
along still snowy ridges
swells of crocuses so blue the light
glissades with the wind
winding fingers through hair
jealous without care

it nudges, pushes
go, go grow
away.

today an owl sweeps a vector across snow
tiny birds eat from the altar of your hand
stand still as the virgin, feel the prick
of their claws, tenuous, delicate
a forbidden kiss.

love without disturbance
in the sanctity of your touch
the thrill of running
so high so light   outside
the moon, melting snow, night
inside, the bed
soft as crocuses.

(2002)

Mari-Lou Rowley

3ʳᴅ Confession

"Birdlime compounded with syllables of your name…"

signet   significant other
at one point in time
an event almost
this disentrailing
rapture trapped and
ruptured
      in public
the snare, a remnant of skin
atrial tremor
fissure

birdlime compounded with syllables of your name
spoken haltingly, phonemes stuck
to incisors, biting bearing
downturn of lips to gravity
syllables embedded in lost history
usurped, home again but not
inhaling
handful after handful of all this wind.

(2002)

Mari-Lou Rowley

4TH CONFESSION

"Do not let my soul be bound to words
by the glue of love through the body's senses."

this chair, window, tree
data transmuted into the moment
of a poem, dative
the pairing of sense to *soul*
bound by words, a process
sticky as the *glue of love*

unbridled beneath a dome of stars
Orion's broad shoulders, jewelled sword
brilliant, potent in Artemis' absence

chastity pins virility to
the wall of night
beguiling in her tucked-up gown
moon goddess rails fury in a quiver
of arrows, blows monsoons
through the body's senses.

(2002)

Allan Safarik

SANCTUARY

Two monks with stooped backs,
shuffling feet, walk in the afternoon
Brittle as dried plants in arid soil
they can barely move against
the slight breeze that ruffles
thin white hair and scruffy beards
Together they have been on duty
serving God for a hundred years

They bear the signs of a long siege
Years have fallen before them
in dim rooms and quiet enclaves
Oppressed by the virtue of solitude
the mind grows a long vegetable
Celery green with pale yellow
blossoms and scraggy brown
roots in the deeper loam

Many beautiful images of St Peter's Abbey remain a vivid legacy in the visual catalogue of the mind. The splendidly treed lanes and grounds of the abbey made walking out each day a marvelous experience. In the hush at the end of August, the newly harvested gardens glowed in the warm sunlight of the late afternoon. In September, flocks of mallards toiled about the itinerant cornfield. One early morning a flock of more than a thousand geese flew in under the cover of the red ball of the sun and gabbled in the grain field nearest the hermitage until mid-morning. On winter nights, I wandered many frozen miles under the icy carpet of glittering stars. A whitetail buck startled me, jumping out from a row of blue spruce trees and bounding over the road into the field beside the soccer pitch. Returning along the road toward the lights, the bell tower and abbey walls stood in stoic brick permanence; sanctuary for the spirit against the bitterly cold night. At St. Peter's, the life of community and contemplation dedicated to the worship of God goes on in a transparent world that encourages and welcomes guests. In this highly structured society under the Rule of St. Benedict, the monks and members of their community live pious lives devoted to service. How ironic that such a community has provided so much solace for writers who pursue the most selfish agenda imaginable: trying to put form and emotion in the shape of language written in symbols on a blank white page.

Allan Safarik

First Winter Storm

All afternoon drinking green tea
in Severin Hall. A few scattered
snowflakes fall against the window
By 4 PM, earth interred in white,
pristine light shines through
the eye hole of the universe
I am out making blotches, erasures,
skid marks on the immaculate
I walk across the snow-covered landscape,
look back at my chaotic prints
The only pattern to mar perfection

What can I do? These masters
of prayer and meditation make
beautiful music in ecclesiastic air
I struggle to write another decent line
The wind whistles through the trees
I breath in the bitter force of it,
relieve the agony of my weakness
I cannot empower the voices in my head
to speak to me about God, only poetry
I kneel in silence upon the white field

(1999-2000)

Allan Safarik

Witness

In the leaden winter, forty below
dark limbed spruce trees with hoary beards
appear ghostly in ice fog
Even the sleepers in the graveyard,
sheltered by frosted hedges,
hear the bell banging on God's door

Down the hall Brother Gerald's canary
begins its morning song of redemption
to its alienated mate, brooding for a lover
Sudden bursts of colour sadder than the wilderness
travel down the polished linoleum

The oleander, in newly opened bloom,
reflected in courtyard windows,
trembles flamingo pink and fragrant
against the drifting veil of snow
It wouldn't last two minutes on the outside

It's a good thing the monks, devotion
and obedience etched in their faces
like an occupational hazard,
are singing prayers for the living
The moment of truth is upon us,
"all the bare fields silent as eternity"

(1999-2000)

Brenda Schmidt

BONE FRAGMENT #5

Paper grey face with no features. Pureed peas running out.

*

Years pass like lives, like things from sheets shaken.
In the days that follow the infinite dead will appear.
It's that time again.
The wind has last night's rain on it. It's all there is to breathe.
Take slow deep breaths, exhale the spirits, don't breathe them back in.
Remember to open a window.

The prairie is perfectly made — you could bounce a dime off it.
I remake the bed, rip the hospital corners apart, set sheets free.
All this way to run a hand over wrinkles,
a career of caring has come to this.
Each day pulled tight, smooth as over-washed cotton —
pull too hard, things rip — it happened

on the bridge, on the way here: memory,
the sand-folded river, a turkey vulture passing over, a July sun
scorching it black.

The entire first draft of *Bone Conduction*, a seventy-one-page poetry manuscript from which my poems in this anthology are taken, was written at St. Peter's Abbey in a two-week period in the summer of 2002. The idea came to me on the first night of the writers/artists colony when a fellow colonist asked why I had left the nursing profession. For the duration of the colony, using a process of walking meditation, I explored guilt and the healing process through the voice of a nurse. In addition to providing the ideal setting for the poems, St. Peter's let me fully occupy the voice, and allowed the voice to fully occupy me, by providing a safe non-intrusive environment in which I could walk, think and write without interruption.

Brenda Schmidt

Out of the Elements

Shed #1

To wander through every building on this monastic farm.
    From holes in walls, haloes.
How dust hangs in radiant light. Through it
              I can almost see you.

There's another farm:
tire tracks on the machine-shed floor,
footprints coming and going.
It's afternoon — men talk farming outside, voices junk-muffled.
Inside, July's heat congregates in corners.

Corners, haphazard piles, fingerprints buried under dirt,
memory black with grease smeared on
cultivator shovels, rolls of canvasses, antifreeze jugs,
some with the bottom cut out,
barrel of springs, two pink chairs on a trolley, paint peeling off,
four black steel lockers from Western Steel Products Limited in Winnipeg,
Number 41, 42, 43, 44, and inside more. None of it belonged to me
until now.

Oil pails, magic mirrors. Look into the future —
things float on the bottom, things dead.
Fallen mouse, hair slicked back in its petroleum grave.
Lit web and thistle seed sit with it.

On the west side a tear in the steel lets light, three molten ovals, beyond
one stone warming in soft yellow glaze.
Among what spiders trap, a few weeds grow. Everywhere
silk in dust camouflage.

The backsides of hundreds of bolts, each square nut webbed to metal seam.
    A mind of spiders.
Shadows curl up against the corrugated steel, against
the million things caught.

Eyes close, voices stop. Outside a diesel growls at the heat,
    engine reverberating.

(2002)

David Sealy

SEANCE IN THE FAR GARDEN

You sense my essence
beyond the shutter's creak
in the push behind a curtain's furrow
dusting across the floor.

I am the toadstool swollen
in the potentilla's shade
the peony's collapse
its petals rusting through the soil

The spider wheedles
One step closer, then give me time
We both know what we are.

This thunder-roll afternoon
elm branches scrabble eaves
one leaf falls.
Set a redwood chair by the garden's end.
Lichen and moss freckle the sundial's face
it's their time now.
A downturned shot glass
holds no greater truth
place it on a rhubarb leaf
its venous runes know before you ask.

Am I your guide
or is it the wind.
My moldy tongue
interred in loam and humus
will never bud bright with lies.
The wind cannot rise
to thread the carragana maze.
You cannot bear to run
a gauntlet of magpies.

The prodigal is tired of returning.
Let us both be ghosts
in our sovereign gardens
haunting perpetual July.

(1999)

A stay at St. Peter's affords me a slow, methodical wake-up call, a revelation of seasons: wildflowers thick along the grid; a cold blast as I clear a windbreak; meteor showers burning through northern lights; chickadees and nuthatches grazing the orchard's wizened apples; a monk hoeing corn rows in midday heat. I lose myself in a cursor blinking on a laptop screen, inspired by the focus and dedication of those touched by this place, all of us nurtured by our particular quests.

Steven Ross Smith

from FLUTTERTONGUE 3: DISARRAY

53

      the idea gone. eating it down at breakfast. with porridge, eggs, and toast. something about the maze. being here. abbeying. adjoining lives. the monks the writers the painters. ordered gestures. the maze is out there, along the road. narrow path among the conifers. you probe and widening takes place. you scribble in silence and lines find their own speaking. the shape of morning is grey, snowflakes dancing. you are forcing. not the snow but the scribbling. you reduce your effort. you play solitaire. last night you dreamt of a distant friend. he'd changed, grown a dark beard. he was sharp and hustling. camera still part of his eye. in the café you and he were talking, lifting cups of coffee to your lips. he was the proprietor, leaning often to the telephone. in the intervals, you watch. in a shadowy *moves inside. bending and a pulling place, spatter and gaffe hooking in. strain* corner a woman, ghostly and furtive rubbed her pale hands. this the first dream in a week of restlessness. perhaps a sign. you shuffle the cards. one week with the self and words, and the bruise heals. one more week and you would be clear. but home calls. those you love. you would plunge deeper into the maze daily and somehow would come out of yourself. but you choose home despite the need for recovery. uncovery. you will return to the world's weight. to watch ecstasy dance through the window, away. the cards refuse to align. news will slip back in. a long way from Fra Angelico's Annunciation. her poised hands. from the time when news was spiritual, a struggling ground. the poise of the angel's hand. today, out there, all is flash and posture, gossip and death. you are here. porridge sweet and sticky. you wash it from your lips. humming. in the café in your head John Prine drones back and forth singing his lawless smile. you grin. the dream washes away. bruises wash away. your hair is wet, face turns up to the spray disguising the tears. in drizzle you hear spirits, the mystics whispering to you. you gather yourself as the bells ring. the monks are kneeling in the chapel, crossing themselves, rising up, breaking into song.

(1999)

I first came to St. Peter's Abbey in 1986 — from Toronto — when I was desperate for writing time I'd been lacking. The quiet and reflective atmosphere led me back into my writing, and then to a life-altering realization that my writing required a deep commitment of time and energy. I enabled that commitment by moving to Saskatchewan — Saskatoon — a year later. And almost every year since then I have attended at least one writing retreat at St. Peter's, and I have kept writing when not at St. Peter's. Each book I have published since 1988 — there have been five — has work in it that was done at St. Peter's. St. Peter's Abbey is inextricably woven into the process of my work as a poet and fiction writer, and occasionally St. Peter's even turns up in the content. There must be magic here.

Birk Sproxton

Lines, Written in Country Graveyards

1. Outcrops

We walk against the winter wind, our chins tucked into the puff and bulk of parkas and scarves. We walk, looking down onto the rutted road, the gate behind us (Hillside Cemetery). Our boots gash tiny islands in the snowcrust, headlands and valleys, a tumbled scramble of boulder-crumbs. The doppler snarl of a light plane rises, then fades.

Look down in summer from a bush plane's snore and you see a Rorschach of lakes, long blots and lean lines, hieroglyphs of the Shield now in winter become bleached streaks running north by north east, caricatures carved in bedrock.

Look ahead in this place and you see blocky granite stories, terse and numbered, laid with a crazy concision that calls you to fill in the gaps. You find yourself minding the stories; the snip and flash of the floating past edited by crunching boots in the present.

The cemetery makes a gap in the bush. It slices along the west side of a rocky outcrop, flattens in the centre and then rises to a crowning outcrop of poplar trees. North and east, the snow slopes gently down toward scattered swamp bush. From over the hill, plumes of smoke announce the city dump. In the middle of the gash, plotted stones stab out of the snow in ruts of rubbled outcrops. A stubble of stone slabs, laid side by side and head to head. (The names and numbers of the friendly dead.)

That first summer I was here everyday for two weeks, and then from time to time in the intervening years, and always in summer. Today, I do not swagger through with a rake over my shoulder, as I once did, but feel my way among the stones, heading for the tell-tale clods of earth.

I remember our raucous complaints about the name of this place. Each day for two weeks we raked the plots smooth and cleared twigs and bits of rock, and yet by the following day rocks had sprung up through the dirt to pock the pool-table surface we wanted. We raked again and again. Nothing seemed to stay under the ground. Should be named Outcrop Cemetery, we said. We raked and raked, preparing for the grass seed and the final plantings to follow. Called ourselves the Boneyard Boys.

To look up and see water or unbroken snow would be good, for to look up is to resist the relentless grave-pull of curiosity or mourning or the simple need to negotiate the gravel and ice and stones. From this angle no lakes can be seen. The absence strikes me as a flaw in cemetery design. People need to see water in summer, or in winter the lake-long sweep of unbroken snow.

My brother Allen arrives first and we cluster around the one who bore us. We drop clots of frozen dirt across the smooth surface of the urn.

2. Riverhurst, Saskatchewan

Contracts here are written in stone. Whatever people may have done in their mobile time, they are now bundled tightly into granite legends — Beloved Son of, or Wife of — as if for all their days they played one role only. No one is called Lover, or Fool, or Bootlegger, or the Egg Woman, or Bobble Bill, the Right Fielder for our Softball Team.

My grandmother has been reduced by a stonecarver's chisel to a single person. "Mary Eade" she has become, the pages of her story turned back simply to her given name and (second) married name. Mary lies with no husband in sight to take offense, neither her first husband, my grandfather, nor the grandfather we knew as Grandpa Fred, to distinguish him we thought from our one true grandfather, whom we knew, we thought.

Mary lies at a safe distance in a separate row (same field) from her in-laws, my paternal great grandparents. The singular truths of their names and dates have been carved in stone. All of them laid out here, in the full splendour of singularity, all having assumed the prone position lying in their beds.

I never met my great grandparents; their death dates were chunked in stone long before my birth. "Father" Albert Sproxton died in 1926; "Mother" Nancy Sproxton in 1915. They comport themselves in seemly fashion, side by side, locked into parenthood.

They surprised me when I first visited, two years ago. I had no idea they were here, laid out so neatly in community of their peers. Grandma Eade I expected to find, Mary, despite what must have been her protestant background. She was the only one I had met and dimly remembered, her small house and the backyard of waist-high grasses, the tiny upstairs rooms, the strange cement sidewalks running flat along flat streets.

The great ones were a blank page to me. Albert and Nancy, let's say, had scratched a living from the dirt of this dry land. Perhaps they had imagined in their future, next year or the next, a world of Ontario green, a flourishing garden bounding out of the soil. Perhaps they dreamt of drawing water from the great Saskatchewan River to the south. Could they have imagined, in the field next to them, the irrigation walkers that stand big-wheeled in the sun, hoops to filter morning light, the blown dirt, looping curves against the gentle hills of the landscape? Surely they did not dream dams and spillways, a gigantic lake backed up to make water and weather for decades. At the river, waves slash into sandbanks, scoop out hollow cliffs, re-map the world.

On my first visit I stopped in the village office for directions. We consulted a black ledger and found row and plot number, names and dates. A pencilled note in the ledger said, "Alice Sproxton. Died Oct 23, 1920." No stone, the village clerk had noted in pencil, no stone to make her grave. A mystery person, this Alice. Was she a child who died of the flu? Did she die in infancy, a younger sister to my father, born 1916? The mayor offered to take me to Albert and Nancy, but I chose to go alone. He pointed to the road. "You can't miss it," he said.

Twice in the summers just before she died I met my grandmother. Mother said one night to stay upstairs and go to sleep, while below my father roared at his stepfather. A mystery. Something, Mother later said, about my father not liking how Grandpa Fred was treating my grandmother.

Grandma Eade now lies beside a child in the Riverhurst cemetery, one row over from Albert and Nancy. At peace? What could that word have meant for the lying ones?

They endured the Great War, the one to end the others following in their fashion, regular as tombstones, and they lasted out the flu that rampaged around the world and many (some) lived through the dispiriting blown dirt of the Thirties and then, again, heard the chuff and thunder of trains loaded not with grain but with men, boys mostly, off again to Europe or Africa, fodder to be chaffed and rent and torn, with Korea on the horizon. Our fodder.

In the corner of the graveyard a tall spruce shakes in the wind. I crouch down, camera in hand, to give the tree stature, to spread the branches into a welcoming embrace of sky, a lone spruce tree in the corner of a country graveyard. There is no church here — this is not a churchyard — only a shed, padlocked as if to keep the residents out, just as the fence tries to keep them in. (In the shed the tools of the trade lean and rest in their fashion.) I crouch to take another photo, enlarge the tree huge against the blue sky. No hulks in the distance, no dark men leap out to grab my throat. Only the tree and rolling hoops of the water walker rusting quietly in the morning sun.

(2000)

St. Peter's Abbey sings for me of fireflies and bells, magpies and poplar fluff, research in town at the poet's corner, wonderful conversations at mealtime with writers and brothers and sisters, long-legged places to walk and wander. St. Peter's allows time to reflect and meditate, an ideal space-time for invention and conjuring, and in that zone I found myself editing old pieces, making notes for new ones, and charged with a need to find out more about family lines, long lines now that run through Saskatchewan from the dry belt to the parkland and the boreal forest and the Precambrian Shield. Like many writers, I am unhomed; at St. Pete's I felt a homely sense of well being that surprised me. The prose poems in this book were brewed in the abbey ambiance, literally prompted into existence by excursions outward to graveyards, to churches and shrines, and back homeward to the abbey to be mulled and warmed. Prose poems, I call them, for the length of the line, the long stretch of family line, the short stab of stoned slabs, poems numbered to make a beginning, poems homaging, homaging, jiggety jig.

Yvonne Trainer

St. Peter's Abbey

This living hand, now warm and capable
Of earnest grasping, would, if it were cold
And in the icy silence of the tomb,
So haunt thy days and chill thy dreaming nights
That thou wouldst wish thine own heart dry of blood.
    ~ John Keats

In my rented room
once the nuns' chapel
I can't even begin
to imagine
how many hands
have turned the knob
to enter:
scanned versions
x-rays
clones
out of focus photocopies of
my own slightly puffy digits

Now I look at my hands objectively
              and remember
the young woman
in medical school
wringing her hands
speaking of her second-year
anatomy class

How it's the hands
the students hate to unwrap
    anything but the hands
    One never knows
perhaps there's a hand
that's sad

beneath the bandages
Perhaps there's a hand
without fingers
or a hand that is mummified
into a fist
with just enough energy left
to deliver one last blow

Or what if
   there's a hand
that reaches back into time
before time
   and pulls us forward
demanding one last kiss?

I spent a week at St. Pete's in both 2001 and 2002. It is a bit of a jaunt — about seven and a half hours from Edmonton — so the journey itself proves a worthwhile experience and a chance to leave city life behind for a while. I particularly find the silence conducive to the writing. It's what I notice first. Second, what I notice is a slowing down of things. The mind relaxes and doesn't need to worry about getting from A to B, or being on time, or having to answer the phone. Robert Graves has an essay called "Baraka" that deals with that element of something so familiar that it carries with it a sacredness. St. Pete's takes me back to early times, when I lived as an only child thirty-two miles from the nearest neighbour with nine cats (most of them orange), a pony, and a shaggy brown dog. The utter simplicity of the farm and surroundings make everything stand out as being sacred and filled with the energy of baraka. The hermit in the woods, and my voyeuristic need to spy on him, brings back memories of childhood stories of reading *Heidi* and her visit to the ole grandfather on the mountain. It's a regressive experience in the best sense of the word, and out of that "going back to what is basic" comes the poetry. And, the "presence" of the other poets who have been there before me adds to a feeling of connectedness to the wider world of poets both present and past. It is as if they too leave a kind of baraka that I can draw on for my own poems. I love the place!

Yvonne Trainer

St. Scholastica

I.

The sky is opening

You are the rain
beating on a hill
at the monastery

Tiger grass grins

Sister to a monk of the abbey
Saint of the sorrows

Shadow
  of
          shadows

Cobble
rock and pebble
wind and breath

tooth in a tent

Fingers are presents
I give you both my hands

Well come

Come in.

II.

The pleasure's mine
Oh seize the day
It's the bird squawking
that makes the
hours turn

but you
don't know
that
yet.

III.

A second becomes
a moment
becomes
an hour
becomes
a day

I read fast
then slow
then fast
and fast
and faster still
Then one word
at a time

savor the syllables
until I am reading
only vowels
Then fast again
and faster
    faster faster
        faster faster still
until
I read
the world
    whole.

Yvonne Trainer

What Makes This

What makes this silence
is not the monk
in his black robe
riding the green lawn tractor
out to the garden

What makes this place
is not the bell
ringing five times per day

nor the buildings
that have stood like bookcases
for almost a century
against a Saskatchewan sky

but the shadows of leaves
on the wall
the shifting patterns of language
their brush of grace
almost not quite blue
fading
into grey
fleeting memory

of a primitive past
before religion
before time
before breakfast

yes.

then.

Paul Tyler

SASKATCHEWAN

When the moon is out it fills the orchard
behind the grey cathedral.
I walk into the field, straw spearing the earth.

At dawn, nervous poplars are yellow with sun,
the trail a cushion
of fallen things. I enter a clearing, lean

on a bough near a fence, this longing
carried toward the horizon,
becomes golden beneath the blue, crisp day.

I sit late in the grass under autumn trees:
we must learn loss like this.
Something must wash the surface bare.

We are strangers here, and here we belong:
the barn quietly sags into shadow,
magpies cackle, shedding green light from their wings.

(1995)

Attending the writing retreats at St. Peter's Abbey is as much about visiting the land as it is about writing. The two seem almost inseparable to me. Whenever walking the grounds of the abbey, or visiting that pocket of life, Quill Lake, I have a sense that I'm becoming part of the landscape. Words respond, but they want to be stated simply to uncover the subtlety of the surroundings. Walking into that sky, seeing distance, you become aware of yourself on the earth. The shape of the prairie around you is a kind of seeking that you take part in just by being there. If the land around St. Peter's Abbey was a distant member of your family, it would be the contemplative one you hear from only occasionally. The one you think of most.

Paul Tyler

Seventeen Poets in a Caravan of Various Trucks and Cars Head into the Wetlands

Quill Lake Nature Reserve, Saskatchewan

We park along a grass-parted backway,
stretch out of the hot seats,
pants tucked into socks, cameras
and field glasses dangling around necks
reeking of citronella and sun screen.
And there's something slightly
goofy about this whole thing, I suspect,
seventeen gadget-riddled poets
treading over a narrow strip of sand
surrounded by reeds and strange yellow birds
warbling at us or not at us at all.
Odd shapes flutter just out of sight,
ducks, a flash of blue under wing,
smacking the water, and sloosh, landing there.
Birds with exotic beaks
like utensils click and woo, others shovel,
some make sounds not even the experts
(of which there are suddenly many) can identify.
All of us, all seventeen word-addicts
heading into the soup of otherness,
this elastic layer of creatures and mud
coating, thinly, the rock of the planet.
Mosquitoes plunge into faces —
which I don't mind, it's only
when I look down at my legs and see
about eight ticks working their tiny way up my pants
that I start wondering why we're here.

"Ticks," I call, thinking
maybe someone might find this fascinating.
But they have ticks of their own
and are not-quite-frantically
brushing them off. It's no wonder
the deer we see stares so long,
her silent ears, so slender,
holding us there for five minutes at least.

Heading back, our heads full of sun,
trying to hold the names of things stuffed in our mouths,
ten or more shell casings
from a shotgun find their way into my sight.
How to fit this into the poem, I wonder,
their steel heads, their empty blue bodies,
these quiet little dislocations.
And still I'm wondering, driving home
seventeen poets kicking up the dust of the road
if those shell casings belong here at all.

(1999)

Elizabeth Ukrainetz

At St. Peter's

(after the psalms)

There's a woman on the banks of the slough,
at the edge of flat fields of new green wheat.

She is huddled in the wind of the new wheat.

On the banks of the slough a magpie is squawking, walking in sponge-wet sand. Dragonflies pencil their sharp blue way, and the new wheat is bending with the wind.

On the surface of the slough, sun glints silver and black on the waves. Grebe hatchlings disappear in the shimmer. The wind ruffles waves from the water and the hatchlings glide by.

A windmill spins between the grid road and the shore, churning the bottom water up. The grebes dive. The magpie flies. The woman bends to the sand, her fingers wet with light.

(2001)

I'd heard many good things about St. Pete's over the years and made a journey of it — two full days — taking the train from Toronto, getting a sense of the size of this country as the rocks and trees opened up into the prairies. Immediately there was a sense of peace and shelter at the monastery. I'd been reading early works, including the psalms, for a year or two prior to the visit so attending the simple and beautiful masses in the chapel made a strong, lovely connection between the written word and the human voice, connecting the centuries with the constancy of human need, celebration, and community. Real cool to see the relic of St. Augustine, too!

Guy Vanderhaeghe

Things as They Are?

A MONASTERY SURROUNDED by fields of lush grain, girdled by dark pines. Iron bells ringing the morning stars out of the skies and the black crows into them. A dusty road at noon, butterflies in the ditches folding brown and yellow wings on purple-headed thistles, stooped monks pulling weeds in a distant garden. A young man greatly afflicted in body but ardent to serve God. A setting and a character for a nineteenth-century story, most probably Russian. Last of all, a writer.

*   *   *

The monastery, like nearly all eccelsiastical establishments in the latter half of the twentieth century, had fallen on hard times. Each year the number of postulants dwindled and the surviving monks grew older, feebler, greyer. The boys' boarding school attached to the abbey was forced to close and farming operations were curtailed. But as the abbot was fond of saying, "New circumstances create new challenges." The monastery welcomed budy Catholic laity seeking to examine and test their souls in solitude, some of whom left substantial testimonials of appreciation upon departing. In time, reports of the monastery's natural beauty and isolation reached the ears of other, more secular-minded individuals eager to make a temporary withdrawal from the world, sort through their lives — "find themselves," as so many of them passionately put it. These, too, the abbey was willing to accept, charging ridiculously small sums for the provision of room and board, unlimited fresh air, and restorative quiet. All that was

---

Although "Things As They Are?" is not a record of anything that *happened* at St. Peter's, it is about a writer withdrawing temporarily from the clamour of the contemporary world and what that withdrawal means to him as an artist. I suppose my own mild sense of being cut off from the quotidian world during a short stint at St. Peter's — multiplied many times — is reflected in the questions that beset this story's protagonist.

asked of these guests was that they behave modestly and decently, and permit the monks to go about their business undisturbed.

It was an old friend, a poet concerned that Jack Greer seemed to do nothing whole-heartedly any more but booze, who suggested a retreat to the Alberta monastery might lend Jack's infamously stalled book the push it needed to get moving again. For the first time in living memory, Greer acted on someone's advice, applied to the monastery, and was accepted.

The monk who greeted him upon arrival at the abbey inspected a tall, bony, angular, sad-faced man, at least forty but probably older, whose hair was cropped so short it was difficult to detect the grey in it. He reminded Brother Ambrose a little of the convict Magwitch in the David Lean film of *Great Expectations* which Brother Lawrence had used to show in English classes in those long ago days when the boys' school was still in operation and he was still a teacher. Of course, Brother Ambrose couldn't know that Greer's hair had been cut only two days earlier to foster a certain disposition. What Greer was aiming at was simplicity, discipline, control. A monastery seemed the place to achieve these things. He was travelling light all around, a pair of Adidas on his feet, six shirts still in Cellophane, and an equal number of tan workpants bearing sale tags packed in his large knapsack. The only things that weren't new were his socks and underwear, a portable typewriter, and a dog-eared manuscript, five and a half years old. For reading he had Chekhov's *Selected Letters*, the *Viking Portable Chekhov*, and a copy of Goethe's *Faust*, nothing more. These were books to clear the head, lift the fog, correct the drift.

Greer was giving himself three months to finish the book and get his life in order. Almost six years ago he had published a first novel that went beyond being a modest success and stopped just short of being truly celebrated. Suddenly agent and publisher began to talk to him about his "career," making him feel like one of those young men who have passed bar exams or been accepted into medical school. But six years was a long time between books and nobody talked to him like that any more. He was a fucking walking disaster and knew it.

But maybe here it would be possible to make himself fit to write again. He would read Chekhov and Goethe, hike hard in the countryside, eat well, sleep better, cut back his drinking. The bottles of brandy clinking in his knapsack were to be strictly rationed, no more than three drinks a day no matter how badly the work went. There was a shot glass for measuring so he couldn't cheat.

Brother Ambrose led him down a seemingly endless corridor, unlocked the door to a room so bare it nearly made Greer shiver, and then carefully pointed out where everything was, desk, closet, chair, bed. It was all obvious but Greer supposed the monk considered the room tour part of his job. In the doorway, before leaving, Brother Ambrose said: "There's only the two of you."

For a second Greer had no inkling what he was talking about.

"There'll be more arriving throughout the summer," Brother Ambrose continued, "but for the time being there's only you and one other gentleman in this wing." Having said that, he departed, leaving Jack to turn his attention to his new home.

There wasn't much to hold it. The walls were painted white. There were no pictures. The bathroom was the sort found in a hospital. On the wall directly above the desk there was a crucifix.

Greer opened a window and lay down on his bed. The scent of damp hay lying in windrows came drifting in, smelling yeasty and sweet. The silence of the building was absolute except when a door closed somewhere at the ends of the earth. Through the open window he heard insects sizzling and thrumming in the hot grass, the ripple of a meadow lark, a hawk's rusty shriek, the dry clattering of a woodpecker, sounds that he had presumed were extinct. He thought of Chekhov and his love for his six hundred acres at Melikhovo. Spring in the countryside had given his favourite Russian hope there would be spring in paradise.

Clean slate, Greer promised himself. New start.

The next morning the tolling of the bells shook him out of sleep, chapel bells summoning the monks to some service. Greer turned on his side and looked out the window while the bells rang relentlessly. A skim of spreading light, a milky flush in the eastern sky told him how very early it was. Abruptly, the bells broke off and in the sudden silence he heard muffled grunts and groans, a dull thumping and scraping outside his door as if something very awkward and very heavy was being lugged down the corridor. Curious, Greer climbed out of bed, eased open his door, and peered out. Except for red exit lights shining at either end, the corridor was in darkness. In the bloody light of the furthest of these exit lights, Greer could see a man starkly silhouetted.

The man hauled nothing down the passageway but himself.

Propped on crutches, he dragged legs encumbered by heavy braces, propelling them forward with violent spasms of effort, groaning as he swung on his crutches and his lifeless legs struck the floor rhythmically, again and again, with a dull, metallic clunk. Throwing himself at the swinging door, he drove it recklessly open with his braced legs, rattled through, and disappeared from sight. Behind the door lay chapel and monastery proper. Was he answering the call of the bells?

Greer hurried back to bed. Although it was June, what he had just seen left him feeling cold.

In the mornings following, Greer found himself waking earlier and earlier in anticipation of the unholy racket in the hallway. It was deeply unsettling, but he could hardly complain about what the unfortunate man couldn't help. Still, Greer was losing sleep and, worse, the whispered mutterings and groans got his working day off to a bad start, lent it a troubling, slightly surreal air.

I came to write a book and instead I find myself starring in a Bergman film, Greer told himself, trying to laugh it off.

But the Bergman film continued, even out of doors. Strolling in the monastery grounds Greer was astounded by the number of elderly, disabled monks he encountered: hunchbacks and clubfoots, the mildly retarded and profoundly disfigured. Meeting handicapped brothers on the gravelled paths, he hurried by them with nothing more than a curt nod of the head. He couldn't help himself. The sight of them, infirmities cloaked in medieval-looking habits, increased his free-floating anxiety. For Greer, the whole place was taking on a gothic air.

He discreetly questioned Diane, one of the women who served in the dining hall reserved for the abbey's guests, about the handicapped monks and she explained. Fifty years ago, Catholic parents concerned about what might happen to a disabled son after they died would encourage him to seek to become a brother in the monastery. If he were accepted, his parents were assured they need never worry about his future; he had a home for the rest of his life and would be taken care of. What Greer was seeing, she said, was the last generation, now old men, left in the care of the Church.

Then one evening when Greer was sitting in the empty visitors' lounge playing a game of solitaire before supper, someone entered the room and dropped himself into a chair. When Greer looked up and saw the crutches and braces, he knew this was the disturber of his sleep, the cripple who groaned his way down the hallway every morning. The surprise was his face.

Greer bobbled his head politely, said hello, and immediately turned his attention back to the cards to avoid staring. The man in the armchair had at one time been horribly burned, so hideously burned that his features had been reduced to an expressionless mask of livid scar tissue that resembled the scales of a reptile. His mouth was a lipless slit, his nose a snake-snout, his blue eyes puckered in flesh as lifeless as Plasticine. He had neither eyebrows, eyelashes, nor whiskers, and the bald dome of his skull was stippled with slick, shiny scars that looked like drippings from a wax candle.

Greer's distaste shamed him, but that didn't make it any less real. He kept thinking how much the man looked like a lizard. No matter how hard he tried to concentrate on the game of solitaire, Greer could sense the stranger watching him, sense the man's ridgity; his blank, fixed face, his legs thrust stiffly out from the chair as if they were planks nailed to his body and not really limbs at all. And Greer began to feel his own body going rigid too, brittle with tension, unease, anticipation.

When the man suddenly spoke to him, Greer started violently. "Pardon me?" he said, confused.

"You're one pitiful solitaire player," the man repeated. Greer looked hard and recognized an ironic, challenging intelligence gleaming in the eyes of the frozen face. The slash of mouth widened and Greer assumed it was a smile.

"Says who?"

"Five of hearts on six of spades! There!" the stranger said pecking at the cards with his fingers. They were hooked like the talons of a bird of prey, several of them lacking nails.

Jack moved the card. "Maybe I ought to surrender the deck to the expert," he said, "and learn something."

The young man held up his hands "I'm a clumsy shuffler and dealer. It takes me a long time to play a game."

"Well, my head obviously isn't in it," said Greer. "Let me lay a game out and you can shift the cards. How does that strike you?"

The fellow extended a claw. "Roland Madox."

Jack reached for it. "Jack Greer," he said.

*   *   *

That night the two men ate supper together in the separate guest dining room. Madox explained he was not a monk yet and was only at the abbey on trial, working in the library until the abbot arrived at a decision as to whether he truly had a vocation. For the present, said Madox, he was free to choose where and with whom he ate. Over the abbey's famous fare — farmer's sausage, sauerkraut, boiled beet tops, and new potatoes, followed by apple crisp and ice cream — Roland Madox told his story. When he was five, he and his grandfather had been involved in a car accident. The old man had been instantly killed when he pulled out into the path of an oncoming fuel truck. His grandson, however, had survived the wreck and conflagration with disabling spinal injuries and third degree burns over eighty per cent of his body. With a kind of perverse defiance Madox mockingly referred to himself as a "fry." According to his self-portrait, perversity seemed second nature to him. The night of the accident, the doctors said he wouldn't see morning. When morning came they didn't give him a week. When a week passed, not another month. On the burn ward everyone expected him to succumb to infection. Nothing doing. He had survived the burn ward, years of hospitalization and rehabilitation. Here he was, twenty-five years old, still defying the odds. He had battled his way through elementary school, endured the adolescent hell of high school, earned a university degree in history. Implausibly, it was in a university philosophy class that he had discovered the existence of God, a startling reversal of what Greer took to be the customary outcome of acquaintance with academic philosophers. Now he was determined to become a monk.

When Greer inquired as to why he had this particular ambition, the answer was simple. "I love God," he said. Adding, "There's not many things I can do as well as the next guy — but praying is one of them."

At last the two men rose and went into the calm sunshine, the blue shadows, the summer stillness which descends on the prairie only after the day's wind has blown itself out in the grass, or the sky, or has lost itself beyond the brackets of earth and horizon. Greer, at that moment, had no inkling of what he had embarked upon.

After ten days, Greer had still to write a word worth keeping. This place, this monastery, didn't seem to be the solution either. All day he exhausted himself with the struggle and when evening came he lay on his bed watching the sky through his window, a sky pale as a bowl of cream. At such times he often thought of Miriam, where she was, how she was, and especially of the night in that quiet street, the Herengracht, outside their hotel in Amsterdam. Miriam, who had stood by him for the four years he was writing the book that was supposed to change his life, and who had remained steadfastly loyal for the three more difficult ones which followed it.

Gazing over the canal, she had asked him exactly what it was he wanted. Because on how many occasions past had she heard him claim that all he wanted was a *book*, one book to prove to himself he was a writer. Well, he had got his book but it hadn't made him happy. Now he claimed it was a disappointment to him. And the new book he was writing disappointed him even more. When was it going to stop? When was he going to get this bad taste out of his mouth?

Miriam told him these things in a calm, agreeable voice, without a trace of the anger she was so richly entitled to. While she did, Greer kept his eyes fixed on the oily, yellow blur of light on the canal, reflections of the windows of the tall, narrow houses that hedged it in, afraid to tell her how afraid he was of failure. A fine, misty rain hung quivering in the air between them like a veil.

He was always complaining that what he wrote didn't measure up. She didn't understand what he meant. Measure up to what? To whom?

He swung round on her, eyes burning. "To me, goddamn it!

It doesn't measure up to me!" he shouted. Embarrassed by this outburst, he turned back to his contemplation of the canal, forearms propped on the railing.

"If that's really the case, Jack," he heard her say, "it seems to me there are only two possibilities. Either you underestimate the quality of your writing, or overestimate your talent. If you want a life, you'd better make up your mind which it is."

The next morning they divided up the currency and travellers' cheques in a café near the Concertgebouw and separated.

It wasn't long before Greer and Madox fell into a routine. By ones and twos more guests began to take up residence in the monastery, but Roland ignored their existence; he clung exclusively to Jack. The two men ate all their meals together, Greer helping Roland load his plate and manage his tray in the cafeteria-style line. In the evenings they played Trivial Pursuit, which Roland always won, earning him the nickname Mr. S.O. Teric from Jack. But it was the hour before supper that was sacrosanct, the hour devoted to solitaire — which Roland happened to be addicted to. As a boy it had been his substitute for Little League and Minor Hockey, later for the Teen Dance, rec-room parties, other excitements.

There were times, however, when Greer grew short-tempered with his new friend. Of course, Greer blamed his frustration with his own work for making him impatient and peevish. He regretted the way he sometimes behaved, comparing the stubborn stoicism with which Roland, in public, silently bore pain, to his own outbursts of irritability. Although each morning Jack lay awake listening to the gut-wrenching noises from the hallway, he couldn't recall a single occasion when Roland had allowed so much as a murmur to escape his lips when they walked together. And the effort to suppress his pain was often evident in his face, the waxy scars taking on a sullen, leaden cast, a shine like the tip of a bullet.

Yet Jack couldn't deny there were things about his new friend that drove him crazy, exasperated him beyond belief. With Chekhov's example before him, Greer was attempting to cultivate the ability to see things lucidly, with nothing more than a pane of the clearest glass to put distance between himself and what he looked at, without even so much as the breath of a lie to mist and cloud the glass for his or anyone else's benefit. The famous objectivity, the pitiless refusal to delude oneself, to see clearly and not lose heart was, for Jack, the mystery of Chekhov's conscience as a writer and a man. The acceptance of things as they are. It was the gift Jack wanted most.

So, naturally, Greer found Roland Madox annoying. It annoyed him the way he gushed about his life to come as a monk, sounding like some bride-to-be burbling about the prospect of a totally fabulously unique June wedding. He talked as if he were on the point of crossing the threshold of some never-never land of unfading, unfailing happiness. Was that likely? Because it was clear to Greer that Roland had not been accepted by the happy band of monks he was so determined to join. They obviously had as little to do with him as possible, grateful to leave him in Greer's company and care. Wasn't it Jack Greer who shuffled his cards, ate with him, listened to his stories, nodded over his plans for the future? Meanwhile his brothers in Christ didn't pay the least attention to him.

Jack resented that. He had come to this place to write a book, not to get saddles with responsibility for another human being. Besides, anyone who had fucked up his own life as badly as he had, had no business letting anybody get in the habit of depending on him. He owed it to Madox to keep him at arm's length.

When the situation became too much for him, Jack Greer took the coward's way out and fled; struck out across country, knowing Roland couldn't pursue him over rough, broken ground. Madox had tried once and taken some bad tumbles over ridges in a freshly cultivated field. Greer, returning to the monastery in the twilight, had found him collapsed in a furrow, panting, dishevelled, dirty, utterly done in. He had had to half carry him back to the abbey.

But if he turned his back on the disappointed man watching reproachfully from the window and strode off in the direction of the shelterbelts and fields, he won a temporary freedom. Two things never altered on these expeditions. There was always brandy in his knapsack and he was always angry; angry about the guilt the figure at the window made him feel, angry at Roland for banking so much on becoming a monk. It wouldn't heal his body, turn back the clock to the time he owned a face. Couldn't he see that?

Past the hot stench of the pig sties, past the black and white cows sedately lowing their way to the dairy barns for milking, past the market gardens, past the rippling fields of wheat and oats, he marched, trying to tramp the fury and frustration out of himself, slashing weeds with a stick, sweating until his shirt clung to his back like a leech. A couple of miles bled the anger out of him. By the time he reached the railway embankment and stood in the cinders looking down at the slough and the ducks, it was spent. In early evening light the flat sheet of water was a mirror. And what does it reflect? Greer asked himself. Bullrushes, sky, cloud, streaks of sun, the wind brushing and wrinkling the surface. Things as they are. Nothing else. The last light of the day is the truest light.

When he had had enough of ducks and water, he headed for the tennis courts. Some of the visitors on retreat passed the evenings there, playing a set or two. They weren't aware he watched. The stand of evergreens planted forty years ago as a windbreak to ring the courts now towered over them, providing cover for a stealthy approach. Slipping from tree to tree, he reached his customary spot. Here the ground was thickly carpeted with dry needles, the resinous air was pleasantly sharp in his nostrils and he could comfortably prop his back against a trunk and view the court through the dark shelter of a screen of boughs. It was in bad shape, the asphalt surface heaved and split by frost, weeds bursting through its cracks, the lines practically obliterated by weather and wear, the net drooping and in need of mending.

Tonight, as they did every evening, middle-aged men and women politely patted a tennis ball and forth across the net. Greer quietly unzipped his knapsack, took out his bottle and glass, and poured his first drink of the day.

There was nothing preventing him leaving the trees and standing at the fence. Nothing except that on his first visit, entirely by chance, he had overheard some of the other guests discussing him. One of them said: "Brother Ambrose mentioned he's a writer — but he is not a *Catholic* writer. He's certainly stuck-up. I have a feeling he's keeping that poor boy from associating with the rest of us. What do you think could be the reason?"

They played on late, until the edges of their shadows on the asphalt began to blur and flocks of sparrows whirled erratically from evergreen to evergreen, preparing to settle for the night. When the players did eventually go, their voices fading off into the darkening distance, Greer realized his hands were sticky with the resin he had nervously picked from the tree bark with his nails.

Then the moon came up as it did in a Chekhov story and shone on the deserted, crumbling court and sagging net while he drank his second and third brandies. As Greer looked at this scene from behind the trees, a moon of loneliness rose in him too, a staring moon, as cold and bright and hard and huge as the one in the sky above.

Knowing first hand the effect disappointment could have on a man, Jack Greer feared for Roland Madox. Wanting to spare him that, he did his best to interject an element of reality into Roland's speculations about his future in the Order. It didn't work. Some days Greer would have sworn Madox was already a bishop.

"The abbot will probably want to make use of my degree," Roland said one afternoon. "I wouldn't be surprised if he assigned me to teaching."

Jack knew he ought to let it pass but didn't. "Teaching where? The school's been closed for five years. Maybe you haven't noticed, but this place is evolving into Palm Springs for the pious Catholic and the budget-conscious bohemian. That's the only growth industry in this place."

"There's the library. He could make me head librarian."

Greer had surveyed the card catalogue one afternoon when he dropped in on Roland. It comprised devotional works, biographies of saints, apologetics, and old high-school texts, the intellectual equivalents of Father Bing Crosby movies. Jack considered it an act of extreme charity to call it a library at all. He raised his eyebrows.

Roland tried again. "Few of the monks have any education. He won't want to let me go to waste. The Order is short of priests. I could be sent to a seminary. I could be ordained."

Greer made no comment on the likelihood of that. The two men sat silently, pretending to be absorbed in a study of the cards spread on the table.

After a bit Roland said, "Why do you have to pick holes in everything? Can't you just be happy for me."

Greer reached for the deck. "It's not up to me to be happy for you. Be happy for yourself."

"What's that supposed to mean?"

"Look," said Greer, "who's fooling who? If you're so crazy about the monastic life, why don't you show any sign of it? Why is it that you eat every meal with me instead of the brothers? Do you think by avoiding them at all costs you're making a favourable impression on the abbot? If you're their kind, why don't you stick with them?"

"I thought we were friends," said Roland. "I eat with you because we're friends."

"Yes," said Jack, "we're friends." He had been on the point of saying something else, something cruel. He had almost said: The reason you choose to eat with me, cling to me, is that one misfit recognizes another. We're both misfits and there's no point pretending otherwise. Things as they are.

Yet he let it drop. At the last moment, Greer had recalled *Faust*, and Mephistopheles' claim to be part of that power which always wills evil and always works good. Was it also possible that there might be uncalculated danger in willing good?

For nearly two days the sky wept grey rain, trapping Greer indoors, further dampening his spirits, deepening his melancholy. Hours at a time he stood at his window, one palm pressed to the glass, watching the dismal curtain of rain sweep the landscape on gusts of wind. Or he lay on his bed, forearm across his eyes; paced up and down the room until his knees ached; rehearsed sentences in his mind that he knew would never find their way to paper. After getting soaked to the skin on his way to lunch the first day of the downpour, he didn't bother to cross the courtyard for meals, it seemed too much trouble.

During the night, the sound of falling rain was magnified in the darkness. He slept in brief snatches, drowsing off to disconnected words, images, thoughts that were not his own but were provided by his reading of the past few weeks. He relived Chekhov's description of Venice, the strangeness which invited a longing for death. Warmth, calm, gleaming stars. The movement of the gondola. The silence of the countryside in a city without horses. This was the silence which surrounded Greer until morning arrived, the bells rang, and Roland struggled his way down the corridor. Suddenly fearful of crying out himself, Greer bit his lips. All morning he did nothing but watch the hypnotic rain. His hands trembled uncontrollably — he hadn't eaten in twenty hours and had no more than a couple hours' sleep the night before. Between eleven o'clock and noon he drank the day's ration of brandy, emptying three shot glasses in rapid succession while standing at the streaming window. For the first time in several weeks he was on the point of losing it, was prepared to dive down the neck of the bottle and hit bottom. Then, suddenly, the rain stopped.

Greer threw on a jacket and rushed outside, as desperate to flee that room as he often was to flee Roland. The problem was where to run. Striking across country was out of the question. The downpour of the past thirty-six hours had flooded the fallow fields, turned them into quagmires, soaked the tall grasses of the pastures. The road he found himself standing in might as well have led nowhere; the nearest town was twelve miles away.

Then he thought of the church. He remembered overhearing Diane talk about it in the dining room, some story about a self-taught artist who fifty years ago had gone from prairie town to prairie town, decorating churches in return for room and board, a kind of Johnny Appleseed of religious art, very likely half-mad. One of his churches was hard by, just two miles up the road. Greer decided to check it out.

The road he tramped through the flat landscape was a grid road, a pencil line on a sheet of paper. The clouds overhead reminded him of ones Miriam and he had seen in Holland, mottled grey and white, so oppressively low and heavy that they left him with the impression he could reach up and stroke their bellies with his hand. Despite there being no wind Greer could detect, the clouds kept rolling and churning, permitting a surprising amount of light to filter through, an odd opalescent light which turned the wet, yellow gravel crunching under his shoes to brass and lent the green of the crops of new oats and wheat an intense, smoky cast.

After Greer had walked for twenty minutes, he saw the church appear on the horizon, a white structure set upon an unexpected knoll rising out of level fields vacant of any other buildings. As he drew near, as the ground rose, tilting his angle of vision upward, the church grew brighter in the strange, beguiling light, more and more luminous against the setting of dark, restless, changeable sky.

Crossing the deserted parking lot, Greer realized he hadn't thought out this visit very well. Surely the church would be locked on a weekday. Yet when he tried the big double doors, one pulled open in his hand. Apparently rural churches could still stand open and unattended. He went in.

The first thing Greer noticed was a peculiar odour suspended in the motionless air, a blurred, sweet scent that struggled to mask a more insistent chemical smell which he associated with science laboratories of his high school days. Stale incense, he supposed.

Greer entered the nave, footsteps echoing hollowly in the empty church. To his right, a depiction of Christ's resurrection was painted directly on the plaster of the wall. To Greer it looked crude, Jesus rising before an incongruous backdrop — a fiery orange sun which inprobably shared a night sky of incredible blackness with a moon and a multitude of blazing stars. The limbs of this God were too white, his hair too blond, his lips too caressingly pink and full. Smiling shyly, he held out to the viewer the red wounds on his palms.

Greer cleared his throat. The strange, nasty, candied odour was stronger than at first. So strong, it was now a taste on his tongue. He began to move down the right-hand aisle from one picture to the next, forcing himself to halt and look. It was some of the most unpleasant, unsettling art he had ever seen. An oyster Saint Sebastian dripped gravy instead of blood; a dead-white Virgin suckled a blue-baby infant.

The emptiness of the church, the hallucinatory pictures, the sickly odour was tightening his breathing, constricting his chest. The smell was everywhere. Linked in his mind to the unnatural complexions of the saints, it was as if he could taste the repulsive-looking flesh itself.

Jack paused to catch his breath. Goddamn it, it wasn't his imagination. The taste *was* in his mouth. Without thinking, he pulled a handkerchief from his pocket, cleared his throat, and spat into it. Then realizing what he had done, gobbed in a holy place, he swept the bare church with a furtive look.

It was then he saw the open coffin before the altar, small and white, resting on a mortician's portable aluminum bier. In a moment of blind shock his mind staggered, then the corpse of the little girl sprang sharply into focus. She had curls. Her upper lip had relaxed, baring tiny front teeth.

The next thing Greer knew he was outside, taking the steps of the church two at a time, plunging across the parking lot, turning into the road in a panicky lope. Clear of the churchyard he tried to curb himself to a walk, but could only manage an undignified, stilted trot. Nor could he stop himself from darting a glance over his shoulder and, when he did, he blundered through a puddle, stumbling and nearly falling.

Looking up, he discovered himself face to face with a huge, coal-black dog. There was no explaining its bewildering appearance; the surrounding fields of grain were still too short in the stalk at this time of year to have hidden the approach of such a big dog, and there were no farmhouses or outbuildings from where it could have come. The two stood staring at each other. The dog did not pad up to make friends, nor slink away. Hollow flanks, matted, muddy coat and sore-looking, crusted eyes, it simply waited, motionless.

A minute, two minutes crawled by and still neither moved a muscle. The blood surged in Greer's temples, he could feel it throbbing in the ends of his fingers. A single thought was running round and round his mind like a toy locomotive on a circular track. *The dog belongs to the little girl. Belongs to the girl. Belongs to the girl. Belongs to the girl.*

And then these words were replaced by others. He heard himself speaking aloud in a wheedling voice. "Go away," he said. "Leave me be. I didn't do anything."

His voice acted as a trigger for the dog. Suddenly it bristled, the hair on its neck rose in a ruff and its head began to weave from side to side with a supple, snake-like menace while it snapped its jaws. The clicking of teeth was the only sound the dog made.

Rabies, thought Greer. *The son of a bitch has rabies.* Frantically seeking something with which to defend himself, his eyes fell on a large stone lying on the shoulder of the road. He bent to snatch it up and roaring wind filled his ears, the stone turned unimaginably heavy in his hands, dragged him to his knees, and for the briefest of moments everything went black. Then his surroundings woozily squeezed back in upon him and he felt the strain of wetness working its way up out of the damp ground and through the cloth of his pants, the gravel biting his kneecaps. Sparking lights, swimming in a cloud, gradually extinguished themselves one by one, and his eyes fastened on the rock, lying where he had dropped it.

The dog. He snatched up the stone and swung it threateningly above his head.

But the dog was gone.

Greer climbed to his feet, hugging the muddy stone to his shirt, and turned slowly around in a circle. The clouds were twisting sluggishly, the green fields running smoothly out to merge with the sky, the church commanding the height. But there was no trace of a dog. Anywhere.

Although he had not been drinking nearly as much as was usual for him, Greer recalled his doctor's warnings about alcoholic psychosis and wondered whether any of this had actually happened. He drew up categories in his mind – this he would accept as real and this he wouldn't. The corpse was probably real because he could not recall a dead child in Chekhov. The black dog was probably *not* real because of the *schwarzen Hund* in *Faust*. Terrified, he went no further, left it at that.

Roland was innocent of modesty. Greer relished the way he was never shy of making himself the hero of his own stories. Greer's favourite was the one about the bicycle. Madox claimed he could ride a bicycle. Before the accident he had been the youngest kid on the street to ride a two-wheeler and after he got out of the hospital he had a goal – to ride again. For six years his mother helped him, outfitted him in elbow pads and a hockey helmet and spent summers running up and down their suburban street, holding his bicycle upright while he fought to achieve a precarious balance.

It was a scandal on the block. Neighbours complained to his father. "Ted, it was ninety-two degrees today and humid. *Humid.* You've got to tell her to quit or she's going to have a heart attack out there on the street. The wife says she can't stand to look out the window anymore. And the kid falls. Lots of times he falls. He's going to get himself hurt."

So far, so good. The writer part of Greer approved of the telling details, the hockey helmet, elbow pads, concerned neighbours, humidity. Where Greer believed Roland went wrong was in his failure to explain how he could pedal a bike with his legs in braces. Still, that was the critic speaking. Greer, the friend, still loved to hear him tell it. He would say, "Give us the one about the bicycle again, Easy Rider," and Roland would willingly oblige, always climaxing the story with the unassisted, joyous sweep down a twilit street, bicycle flying through an autumn evening, scattering fallen leaves while Roland whooped his delight and his mother did an impromptu jig on the sidewalk in honour of his recovery of solo flight.

By now, Jack, realizing it was hopeless, had given up even the pretence of trying to write. As a result, he found himself spending more and more time in Roland's company, often filling the long hours of the day by assisting him in the library. While they sorted and shelved books, Roland talked excitedly about his plans. There was nothing new in this. But the insistent, urgent way he spoke was new, as if he was trying to reassure himself, as well as convince Greer.

Something else was new. Greer started to drop hints about himself and his past. On several occasions he even casually mentioned her name: Miriam. With Roland, who was a stranger to their history, he could do this because her name signalled nothing, set off no warning bells. To speak of her in this off-hand fashion helped Greer feel she was somehow a normal, everyday feature of his life, simply there. And that released in him a quiet, calm affection for her memory that had been impossible to experience whenever he spoke of her with anyone who had known them together, in the old days, and knew the score.

Mostly, though, it was Roland who talked, more and more often going obsessively over old ground. The doctors had thought he wouldn't last the night — but look at him now. Nobody had thought he could come so far. He had a degree in history, he could ride a bike, he had learned Latin. The rest went unsaid — that he would become a monk. Even though the decision wasn't his to make but the abbot's.

It was obvious the uncertainty was playing on his nerves.

"I'm not going to give him much longer," he said one afternoon over solitaire.

"Who?" said Greer.

"The abbot."

"You ask me," Jack said, "no news is good news."

"How long does he think he can keep me dangling?" Roland pleaded. Greer avoided his eyes and shrugged.

Two days after this, Greer missed Roland at breakfast. He didn't think anything of it, but later that morning when he dropped by to give his friend a hand he was surprised to find the door of the library locked. Assuming that Roland must be ill, Greer didn't look in on him so he wouldn't disturb him if he were resting. Instead, he returned to his own room and found Brother Ambrose waiting there with a request that he accompany him to the office of the abbot.

The abbot turned out to be a wisp of a man with greying sandy-coloured hair like a shock of November grass, and a parchment complexion. Inviting Greer to take a seat, the abbot settled himself fussily, chair creaking.

"How's the writing going, Mr. Greer?" he asked as a conversation-opener.

"It's going," said Greer.

"You understand — I get so little time to read — it's difficult to keep up." An apology for being unfamiliar with Greer's work.

"Of course," said Greer.

"But Trollope," said the abbot. "I have a weakness for Trollope. The clerical novels," he qualified.

Greer nodded.

"And you, Mr. Greer," he inquired politely, "you have a favourite writer?"

"Checkhov."

"Ah," said the abbot and stared off into space, palms pressed together in a prayerful attitude. "I have the greatest respect for your profession, Mr. Greer. Writing. You can touch so many people, do so much good."

Not bloody likely, thought Greer.

"But, as you have probably guessed, I didn't ask you hear to discuss writing — no, something else entirely," said the abbot, abruptly becoming business-like.

"Yes?"

"Several of the brothers have noted that you are a special friend of Roland Madox." He waited for confirmation.

Greer didn't care for the adjective "special." It sounded like an accusation of immorality. "A friend, yes," he said.

"Then I would like to ask you a favour," said the abbot.

"What king of favour?"

"I understand you have a car?"

"Yes."

"As you many imagine, none of us here owns a car. If you could drive Roland to the city tomorrow to catch his flight, it would be most appreciated. Of course, the abbey would be glad to recompense you for gas and incidentals." He hesitated delicately. "And having a friend see him safely off – it would ease our minds."

"Roland didn't say anything to me about going anywhere," said Greer, mildly alarmed.

"We felt is best that he leave immediately. I have been in touch with his father and he has purchased Roland a ticket home to Winnipeg. It will be waiting for him at the airport."

"I don't understand why you're banishing him," said Greer. "Don't you have any idea what this meant to him?"

"You may not be aware of it, Mr. Greer, but in the last five years Roland has made at least six attempts to be admitted to monasteries across the country. None would accept him." The abbot shook his head sadly. " He is a troubled young man."

"More remarkable than troubled," said Greer.

The abbot scrutinized Greer shrewdly for a moment. "You're angry with me, Mr. Greer," he said. "But perhaps you don't know all the facts of the case."

"I didn't realize it was being treated as a case," snapped Greer.

Overlooking this, the abbot continued in a patient voice. "This is the second time Roland has been with us. The first time was two years ago when the old abbot was still alive. It was not a happy experience for all concerned. I do not know what he has said to you, but I allowed him to return only on the understanding that he would not be considered for admission to the Order. That was made unequivocally clear. It was done as a favour to his father. He hoped that if Roland was provided with some small job he could manage, it might prove helpful to him. Mr. Madox is a layman of some standing in the Church, well respected. However, I may have made an error of judgment in obliging him."

Greer was confused. "But Roland's father isn't a Catholic," he protested. "Roland told me himself he converted to Roman Catholicism against his parents' wishes when he was at university."

"You see what I mean?" said the abbot. "Roland was born a Catholic. But that does not suggest the spirit of independence he likes to project. So he altered the facts to conform to his picture of himself. Mr. Greer, not everything is quite as Roland portrays it. Yesterday he was in my office, demanding I come to a decision about admitting him to the Order." The abbot paused. "It was in the nature of an ultimatum. Now he knew when he came here there was no possibility of my accepting him. Yet when I reminded him of this he seemed astonished, as if I had gone back on my word. He made threats."

"Threats?"

"Threats," repeated the abbot enigmatically. He took a deep breath. "At present he is very angry and wants nothing to do with any of us — the religious, I mean. It would be difficult for any of us to accompany him. You see our problem. But if someone he likes and trusts could take him to the airport, it would be most helpful. Would you be so kind as to do us this favour, Mr. Greer?"

"When's his flight?"

"Tomorrow afternoon, five-thirty. Air Canada Flight 183," said the abbot.

Greer got to his feet. "All right," he said. At that moment, he felt sad and injured and angry, a little like the father asked to remove from school the boy of whom he is so proud.

As Greer drove, he glimpsed, out of the corner of his eye, metal machinery sheds, dull-red granaries, farmhouses with bug satellite dishes in their front yards stuttering by. Meanwhile Roland was in a passion, body jerking and twitching in the seatbelt. "Justice is all I asked," he said bitterly, for what seemed to Greer the thousandth time. "Justice. Who did Christ hold his arms out to if not the crippled and the blind? And nor the Church turns its back on us."

Greer felt sorry for him, sorrier than he could say. He had tried to take the line with Roland that he was well out of it, look what he had been saved from — chastity, poverty, obedience. Who needed it? But Roland wasn't buying it, nor was Greer exactly surprised. In his experience, of all slighted parties, the refused were the least responsive to reason. Maybe because refusal so intimately connected injury with humiliation. It isn't an easy thing to swallow, the news that someone doesn't want you. Greer had found that out with Miriam.

They arrived in the city with nearly three and a half hours to spare before Roland's flight was scheduled to leave. It was Jack's plan to mark his friend's departure by treating him to a farewell lunch. Greer wasn't certain of the ins and outs, the rights and wrongs of it, but he knew Roland felt genuinely betrayed at being given the push by the abbot. The least somebody could do in this situation was to give him a proper send off. The restaurant Greer chose for this was the Golden Wok — on the recommendation of Diane — who provided him with directions to find it. The Golden Wok turned out to be an establishment more upscale than the type Greer usually frequented, the décor insistently bellowing "Chinese Experience" — brass gongs, plaster lions, kites, ornamental screens, a multitude of fire-breathing dragons. *Early Shanghai Whorehouse*, Greer thought, surveying the scene.

They had arrived late for lunch and the dining room was almost empty. As Jack and Roland were escorted to a table, they passed the only other diners, a large party of what appeared to be office workers marking some festivity, perhaps the birthday or retirement of a co-worker. Each of the ladies had a pastel-coloured cocktail — a grasshopper, brown cow, or daiquiri — set in front of them and were having a high old time noisily joking and cutting-up in front of their indulgently smiling male bosses. But as he and Roland went by, the noise of clattering cutlery nervously subsided and the shrill, high-pitched laughter died.

Roland paused, shifted his crutches as if to move on, reconsidered, swept the uneasy gathering with a long cool stare and said, "You're all wondering, no doubt. I'm Jim Morrison — the Lizard King."

If there was anything Jack Greer hated, it was public embarrassments. "Jesus Christ," he said angrily, trailing after Roland as he lurched haughtily to their table on his crutches. "What was the point of that?"

"I detected a certain morbid curiosity," said Roland. "I tried to satisfy it."

Greer was at a loss how to respond. All he managed to do was mumble, "Jesus Christ."

"Any guess as to why I prefer a monastery?" asked Roland.

Behind him Greer could feel a distinct chill of disapproval, hostile whispers. Someone said, "A person expects to be able to go out and have a nice time and enjoy yourself. We're supposed to accommodate those people — but what effort do they make to accommodate us?"

Greer partly blamed himself for the incident. Christ, how could he be so stupid, bringing Madox into a place like this! That's all Roland needed, another humiliation. Why hadn't he taken him to a drive-in where they could have eaten in the privacy of the car, rather than this hang out for the blue-suit crowd?

Perhaps his discomfort made him try too hard. He insisted on ordering too many dishes, dismissing Roland's protests with, "A taste from each then. We'll have a taste from each. And besides, what do you care? I'm paying." He called for a pitcher of beer and proposed a toast. "To your future," he said, lifting his glass. It was, on reflection, ill-advised because once they drank, the unspoken question hung between them. What was Roland's future?

Roland tried to answer. "There are monasteries all over the States," he said. "Dominicans in Vermont, Cistercians in Kentucky, lots more. I'll keep knocking on doors. I'll keep trying. You've got to keep trying."

"But not right away," cautioned Greer. "You'll have a rest, catch your breath, won't you, before you start this all over again?"

"A couple of days maybe," said Roland. "Then the old man can buy me another plane ticket, or bus ticket, and see I get wherever I'm going. He owes me after this."

"And where will you be going?" asked Greer.

"Wherever there's a chance. I still have a long list of possibles to work through."

"Tell me," coaxed Greer. "Why did the abbot hustle you off so quickly? What did you do?"

Greer believed he saw Roland smile. "I told him that if he didn't accept me I'd pick up where the accident left off twenty years ago. Douse myself in gasoline and set myself on fire. Like the buddhist monks did in Vietnam. As an act of protest."

"And he believed you? He didn't know it was a joke?" said Greer.

Roland held out his empty glass to Greer. Jack filled it, topped up his own. He found Roland's reluctance to answer disconcerting. "It was a joke, wasn't it?" he demanded.

"Oh yes, a joke," said Roland. "For the time being at least. But it's always wise to reserve the right to the last laugh, isn't it?"

The waiter arrived with their lunch, plate after plate of dumplings, Cantonese chow mein, Kung Po chicken, Szechwan shrimp, curried beef, ribs with black bean sauce. Both men welcomed this interruption of what had been verging on an uncomfortable conversation and dug into the food, exclaiming over the dishes, heaping their plates, pretending to argue over the division of the shrimp. Roland was even making a gallant attempt to manipulate the chopsticks in his claw. Finally, he tossed them aside, picked up a rib, and began to gnaw it. "It's like the beer commercial. It doesn't get any better than this, does it, Jackie?" he asked, mumbling around the bone.

"A subtle reminder," said Greer, signalling the waiter to bring another pitcher. He had already exceeded his daily quota of booze, but this was different. This was his friend's going-away party. Greer was beginning to feel better than he had in weeks, exhilarated like a kid on a holiday. Today he need feel no guilt for not writing, need not ask himself why he failed whenever he tried. For the first time he realized how the dreariness, the sameness, the regimentation of life in the monastery had been weighing on him. He was becoming a little giddy. So was Roland.

Green asked, "Did you hear the one about the absent-minded priest who put his hand in his pocket and said, "Plums, plums? When did I buy plums?"

Roland began to giggle. He picked up his chopsticks, held them to his forehead, and waggled them like antennas. "Worker ant. Clerical division. Library," he said.

Greer collapsed with laughter. Roland winked at him, cocked his head in the direction of the other table. Greer glanced over his shoulder. One of the daiquiri-drinkers was staring at them with an indignant, offended expression. She leaned over to her neighbour and said something. The other woman primly nodded her agreement.

The second pitcher had emptied in no time at all. Madox ordered more. "This one's on me," he said. "I ought to contribute something to the party. Besides my charming self."

After the third pitcher arrived they went quiet, sat looking at their glassses. Suddenly Roland asked, "And you, Jack, what does the future hold for you?"

"More of the same, I suppose," he replied evasively.

"You mean writing," Roland prodded.

Greer shrugged.

"So what do you want to write next?"

Greer shifted on his chair. This talk of writing was turning his mood self-abusive and self-accusing, qualities which Miriam had deplored in him and which had never failed to infuriate and upset her. "I'll tell you what I want to write," said Greer with a bitter smile. "A Chekhov story. He left an outline for one he never got around to writing himself. It's a natural for a guy like me. The story concerns a brown-noser, the son of a serf or small shopkeeper raised to respect rank, kiss priests' hands, worship others' ideas, play the hypocrite before God and his betters because he cannot forget his own insignificance. Anyway, that's roughly the way Chekhov describes his character." Greer paused. "Change a few details — the son of the serf business, kissing the priests' hands — and Chekhov is describing Jack Greer. Except for one other difference. In Chekhov's story the young man presses the bad blood out of himself one drop at at a time until one morning he wakes up with human blood running in his veins. That's the one essential difference between me and Chekhov's character."

All the time he had been delivering this sardonic discourse, he had kept his eyes fixed on his glass of beer while he slowly rotated it, grinding it into the tabletop. It came as a complete surprise to him when he looked up and encountered a stony stare of unrelieved, naked animosity.

"Well," said Jack, "it's just a story I thought might be interesting to write. You don't have to agree with me."

Madox erupted. He shouted that he knew who Greer was really talking about. Who kissed priests' hands? Who was the hypocrite before God? Who was a slave? Who worshiped others' ideas? Fuck him. He was wrong.

All Roland's convictions had been arrived at on his own. And he *had* convictions, which was more than Greer could say. Another thing. He was getting pretty damned pissed off with Greer and his snide remarks about his religion. His religion was nobody's business but his own.

The more Greer tried to assure him that he had not been talking about him at all, that it was a terrrible misunderstanding, the more furious Madox became. At first Greer didn't realize what was wrong: the immobility of Roland's face helped hide the fact that he was drunk. It was the swearing that tipped him off — Roland was not a swearer — and the rage, the rage born of utter frustration, his voice booming out asshole, dicklicker, cunt, cocksucker throughout the dining room. "So fuck off and mind your own fucking business, why don't you?" he ended by shouting.

Greer felt a tap on his shoulder. A man from the table of merry makers, silver-haired, distinguished, stood over him. His face was beet-coloured. "I don't know what your friend's problem is," he said in a tone that is acquired only after years of handing out orders to subordinates. "But if you're going to take him out in public he ought to control himself. His language and behaviour is offensive to the ladies. Please make him stop it." Before Greer could collect himself to reply, the executive turned briskly on his heels and marched smartly to his table, several of the women greeting their champion with approving looks.

Greer rose to his feet.

Roland had suddenly regained his composure. "Forget it, Jack," he said in a calm voice. "One way or the other, it's always the same. Sit down."

"No," said Greer. "I won't forget it." At the same time he wondered what had come over him. He hated scenes.

Some minor awkwardness with his chair alerted Greer that he too might be suffering the influence of alcohol. Concentrating on carrying himself in as dignified a manner as possible he approached the table. There was a stir. The gentlemen in authority squared his shoulders in an expensive blue suit and ran a hand down the length of his tie, appeared to be readying himself to stand but, in the end, settled for defensively shoving his chair back from the table a few inches.

Greer halted directly in from of him. "Why don't you tell him yourself?" he said.

"What?" said the man sharply, taken aback.

"You want him to shut up, why're you talking to me? I'm not his babysitter. Come on back to the table and say what you have to say to him directly, man to man. He is a man, if you haven't noticed. Then he can tell you to go fuck yourself to your face."

"This is ridiculous," said the suit. The comment was meant for the table, not Greer.

"He's not an idiot," said Jack. "He can understand you perfectly well." Greer began to motion the man out of his chair. "Come on over to our table and give him a piece of your mind, such as it is."

"I don't know what's wrong with your friend," he said, "but you're drunk."

"Really," said Greer, "won't you speak to him? An old-fashioned Dutch Uncle talk would mean the world to him. To both of us actually." He leaned forward. "Just a few pointers on life and how the best people behave in Chinese restaurants."

Roland, following this performance eagerly, was excitedly trying to rise from his chair. "Come on over," he suddenly shouted, beckoning with a crutch. "I never had a conversation with a fucking doorknob before!"

"You see," said Greer, "he would love to chat. Won't you spare him a minute, up close and personal?"

"Hey, the red baboon's ass in the blue suit!"

All around the table there was general consternation, people were getting hurriedly to their feet, fishing, for purses underneath chairs, exchanging whispers and agitated glances. One of the junior-looking executives from the far end of the table was squeezing his way past the ladies, hurrying to reinforce senior management. In the high polish of a nearby gong Greer caught a glimpse of himself, his cropped head sinister, a model for the escaped convict, gallery slave, Magwitch, Jean Valjean. Little wonder respectability was beating a retreat.

"Anything I can do, Mr. Tyler?" asked the young man, eager to ingratiate.

He was ignored. "I'd watch my step if I were you," said Mr. Tyler to Greer. "If you two insist on making public nuisances of yourselves you'll get mixed up with the police. That's just a friendly warning."

Roland was standing now, swaying as he tried to disentangle one of his crutches from the chair legs. "Hey, Jack," he bellowed. "Need any help with those two?"

To Mr. Tyler, Jack said quietly, "I think you've confused public nuisances and misfits. The two of us are misfits. Get it right, why don't you?" From behind, he felt the hands of white-jacketed Chinese waiters closing on his arms.

Public disgrace, getting tossed out of a restaurant, had them howling all the way to the airport, laughing school boys recounting and reliving a stupid prank. Self-appointed rogues and rascals, they swaggered through the terminal. The shared adventure heightened the emotion of the leavetaking, Greer impulsively throwing his arms around Roland's neck at the gate, Roland letting one of his crutches fall to the floor so he could thump his friend's back. "Have a good flight," said Greer, his voice tight. "Wherever it takes you."

"You too, Jack," said Roland.

Only after Roland passed through security did Greer remember that he meant to ask his friend whether it was really true that he could ride a bicycle.

Out in the parking lot Greer stood under the hot glare of the afternoon sun listening to the jets take off. He had felt nothing like this in years, was still keyed-up, wildly elated. A plane soared into the summer sky, its engines whining. Greer checked his watch. Five-thirty. That would be Roland on his way. Jack closed his eyes. He realized he would never see his friend again but he knew how he wished to hold Roland Madox in his mind. Forever like this, in reckless pursuit of his destiny. The bicycle, swift ghost in the gloom of an October evening, rubber tires whirring madly on the pavement, the roar of a jet under a cloudless blue canopy. The same headlong rush against the odds.

Mad, whirling monk, thought Greer. And then it was he remembered that Chekhov had had his monk too. Greer had never been able to make head nor tail of the story "The Black Monk" because this fantastic, dreamlike fable was like nothing else Chekhov had ever written. As unlike his other stories as the monastery in which Greer had spent the past month was unlike the outside world.

In Chekhov's story, a brilliant young man by the name of Kovrin becomes obsessed with the legend of a black-robed monk who, a thousand years ago, wandered the wildernesses of Syria and Arabia. The mirage of this black monk was projected onto a lake many miles distant and this mirage produced a second mirage which had produced a third, and so on, until the image of the monk had flown all about the world, to Africa, to Spain, to India, to the Far North, perhaps even beyond, to Mars, to the constellation of the Southern Cross. But the legend held that after a thousand years the mirage would return to earth and make itself known to men. Which it did to Kovrin, in the form of a cyclone whirling across the Russian landscape, a cyclone which transformed itself before his eyes into a monk who addressed Kovrin — something that optical illusions are not supposed to do. The message which it whispered to him was that he was a genius.

Exhalted by this news, in the months that follow, Kovrin discovers the sweetness of life. He falls in love, enjoys his wine and cigars as never before, works on his philosophical investigations with unremitting energy and purpose, is filled with inexpressible joy. But one night his new wife awakes to find him sitting in their bedroom talking to an empty chair. Only Kovrin sees the black monk seated there.

He is handed over to doctors to be cured of his delusion. After treatment, the black monk ceases to appear to him. Kovrin is a changed man, but scarcely for the better. Where once he was interesting and original, now he is cruel and listless, a mediocrity. He quarrels with his wife and insults his father-in-law. The marriage falls apart, Kovrin and his wife separate.

Then one night in a resort hotel, Kovrin hears a song which reminds him of the black monk's first visit to him. Filled with the rapture of anticipation he sees a black waterspout forming across the bay. The waterspout sweeps down upon him and the monk materializes. He chides Kovrin for passing his last two years so sadly and barrenly, all because he refused to believe the monk's message. Kovrin, in ecstasy, cries out for his wife, cries out for the work he gave his youth to, cries out for the beautiful garden which had been his dead father-in-law's single passion and, in crying out, his tuberculosis-ridden lungs begin to haemorrhage. In the morning he is found dead.

Yes, said Greer to himself, slowly walking up and down the parking lot. Yes, yes, yes. Things are as they are. But did things outside a man or woman simply mirror things *inside*? On the drive back to the abbey he, like Kovrin, began to recall the past. A gentle rain in Amsterdam. The harsher rain of last month, a muddy dog, a dead child in a church, the ringing of bells, Roland groaning down the corridor to kneel before something Jack could not imagine.

*　　*　　*

Two months later, Greer was present to watch the monks harvest their crops. what had been green was now yellow, the roads were dust, the pines soared even darker against the hot blue sky of August. It was good to walk among the heaped and bristling swaths like Chekhov in his beloved Melikhov, to have begun a nineteenth-century kind of story.

Bernadette Wagner

Calling

bells mark our time in this
place that honours life
lived in devotion

you escape insanity
me, another reality. our sharing
carillons
coming closer

a lingering touch   brush
of tingling skin

too dangerous, this connection
to volatile to explore...
                         this ringing

(2002)

Time spent at a Writers/Artists Colony at St. Pete's is sacred. It's an opportunity to set aside the outside world and to honour my craft. In a world gone weird on consumerism, greed, and violence, that's not always an easy task. The sense of calm and peacefulness, the silent working hours, and my own commitment help me to explore new possibilities, to consider options or to work at that one piece that's been niggling me for months. I also appreciate the camaraderie of other writers and artists. Finding community, becoming friends with other writers, being part of the writing community in Saskatchewan and Canada is good for me and for my poetry. Oh, and I love the rhubarb and raspberries!

Bernadette Wagner

Specimens from the Abbey 2002

a palindromic year
a winter week

to bridges that span run-off creeks
miniature pine boughs and cones falling

chickadees lighting on outstretched hands peck peanuts
from a pile of grains and legumes

behind the rink on snow stamped down by walkers wondering trails
string of numbered tickets admitting one lie

sky-blue

string of numbered tickets admitting one lie
behind the rink on snow stamped down by walkers wondering trails

from a pile of grains and legumes
chickadees lighting on outstretched hands peck peanuts

miniature pine boughs and cones falling
to bridges that span run-off creeks

a winter week
a palindromic year

Joanna M. Weston

Sunrise Walk at St. Peter's

boots crunch frost
hard at -26

crystals matt
wool-covered mouths

while brilliance strips
earth of definition

floods gold-blue dazzle
over morning

we walk dark
shadow-sprung

dawn-struck
into silhouette

(2000)

It's the solitude of the rooms, the camaraderie in the dining room, the companionship of other writers, and the cold outside that makes the words flow at St. Peter's — I believe. It's also the support of the monastic community, the wide landscape, the chickadees, the time and space in which to focus and write my interior world. "Sunrise Walk at St. Peter's" is that morning walk, right after breakfast, with Shelley and Honor, getting my daily exercise before the real work began, and entering a revelation of light, colour, and prairie cold! "Two Cemeteries" puts together the time I first saw my father's grave in the war cemetery near Caen, France, and the first time I entered the cemetery at St. Peter's and was stunned (actually "gobsmacked" is a better word) by the resemblance between the two places. Went back to my room and wrote a poem. Heard Dave Carpenter read a poem about his father that evening — and I realized I'd written the wrong poem. Got to my room and wrote "Two Cemeteries."

Joanna M. Weston

Two Cemeteries

(St. Peter's, Muenster, and Caen, France)

regulated rows
uniform tombstones
intone names and dates

this is where my
father's war has ended

>close my eyes
>and there are roses
>on each grave
>mown velvet grass
>over battledress   and gun
>with fields laying plain chant
>beyond the battalion
>of cross, star and crescent

I am looking at enclosure —
tranquility
in requiem of snow

memorials lie, black
on white stone
contained by hedge
and ministry of wind
over royal priesthood

>yet — do the brothers lie in Brittany
>on a hill of blazing canticles —
>soldiers there transfigured?

here, my father lies
patriarch in this garrison
of Christendom

I, now, beneath this overcast
have another sky
and lose a summer father
in a funeral
whose psalm
is wind and frost

(2000)

Christopher Wiseman

Dead Angels

No more dancing on heads of pins
Or sunning themselves on sunlit clouds,
No more celestial music in our dreams,
Bending near the earth with harps of gold,
Standing high with trumpets over congregations.
And something else will have to be assigned
To be the Guardian of childrens' souls
And give protection from nightmares or hunger,

For these are dead angels I look at
In a monastery storeroom, where a key
And curiosity have led me. Half-dark,
The air hot and thick, blinds drawn on the sun,
Here, among assorted relics of the years,
Among fly corpses and damaged furniture,
Are four angels in a corner, line astern,
Tilted awkwardly together in the silence.

I'm not surprised the monks didn't smash them.
I couldn't. It would be desecration,
Seeing the blue robes, the Victorian doll
Faces, the white and pink and gold,
The long feathered wings furled right down
Their backs. But see the thick dust coating
The bright blue eyes and caught in the folds
Of feathers. A shock. There's been a great fall here.

These presences should never turn to dust,
Nor be piled up, grounded, silenced, abandoned
In such a place. What monstrous innodation!
Compelled, I move around. In the shadows
The wings are deformities, turning them
Suddenly into cruel ugly three-foot birds,
All their softness gone, except in imagination's
Memory. Lilies that fester. I think of Rilke

And wait for pity to come, real compassion,
For this is wrong. These are images of light,
Of higher places, the miraculous. These
Are the singing from other worlds, the poems,
The glory shining round. Demystified, they
Stare unblinking in a clog of dust and cobweb,
Sad forsaken spirits who have filled our books
And paintings, cast gold on our history,

And can never be obsolete, for we all crave
To be spirit, to shuck off the dying animal,
To fly amazed, atheist or believer, in high music,
Transfigured and graceful. We hate
Our gross misshapen entanglements,
Our crude limitations, and look for what
Angels signify — light in darkness, music,
And brightness linking us to something else.

But I wonder if it isn't in some way
Salutary to find places like this
And contemplate how glory turns to dust,
Free flight to helpless immobility.
Perhaps we should know about dead angels,
Dead dreams, dead music, all the airless rooms
Where lambent hopes end up, and beauty, and see
How far we've fallen from the celestial,

How heavy we are, how mired, how *lumpen*.
I don't know. One last look. They smile their dusty
Doll-smiles. The shadows play tricks. A lone fly
Lurches heavily behind a blind. I must leave,
Full of dark obsequies. But then, as
I step outside, bright birds, blue and white and gold,
Unfurl their wings and swoop and soar in a great
Cloud, their songs pealing and belling

In pure enormous harmonies, not strange
To the heart, and I lift my eyes up high to them,
My spirit soft and open to the summer,
And compassion finally breaks for what
Is behind me in that room of death,
Compassion breaks as if I were released,
And it is wide as all the sky and glorious.
I stand astonished, half blinded by the sun.

(1987)

St. Pete's in July is often extremely hot, overarched by an enormous sky, the air full of a massive heat, birds everywhere. A brightness remarkable in the curious oasis on the prairie. I have been an appreciative guest there six or seven times and have always found it a marvellous place to write and concentrate, as well as to relax with good company. It was, therefore, slightly surprising that two of us found ourselves in the huge locked storeroom in the main building, a strange world of gloom and relics and silence — a secret cave, almost, out of the climate and the feeling of the rest of the monastery. There were many strange things there — old furniture, the first telephone switchboard of St. Pete's, pictures, books, written records, rolls of carpet, photographs (like memories inside a head), all jumbled together in the half-dark smother of airlessness, relieved by the occasional fly purring and clattering in the closed blinds. And then there were the plaster angels. Stacked in a corner, oddly incongruous, hypnotizing, half-human in size, their sad blind dust-filled eyes followed us everywhere. The poem starts in semi-comic exaggeration — the way I thought it would continue — but then it pulls me out into a long meditation about different sides of experience, about what produces art, perhaps (laced with small references to Shakespeare, Larkin, Yeats, Rilke), the human need for transcendent experience, until, finally, back up the rabbit hole again, leaving those dead things behind, they become stunningly and redemptively alive again in the birds and sun and sky. The final lines of this poem, as perhaps befits that special place, are, I believe, the most celebratory I have ever written.

Jan Zwicky

STUDY: ASPEN

Shade that wears itself
lightly in the morning breeze,
and at noon, the sad sleep
of its little pointed leaves.
Such a sweet haze
folds along the gully's flank
in May.

(1998)

The Rule of St. Benedict enjoins its adherents to listen with the ear of the heart. This, it seems to me, is also one way to describe the discipline demanded of poets. The abbey thus provides an environment that effortlessly, unselfconsciously, focusses one of the deepest aspects of poetic practice. I am grateful beyond measure for the sense of coming home that St. Peter's always provides.

Jan Zwicky

Small Song: Blue

The sky today
is a single
perfect sound, an open
throat, the now
that's everywhere
and all of time
there is —

the sky, perhaps,
Parmenides
looked up into and said
what is for being
is for thinking, too.

I guess I better
wear a hat.

(1998)

Jan Zwicky

Study: Reeds

The light is weight, it it
a mane of sleep.
See how it lies there, fallen
in the rushes. The afternoon
has pressed it,
tousled, stiff as taffeta,
and matted it: the sleeping reeds
are ribbons
of green and tawny light.

And at their white roots
water ripples once,
is motionless.

(1998)

Jan Zwicky

Small Song: Prairie

Wood light, meadow light,
the fencepost silver
in the afternoon's long stare;
beast light, the satin flash
of horserump or the brown hand
in the saskatoons;
cloud light and willow light,
the dead light of the salt marsh
and the hammered brilliance
of the dugout under wind;
even the rain in its night singing,
the night rain in its forgetting,
is a kind of light.

(1998)

Contributors' Notes

Patricia Abram's poetry has appeared in literary journals and anthologies; her fiction has appeared in *Two Lands: New Visions*, an anthology of short stories (Coteau Books, 1998). Her first collection of poetry, *The Ink of Light*, was published by White Mountain Publications in 2000. She currently lives in southern Ontario.

Susan Andrews Grace's most recent book of poetry was *Ferry Woman's History of the World*, which won the Saskatchewan Book of the Year Award in 1998 and was short-listed for three other Saskatchewan awards. She's a founding faculty member of the Nelson, BC, Fine Art Centre, where she teaches creative writing.

Kimmy Beach's second collection, *Alarum Within*, was published by Turnstone Press earlier this year. Her first book, *Nice Day for Murder: Poems for James Cagney* (Turnstone) was released in 2001. Kimmy travels from Red Deer, Alberta, to St. Pete's twice a year.

Madeleine Beckman, poet/fiction writer, is the author of *Dead Boyfriends*, a poetry collection (Linear Arts Books, 1998). Her second collection, *All You Can Eat*, is forthcoming. She teaches creative writing at New York University and is writer-in-residence at Stern College for Women.

Jacqueline Bell lives in Edmonton. Her first book, *burning for it*, was published in 1998 by Rowan Books. She has attended two poetry colloquia at St. Peter's.

Sheri Benning's first book, *Earth After Rain*, won two Saskatchewan book awards in 2002: the Anne Szumigalski Poetry Award and the First Book Award. She is currently completing her creative Master's in English at the University of New Brunswick. She was a student at St. Peter's College from 1996 to 1998.

Erin Bidlake is an east coast poet living in Calgary. She attended the Sage Hill Poetry Colloquium at St. Peter's in 2001. Most recently she has published poetry in *Grain*, *Malahat Review*, and *Prism*.

Ronna Bloom has published two books of poetry, *Fear of the Ride* and *Personal Effects*. Her third, *Public Works*, will be published by Pedlar Press this year. She lives in Toronto.

Annette Bower writes short stories from Regina Beach, Saskatchewan. Her writing is a mid-life adventure full of challenges and joys.

Beverley Brenna is a Saskatoon poet, writer and teacher who has published three children's books.

Laura Burkhart writes fiction and poetry. Most of the time she lives in Regina.

Alison Calder lives in Winnipeg, where she teaches literature and creative writing at the University of Manitoba. She's originally from Saskatoon.

Anne Campbell is the Regina author of four collections of poetry: *No Memory of A Move*; *Death Is An Anxious Mother*; *Red Earth, Yellow Stone* and *Angel Wings All Over*. Her poems, stories and non-fiction are published in journals and anthologies, and her musical collaborations (with Tom Schudel) played world-wide.

Warren Cariou was born and raised in Meadow Lake, Saskatchewan, which is the subject of his most recent book, *Lake of the Prairies*. The piece in this anthology is the first chapter of his novella "Lazarus," published in his first book, *The Exalted Company of Roadside Martyrs*. He lives in Winnipeg and teaches at the University of Manitoba.

David Carpenter writes novels, essays and poems full-time in Saskatoon. A collection of his poems is due out in fall 2003. His father was born in Regina during the year of this province's birth, 1905. His mother was born five years later in Moose Jaw. They met in Saskatoon, where David was conceived. "An accident," both parties have claimed. The responsibility for his escape into our world is still being hotly debated.

Sara Cassidy writes poetry and children's picture books in Victoria, where she lives with her husband and two children.

Hilary Clark, originally from Vancouver, has lived with her family in Saskatoon for the last thirteen years. She teaches English and women's studies at the University of Saskatchewan and is the author of three books of poems: *More Light* (Brick Books, 1998) and *Two Heavens* (Hagios Press, 1998) and the most recent, *The Dwelling of Weather*, which came out from Brick Books earlier this year.

Marlene Cookshaw is the author of four books of poems, most recently *Shameless* (Brick Books), which was short-listed for the 2002 Dorothy

Livesay Poetry Prize and the Pat Lowther Memorial Award. She lives on Pender Island and in Victoria, BC, where she edits *The Malahat Review*.

Gloe Cormie's first collection of poems, *Sea Salt, Red Oven Mitts and the Blues*, published this year by Augustine Hand Press, was short-listed for The Eileen McTavish Sykes Award for Best First Book. Her poems have been published in several literary magazines and anthologies, and on CBC radio. She lives in Manitoba.

Lorna Crozier, born in Swift Current, Saskatchewan, now teaches at the University of Victoria. *Inventing the Hawk* won the Governor-General's Award for Poetry in 1992. Her latest book is *Apocrypha of Light*, published by McClelland & Stewart in 2002, from which her poems in this book first appeared. It was a finalist for the Pat Lowther Memorial Award.

Lynn Davies' first collection of poems, *The Bridge That Carries the Road*, was short-listed for the Gerald Lampert Memorial Award and the Governor-General's Award in 1999. She lives in New Brunswick.

Degan Davis spent four months living at St. Pete's after his travels through Asia. His poetry has appeared recently in *Exile*, *Grain* and *Descant*. He is currently writing a memoir/history of Japan on the theme of hiddenness.

Adam Dickinson's first book of poetry, *Cartography and Walking*, was published by Brick Books in 2002. He lives in Edmonton where he is currently pursuing graduate studies at the University of Alberta.

Sharon Abron Drache is the author of three books of adult fiction, including *Ritual Slaughter* (1989), children's stories, and numerous book reviews and feature articles to newspapers including *The Globe and Mail*.

M.A.C. Farrant is the author of seven collections of satirical and humorous short fiction, most recently *Darwin Alone In The Universe*, published in 2003 by Talonbooks, and a memoir, *The Turquoise Years* (forthcoming from Annick Press). She is the West Coast organizer and host of the annual Canadian small press ReLit Awards.

Dorothy Field is a visual artist working with handmade paper for sculpture and artist's books on Vancouver Island. Her poetry has appeared in numerous Canadian journals. She is the author of a children's book and co-author of a book of garden letters.

Linda Frank lives and writes from Hamilton Ontario. Her first book of poetry, *Cobalt Moon Embrace*, was released by BuschekBooks in 2002.

Myrna Garanis has lived in Alberta for over thirty years, with plenty of family-visit highway miles racked up between Edmonton and Saskatoon. She's working on a book of Saskatchewan expatriates, documenting, via its contributors, the impact of a Saskatchewan "tattoo" on those who think they've left.

Connie Gault lives in Regina where she writes fiction and plays. Her most recent story collection is *Inspection of a Small Village*, published by Coteau Books in 1996.

Sue Goyette of Cole Harbour, Nova Scotia, attended the 1999 Nature Writing and Wilderness Thought Colloquium at St. Peter's. She is the author of a book of poems, *The True Names Of Birds* (Brick Books, 1998) and a novel, *Lures* (HarperCollins Canada, 2002). Her second book of poems, *Undone* will be published in Spring 2004. She is currently working on her second novel.

Heidi Greco, an editor and writer, lives south of Vancouver in a house with lots of trees around it. Her poems have been published in many magazines and anthologies; she also writes book reviews for newspapers and magazines. Her collection of poems, *Rattlesnake Plantain*, was published by Vancouver's Anvil Press in 2002.

Frances Greenslade has an MFA in creative writing from the University of British Columbia. Her first book, a travel memoir called *A Pilgrim in Ireland: A Quest for Home*, won the Saskatchewan Book Award for nonfiction in 2002. She now lives in Regina.

Catherine Greenwood's collection *The Pearl King and Other Poems* will be published by Brick Books in 2004. She lives in Victoria with a cat named Prudence, who was born in a straw-bale manger behind the monastery workshop.

Maureen Scott Harris is a poet and essayist who grew up in Winnipeg and has lived in Toronto since the mid-60s. Her book *A Possible Landscape*, published in 1993, is out of print. A chapbook, *The World Speaks*, came out this year from Junction Books.

Julia Herperger lives in Saskatoon. She's had poems published in journals, such as *Grain* and *Arc*, and broadcast on CBC radio. She received a scholarship to the Sage Hill Writing Experience, a grant from the Saskatchewan Arts Board, and is currently at work on her first collection.

Trevor Herriot is a Regina naturalist and writer. His first book, *River in a Dry Land: a Prairie Passage*, took several national and provincial awards and was short-listed for the 2000 Governor-General's award for non-fiction.

Gerry Hill was born and raised along the Trans-Canada Highway in southern Saskatchewan. He teaches English at Luther College, University of Regina, and parents three fabulous kids. His third poetry collection, *Getting To Know You*, will be published this year by Spotted Cow Press.

Kitty Hoffman is a Victoria writer and lecturer. She is a winner in the 2003 Short *Grain* contest for creative nonfiction. Her articles and reviews have appeared in numerous newspapers and magazines.

Maureen Hynes has published two books of poetry: *Harm's Way* (Brick Books, 2001) and *Rough Skin* (Wolsak and Wynn, 1995), which received the League of Canadian Poets' Gerald Lampert Award. She is the poetry editor for *Our Times* magazine and creative arts editor for *Atlantis*. She is now based in Toronto.

Barbara Klar's books are *The Night You Called Me A Shadow* and *The Blue Field*, both of which owe part of their existence to retreats at St. Peter's Abbey. She was the 2002 recipient of the Wallace Stegner Grant for the Arts, a one-month writer-in-residency in Eastend, Saskatchewan. She lives and writes west of Saskatoon.

Myrna Kostash is a full-time writer in Edmonton who is working on a book of creative nonfiction, *Memoirs of Byzantium*. Her many books include *All of Baba's Children*, *The Doomed Bridegroom* and *The Next Canada*. She's just finished a stint as writer-in-residence in Saskatoon.

Judith Krause is a Regina poet, editor and teacher. Her most recent poetry collection is *Silk Routes of the Body* (Coteau Books, 2001).

Katherine Lawrence writes from Saskatoon. Her first collection of poetry *Ring Finger, Left Hand* (Coteau Books) won the Saskatchewan Book Award for best first book in 2001.

Ross Leckie is director of creative writing at the University of New Brunswick and editor of *The Fiddlehead*, one of Canada's finest literary journals. His most recent book of poetry is *The Authority of Roses* (Brick Books, 1997).

Tim Lilburn is the author of six books of poetry, the most recent being *Kill-site*, published this year by McClelland & Stewart. He is also the writer and editor of several collections of essays, the latest being *Thinking and Singing: Poetry and the Practice of Philopsophy* (Cormorant, 2002). He lives in Saskatoon and teaches at St. Peter's College.

Jeanette Lynes is the author of the 1999 poetry collection *A Woman Alone on the Atikokan Highway*. She has two books of poetry forthcoming this year: *Left Fields* (Wolsak and Wynn) and *The Aging Cheerleader's Alphabet* (Mansfield Press). She received the 2001 Bliss Carman Poetry Award. She lives in Antigonish.

Hannah Main-van der Kamp is a seasonal resident in BC's Desolation Sound. She considers contemplation to be her true vocation.

Dave Margoshes is a Regina fiction writer, poet and editor. His most recent books are the novel *Drowning Man*, published this year, and a collection of poetry, *Purity of Absence*, which came out in 2001.

Mary Maxwell lives in Saskatoon. Her poetry and non-fiction have been published in various literary magazines and anthologies. She is currently working on a collection of prose poetry.

Don McKay's books include *Vis-à-Vis: field notes on poetry and wildness* (2001), *Another Gravity* (2000), and *Apparatus* (1997). An esteemed editor and workshop leader, he's won the Governor-General's Award for poetry. He currently lives in Victoria.

Arlene Metrick is a New York City poet (currently living in India) who has travelled widely, including to Saskatchewan. Her poem in this anthology is one of her few published works.

Erin Michie has published non-fiction and poetry in various magazines and written for performance. She lives in Calgary, Alberta.

Jane Southwell Munro lives on Vancouver Island. Her third collection of poetry, *Grief Notes & Animal Dreams*, was reprinted by Brick in 2002. These poems are from *Point No Point*, a new manuscript.

Brenda Niskala is a fiction writer and poet living in Regina. Despite being a chronic underachiever, she plans to have a book of short fiction out soon. Her last publication was *Emma's Horizon* (2000), a HagPapers chapbook.

Jacqueline Osherow is the author of four books of poetry, most recently *Dead Men's Praise* (Grove Press, 1999). The Salt Lake City poet has been awarded fellowships from the John Simon Guggenheim Foundation and the National Endowment for the Arts, and won a number of prizes.

Miranda Pearson is a graduate of the University British Columbia's MFA Creative Writing Program. Her poems have been published widely in literary journals and her first book, *Prime*, appeared in 2001. She lives in Vancouver but makes occasional escapes to Saskatchewan where she is involved in a quiet but long-term relationship with the sky.

Elizabeth Philips is the author of three collections of poetry, most recently *Beyond My Keeping* (Coteau Books, 1995) and *A Blue with Blood in It* (Coteau Books, 2000). Both collections received the Saskatchewan Poetry Award for their respective years. She was the editor of the literary magazine *Grain* from 1998 to midsummer 2003. She lives in Saskatoon.

Alison Pick's first book of poetry, *Question & Answer*, was published by Polestar this year. She is the winner of the 2002 Bronwen Wallace Award for Poetry and the 2002 Alfred Bailey Manuscript Prize from the Writers Federation of New Brunswick. After two years of travelling and writing on the prairies, including several stays at St. Pete's, she and her partner Degan Davis have settled in St. John's, Newfoundland.

Ruth Roach Pierson, trained as an academic historian, retired from teaching in 2001 in order to devote herself full-time to poetry writing. *Where No Window Was*, published by BuschekBooks in 2002, is her first book of poems. She lives in Toronto.

Joanna A. Piucci is a poet and fiction writer living in New York City. Her work has appeared in many American literary magazines. Her short play, *Sunday, Sugar*, was produced in New York City as part of the 2000 Love Creek Short Play Festival and selected for *Best Stage Scenes of 2000* (Smith & Kraus, 2002).

Marion Quednau, a poet and novelist living in Mission, BC, attended a fall poetry colloquium with Tim Lilburn at St. Pete's in 1998. The next year she won a League of Canadian Poets award for her chapbook *Kissing: Selected Chronicles*. Her poetry has been published in a number of magazines and anthologies, most recently in *The Common Sky: Canadian Writers Against the War*.

William Robertson lives in Saskatoon and teaches English in Prince Albert, Saskatoon, and at St. Peter's College. He's published three books of poetry, most recently *Somewhere Else* (Coteau, 1997).

Mari-Lou Rowley is a poet and science/corporate writer originally from Saskatoon and now living in Vancouver, after stints in Edmonton and Toronto. Her collections include *a Knife a Rope a Book* (Underwhich Editions), *Interference with the Hydrangea*, to be published this fall by Thistledown Press, and *Viral Suite* (forthcoming from Anvil Press).

Allan Safarik lives in Dundurn, Saskatchewan. He is the author of ten books of poetry including *Bird Writer's Handbook* (Exile Editions, 2002). In 2000, while writer in residence for Humboldt and district, he found weekly refuge at St Peter's Severin Hall. His poems in this anthology are from a manuscript entitled *Blood Of Angels* that will be published by Thistledown Press next spring.

Brenda Schmidt is a writer and artist in Creighton, a mining town in northeastern Saskatchewan. Her first collection of poetry, *A Haunting Sun*, was published by Thistledown Press in 2001. Poems from a new manuscript have appeared in many literary magazines and the anthology *Running Barefoot: Women Write the Land* (Rowan Books, 2001).

David Sealy is a freelance writer/playwright/Hansard staff member/proofreader/community worker/newsletter editor. He juggles slash marks in Regina.

Steven Ross Smith writes poetry and fiction and explores the realms of sound and performance poetry. His latest books are *fluttertongue, Book 1, The Book of Games* (Thistledown Press, 1998) and *fluttertongue, Book 2, The Book of Emmett* (Hagios Press, 1999). He can be heard on *Carnivocal*, a CD anthology of Canadian sound poetry. He is also executive director of Sage Hill Writing Experience.

Shelley Sopher is a Regina-based artist. Her most recent photographic installation, *The Garden*, which was shot in the grounds of St. Peter's, will be in a touring exhibition from 2003 to 2005. She worked in publishing for a number of years, currently co-ordinates the Saskatchewan Writers/Artists Colonies and considers St. Pete's to be her second home.

Birk Sproxton writes from Red Deer, Alberta. Editor of the best-selling collection *Great Stories from the Prairies*, he is author of the novel *The Red-Headed Woman with the Black Black Heart*. He is currently writing a sequel to his long poem *Headframe*.

Yvonne Trainer has recently published a collection of poems titled *Tom Three Persons*. She was also a recent recipient of the Edmonton Arts Trust Fund Award for Writing. She is completing a Ph.D. from the University of Manitoba English Department.

Paul Tyler's poems have appeared in Canadian and US literary magazines. He currently lives in Ottawa, but his favourite province is Saskatchewan.

Elizabeth Ukrainetz is a Toronto writer working on her second novel.

Guy Vanderhaeghe is the author of four novels, three collections of short stories, and two plays. He is a two-time winner of the Governor-General's Award for Fiction. His most recent book is *The Last Crossing* (McClelland & Stewart, 2002), which was chosen Fiction Book of the Year by the Canadian Booksellers Association.

Bernadette Wagner of Regina completed an apprenticeship in the Saskatchewan Writers Guild's Mentorship Program, and received the W. O. Mitchell Bursary Award to the Sage Hill Writing Experience and a Saskatchewan Arts Board Individual Assistance grant in 2002. The support and recognition has strengthened her resolve to continue crafting poems.

Joanna M. Weston, born in England and now living on Vancouver Island, has had poetry published in numerous anthologies and journals, and a middle-reader novel *The Willow-Tree Girl*, online at www.electricebook publishing.com/publishing/childrens.html.

Christopher Wiseman has published nine books and a *Selected Poems* will appear in 2004. He has lived in Calgary since 1969, and taught English and creative writing at the University of Calgary for some thirty years before taking early retirement. His most recent poetry collection is *Crossing the Salt Flats* (Porcupine's Quill, 1999).

Jan Zwicky's most recent collection is *Songs for Relinquishing the Earth*, which won the Governor-General's Award for poetry. *Wisdom and Metaphor* will appear from Gaspereau Press this fall. She currently teaches at the University of Victoria.

PERMISSIONS

Some of the work in this anthology has appeared previously in other books. Permissions to use them, from the authors and publishers, is gratefully acknowledged:

The piece by Warren Cariou is the first chapter of his novella "Lazarus," which first appeared in his book *Exalted Company of Roadside Martyrs* (Coteau Books, 1999); reprinted with permission of the author and Coteau Books.

"A Piece of Quartz Crystal," by David Carpenter is from *Courting Saskatchewan*. Copyright © 1996 David Carpenter, published in Canada by Greystone Books, a division of Douglas & McIntyre Ltd. Reprinted by permission of the publisher.

"Moment" by Hilary Clark first appeared in her book *The Dwelling of Weather* (Brick Books, 2003); reprinted with permission from the author and Brick Books.

"St. Peter's, Thanksgiving" by Marlene Cookshaw first appeared in her book *Double Somersaults* (Brick Books, 1999); reprinted with permission from the author and Brick Books.

"The Divine Anatomy" and "A Prophet in His Own Country" by Lorna Crozier from *Apocrypha of Light* by Lorna Crozier. Used by permission, McClelland & Stewart Ltd. *The Canadian Publishers*, (2002).

"The Doorway to St. Scholastica" and "When Doves Cry" by Linda Frank first appeared in her book *Cobalt Moon Embrace* (BuschekBooks, 2002); reprinted with permission from the author and BuschekBooks.

"The Fat Lady with the Thin Face" by Connie Gault first appeared in her book *Inspection of a Small Village* (Coteau Books, 1996); reprinted with permission of the author and Coteau Books.

The selection by Frances Greenslade is from *A Pilgrim in Ireland* by Frances Greenslade. Copyright © Frances Greenslade 2002. Reprinted by permission of Penguin Books Canada Limited.

"North Central Baseball League...." by Gerry Hill first appeared in his book *Getting To Know You* (Spotted Cow Press, 2003); reprinted with permission of the author and Spotted Cow Press.

"Clang" and "Dance Pavilion" by Maureen Hynes first appeared in her book *Harm's Way* (Brick Books, 2001); reprinted with permission from the author and Brick Books.

"Devotions" and "Retreat" by Judy Krause first appeared in her book *Silk Routes of the Body* (Coteau Books, 2001); reprinted with permission of the author and Coteau Books.

"Three Weeks" by Barbara Klar first appeared in her book *Blue Field* (Coteau Books, 1999); reprinted with permission of the author and Coteau Books.

"Why Prairie Barns Are Red" by Hannah Main-van der Kamp first appeared in her book *The Parable Boat* (Wolsak and Wynn, 1999); reprinted with permission from the author and Wolsak and Wynn Publishers Ltd.

"Northern Lights" by Don McKay from *Another Gravity* by Don McKay. Used by permission, McClelland & Stewart Ltd. *The Canadian Publishers*, (2000).

"Wild Mint" by Elizabeth Philips first appeared in her book *A Blue with Blood in It* (Coteau Books, 2000); reprinted with permission of the author and Coteau Books.

"Below 'Imponderable,' A Yellowed Iris" by Ruth Pierson first appeared in her book *Where No Window Was* (BuschekBooks, 2002); reprinted with permission from the author and BuschekBooks.

"Hunting Truffles" by William Robertson first appeared in his book *Somewhere Else* (Coteau Books, 1997); reprinted with permission of the author and Coteau Books.

"Things As They Are?" by Guy Vanderhaeghe from *Things As They Are?* by Guy Vanderhaeghe. Used by permission, McClelland & Stewart Ltd. *The Canadian Publishers*, (1992).